The Twilight Zone
and Philosophy

Popular Culture and Philosophy® Series Editor: George A. Reisch

For full details of all Popular Culture and Philosophy® books, visit www.opencourtbooks.com.

Popular Culture and Philosophy®

The Twilight Zone and Philosophy

A Dangerous Dimension to Visit

EDITED BY

HEATHER L. RIVERA AND
ALEXANDER E. HOOKE

OPEN COURT
Chicago

Volume 121 in the series, Popular Culture and Philosophy®, edited by George A. Reisch

To find out more about Open Court books, visit our website at www.opencourtbooks.com.

Open Court Publishing Company is a division of Carus Publishing Company, dba Cricket Media.

Copyright © 2019 by Carus Publishing Company, dba Cricket Media

First printing 2019

Printed and bound in the United States of America.

The Twilight Zone and Philosophy: A Dangerous Dimension to Visit

This book has not been prepared, authorized, or endorsed by the creators or producers of *The Twilight Zone*.

ISBN: 978-0-8126-9989-0

Library of Congress Control Number: 2018949963

This book is also available as an e-book (ISBN 978-0-8126-9993-7).

Contents

Dare to Enter the Zone

ALEXANDER E. HOOKE AND
HEATHER L. RIVERA

> I sought great human beings. I never found anything but the *apes* of their ideal.
>
> —FRIEDRICH NIETZSCHE, *Twilight of the Idols*

Imagine you're travelling through another dimension—the infancy of television. It's the 1950s when television is entering American households to offer game shows, suburban sitcoms, and sundry programs to keep toddlers entertained. Though universities tried to seize the educational uses of TV, their efforts quickly succumbed to commercial interests. Parents and teachers soon complained that the TV set was an "idiot box." Newton Minnow, head of the FCC, condemned TV as a gateway to a "vast wasteland." It will corrupt young minds and vulnerable teens. TV culture, according to this growing and outraged consensus, threatens to destroy civility and family values.

Then came *The Twilight Zone*. Suddenly television viewers were encouraged to think. In a mere thirty minutes we were invited to enjoy twists and turns, contemplate absurd endings, figure out the interplay of the narratives and the scenes. For the next five seasons millions of us had our minds captivated by a prisoner falling in love with a robot, a woman encountering herself as a child, aliens plotting the consumption of human flesh, hapless individuals making deals with death or the Devil. We witness a slot machine calling out to a tormented gambler by name, mannequins coming alive, and a banker who suddenly finds he can read other people's minds.

The Twilight Zone remains one of the most revolutionary televisions shows of all-time. Most polls rank it among the top ten important programs ever. To classify it solely as part of the science fiction genre is misleading. While *The Twilight Zone* certainly embraces current sciences and emerging technologies, they are featured insofar as they help address enduring philosophical themes, such as Who am I? What are we? What is our relation to truth, love, death, beauty, or good and evil?

In an Indiana newspaper, the show's creator Rod Serling explained, "*The Twilight Zone* is about people—about human beings involved in extraordinary circumstances, in strange problems of their own or of fate's making." This outlook has endured and influenced a variety of offspring, including today's quite popular *Black Mirror* series, where ubiquitous smart phones, micro-cameras and neurological transplants haunt human hopes and fears. Serling himself reminds us of a reincarnation of Socrates, the gadfly of Athens. Many of the episodes can be seen as thought experiments where the promises offered by experts and the elite are exposed as cosmic tricks or jokes played by divine and demonic powers dishing out fortune and misfortune.

Consider how Serling presents human beings and their fates. The promise of eternal youth, for example, presents a twenty-five-year-old husband (cosmetically rejuvenated) looking forlornly into the eyes of his dear seventy-year-old wife. The hopes to protect our family from a nuclear bomb attack lead to a brutal confrontation with our neighbors, who selfishly neglected to build their own shelters. A toy telephone entices a young boy to die so he can be with his recently departed grandmother. Space ships take their passengers to transcend human horizons, but invariably the results find a darker humanity.

As with Socrates, there are disputes over Serling's essential beliefs. At times he is an optimist. More often he is the cynic, pessimist, realist, or merely an inquirer into human frailties and self-delusions. "Time Enough at Last" is one of the most endearing episodes of all. As the sole human survivor of a nuclear catastrophe, Henry Bemis finally has the chance to read all the books he wants without the annoyances of his fellow creatures. Most of us can only admire his quirky but intense character. Yet the fate that befalls with his glasses is such that, in the words of Marc Scott Zicree, "few can watch it and not be seduced by its simplicity and its pathos."

The episode "The Hunt" casts a different light on humanity by playing on the sentiments of every dog-lover. An old man and his mutt Rip dive into a pond, only to ascend into a place where no one seems to recognize them. The familiar faces believe that the old man has died. So he assumes he is dead and looking for heaven along Eternity Road. A young man welcomes him, but says no dogs allowed. It turns out that the young man was actually directing the man into Hell, and he knew that faithful Rip would have smelled the danger immediately and lead his owner back to Eternity Road. The old man soon meets a real angel who welcomes him and Rip to Heaven. "You see," the angel says to him, "A man, well he'll walk right into Hell with both eyes open—but even the Devil can't fool a dog."

We viewers eventually see how Serling's creation shares the disappointment of Nietzsche in the above epigraph. What we seek and what we find rarely mesh. We are as rational as we are irrational, good-hearted and malevolent, hopeful and despondent. So many episodes depict characters embracing the ideal of friendship, justice, truth, loyalty, passion, or trust. At the same time, viewers see the treachery of human beasts. They kill over gold, sell their souls for the promise of eternal life, befriend the Devil, compromise with the Grim Reaper, or trust a machine rather than another human.

This dramatic and intellectual tension underscores Serling's creation. He and his talented writers, producers, directors, and actors were able to address this tension between our ideals and the futility of achieving them that made viewers chuckle, grin, nod our heads in amazement, or simply laugh at another absurd ending. Yet part of this humor continues to have an enduring edge in *Twilight Zone* and its reincarnations such as *Black Mirror.* Here Serling and Nietzsche join forces—we again realize that we're laughing at the apes of our ideals. We are the species that laughs because we are the species most deserving to be laughed at.

The following writers have dared the boundaries of our knowledge and imagination by offering still new signposts for viewers and readers trying to negotiate their way through the joys and despairs of a strange dimension. They offer the most recent enticements and cautions for abandoning our comfort zone. They help us to find our way in the Twilight Zone.

First Dimension

Facing the Zone

1
Lost in Time

Elizabeth Rard

At the beginning of "The Rip Van Winkle Caper" four men have just pulled off the heist of the century: they have stolen one million dollars' worth of gold bricks. Now, as they stand in a cave full of metal and glass containers and fancy computer equipment with impressive knobs and flashing lights, it begins to dawn on them that in order to get away with the crime of the century they will have to lay low for a century—literally.

The ring-leader of their group and resident mad scientist, Farwell, explains that in order to be sure that the heat is off before they divide up the spoils of this caper they will need to go into suspended animation for one hundred years. His comrades are initially skeptical of this rather unorthodox plan, but as Farwell explains that the suspended animation pods will keep the four men alive and healthy (and not aging) for the duration of the wait, and that they will awake rested and safe, feeling as if they have been asleep for mere minutes, they begin to reluctantly agree to the plan. They lie down in the pods, flip the switch, and (with the exception of poor Erbie, whose chamber was damaged by a falling rock) awaken a hundred years later feeling as if they've only been asleep for a few moments. Of course, the three survivors end up killing each other right before it's revealed in an all too predictable ironic twist that gold is now manufactured, and hence worthless.

We might be tempted to think that the characters involved in this story have time-traveled. After all, this adventure takes place on two different days separated by one hundred years. This would be a mistake however. The events of "The Rip Van Winkle Caper" caper don't amount to genuine time travel. To see why, consider what happens every night when you go to bed. From your perspective, no time passes between when you fall asleep and when you wake up. However, if someone were to creepily sit in the corner of your room and watch you sleep they would observe that you were present at every single moment between 11:00 P.M. (when you fall asleep) and 7:00 A.M. (when you wake up screaming because you realize that someone is sitting in the corner of your room watching you).

The important thing is that it takes your body eight hours to make the trip, the exact amount of time that passes while you are sleeping. Likewise, if someone extremely long lived were to hang around the cave from the moment our gold thieves go into their chambers and watch until the moment they emerge, what this person would observe would be that their bodies are there at every single moment for the entire hundred years. In other words, it takes the bodies of the gold thieves a hundred years to make it to one hundred years in the future. The fact that the thieves are not aware of the passage of time no more means that time travel has occurred than it does when you sleep through the night.

So, what's required for genuine time travel? Philosopher David Lewis describes the requirement as involving a discrepancy between time and time. When we normally move forward in time (which we seem to be able to do just by existing in a universe with a temporal dimension) the amount of time that it takes our body to travel from 10:00 P.M. to 10:05 P.M. is five minutes, which is exactly the amount of time that actually passes. In other words, the departure and arrival time equal to the duration of the journey.

When someone engages in genuine time travel there is a discrepancy between the amount of time the journey takes them and the amount of time between their departure time and their arrival time. So, if Farwell had built time machine pods rather than suspended animation pods then only a few moments (at most) would have passed for the four men between the point in time that they started their journey in 1961 and the point in time that they finished their journey in 2061. However, the temporal distance between these times is one hundred years. So, since a few moments is a different amount of time than a hundred years, the four men would have engaged in time travel.

The definition would work just as well for time traveling adventurers that headed into the past rather than the future. Imagine someone gets into a time machine in 1961, waits for a few moments, and steps out in 1861. Again, while the journey took only a few moments for our traveler, there is one hundred years between the point of departure and the point of arrival. Hence again we have a genuine case of time travel. Whether we chose to measure the passage of time in this case as one hundred years or negative one hundred (because we're going backwards) will make little difference in most cases. The only time it would matter is if we have someone who is traveling back in time but at a rate that matches the forward rate (so it takes me one minute from my point of view to travel one minute backwards in time). However, our definition is more than enough to allow us to identify several instances of genuine time travel to consider. While our gold thieves are not time travelers in any interesting way, there are many others who have journeyed off into the various dimensions of time and space that can only be accessed in the Twilight Zone.

A man can be lost not only in terms of maps and miles, but also in time . . . in the Twilight Zone!

In the episode "Last Flight" Flight Lieutenant William Terrance "Terry" Decker gets into a fire-fight against seven German planes with his comrade Mackaye. Terry's not a bad guy but he is a bit of a coward. Seeing that they are outnumbered (and fearing that he will inevitably be shot down) Terry flees the fight and flies his plane into the relative safety of a large cloud. He makes his way to an American Airforce base somewhere in France. Upon landing, he checks in with the men stationed at the base. Terry quickly realizes that there was something very strange about this particular flight. While the fire-fight he just left took place in 1917, he learns that he has arrived at the Airforce base in 1959. A journey that took perhaps a few hours for Terry has placed him approximately forty-two years in the future. Terry is a time traveler!

As he is questioned by the personnel at the base (who have taken him into custody because, after all, he's claiming to have traveled more than forty years into the future) he discovers that the other man in the fire-fight, Mackaye, is still alive in 1959. In fact, Mackaye was a hero during World War II who saved hundreds (perhaps thousands) of lives. But how could this be? When Terry left he was sure that he was leaving Mackaye to his death. There's no way that even a great pilot could survive against seven German planes.

As Terry marvels at the seeming impossibility of Mackaye's survival and wonders how he could have escaped without aid a peculiar thing dawns on him. Mackaye must have had help, and the only reasonable conclusion was that the help must have come from Terry himself, at a point in time after Terry fled the flight. Once Terry is convinced that he (in 1917) returned to the fire-fight he realizes what he has to do. The only way Terry can save Mackaye in 1917 is if he gets in his plane and somehow makes it back to 1917. Failure to go back and do the action that the history of 1959 includes will have the effect of changing history, and in some rather extreme ways. After all, Mackaye saved hundreds of lives, and each one of those people have gone out into the world and done things since the time they were saved. If Mackaye dies in 1917 then not only are all of his actions since 1917 undone, but in addition all of the actions that the people he saved have done will be undone. It's probably impossible to determine where the causal ripples would stop.

This is not what happens in Terry's case, however. Inspired by his conviction that he has already saved Mackaye in the past (and motivated by his fear of what will happen if he now fails to return to save him) Terry escapes custody and flies off in his biplane, destined to sacrifice himself for his friend back in 1917. In this particular case, nothing is changed as a result of time travel. Terry always saved Mackaye in 1917, and Terry always appeared in 1959 prior (from Terry's point of view) to saving Mackaye.

Now we do get a bit of a causal loop in this particular case. What is a causal loop, you might ask? We normally think that every event has a cause. Hence if my bike tire pops there must be some cause (perhaps my tire ran over a sharp piece of metal). If I am hungry I eat a cupcake and that causes me to feel full. If I sink the eight ball in the pocket this is caused by the cue ball hitting the eight ball at the right angle, with the right force and such, which was caused by my hitting the cue ball at the right angle, with the right force and such.

Now we normally think that a cause has to happen before the event that it causes. I have to hit the cue ball before it can knock the eight ball into the pocket. I have to eat the cupcake before my belly feels full. But with the possibility of time travel there is suddenly more than one way that one event can happen before another. Let's say that I'm again playing pool. I begin the game by breaking up the triangle of balls on the table. We'll call this event *break*. Let's say that *break* happens at 9:00 P.M. (a most reasonable hour to begin a pool game). Of course (and after much knocking around of balls by me and my opponent) the game ends in my sinking the eight ball. We'll call this event *sink* and we'll say that *sink* occurs at 9:17. Now, from my point of view (and from the point of view of normal time) *break* occurs seventeen minutes prior to *sink*. But let's say that you walk in at 9:16 and happen to see my winning shot, although you have not seen the rest of the game. After witnessing my winning shot at 9:17 (and perhaps buying me a congratulatory beer) you decide at 9:30 that you would like to see the first part of the game. Fortunately, you happen to have a time machine that you purchased at that new (and not at all sinister looking) curiosity shop that just opened across the street, and you pop into the time machine at 9:30 and instantaneously (from your point of view) step back out of your time machine at 8:59, allowing you to watch me break at 9:00. So, from your point of view *break* happens about fourteen minutes after *sink* occurs. So now we have one event (*sink*) that in a sense happens both before and after another event (*break*).

In a causal loop, we have two events which end up being each other's cause, because in a real sense each event is prior to the other event. In Terry's situation, we can identify two important events. Terry learns (in 1959) that he saved Mackaye in the past. Let's call this event *learn*. *Learn* occurs in 1959. In addition, Terry actually saves Mackaye in 1917 because he knows that he is supposed to save Mackaye. We can call this event *save*. *Save* occurs in 1917.

Clearly *save* causes *learn* because in order for the Air Base personal to be able to tell Terry in 1957 that Mackaye is still alive (thus giving Terry the information he needed to infer that he must have saved Mackaye) it must be the case that Terry has already saved Mackaye. And since *save* happens in 1917 and *learn* happens in 1959 save clearly happens before *learn*. Now the reason this creates a loop is that *learn* also causes *save*, since it's Terry's knowledge that he will save (has saved?) Mackaye that motivates him to travel back in time and risk his own life to save Mackaye. In addition, *learn* happens before *save* from the point of view of Terry. So, *learn* causes *save* and *save* causes *learn*. Causal loop achieved!

Now this might seem very odd, and it raises questions that may be unanswerable, such as what causes the causal loop to occur in the first place. But importantly there is no inconsistency in this loop. No events change. There is one consistent timeline in which in 1917 Terry leaves a firefight to travel to the future and then returns moments later save Mackaye. Later in 1959 Terry lands at an Airforce base in France, learns that he is supposed to save his comrade in the past, and then steals his own plane so that he can travel back in time. But if time travel is possible we shouldn't expect all time travel events to play out so perfectly, should we?

A desperate attempt to alter the present . . . in the Twilight Zone!

In the episode "No Time Like the Past" the twentieth-century scientist Paul Driscoll does what any reasonable person who lives in a world full of war, weapons, and radioactivity (and who happens to have access to a time machine) would do: he tries to go back in time and change things in order to make the world a better place. And what would someone with a time machine try to do? Kill Hitler of course! In addition, he hopes to warn the citizens of Hiroshima of the impending attack, and to avert the torpedoing of the *Lusitania* by the Germans. But this raises an interesting question, one which should be considered by anyone intending to time travel with altruistic (or even nefarious) intentions. Setting aside whether or not we should try to change the past, is it even possible to change the past?

There is a fairly convincing argument that it must be impossible to change the past. If it were possible to travel back in time and change the past then at some point someone would travel back in time and try to kill their own grandfather. For some reason philosophers usually assume that the two main goals of time travel would be kill Hitler, followed by kill your grandfather.

Sidestepping the clear moral reasons to avoid traveling back in time to kill your grandfather, it seems to literally be something that would be impossible to do. Imagine you manage to travel back in time and locate your grandfather at a point in time prior to him having any children of his own. Somehow you overcome your moral reservations and take dead aim at your grandfather, pull the trigger, and watch as his now lifeless body falls to the floor.

Here's the problem. If you grandfather dies prior to having children then he will never father whichever one of your parents he is responsible for. This means that one of your parents will never exist, making it impossible for you to be born. Which means you will have never existed and should be completely erased from history. But if you never existed then you certainly weren't around to travel back in time and kill your grandfather. Thus, your grandfather should be just fine since no one was there to shoot him. But then you do exist and are free to travel back in time and shoot him . . .

This situation surely must be impossible. But does that mean that time travel is also impossible? David Lewis, who gave us our initial definition of time travel, argues that if time travel is possible then any action that would lead to the creation of a paradox (or an impossible situation) would be prevented by some ordinary occurrence. The time traveler's gun could jam, or the time traveler could get distracted at the last minute. Perhaps a stray banana peel could thwart the time traveler and add a bit of much needed levity to the situation. The upshot is that whatever the time traveler does they will not be able to change the past in any way that would prevent them from originally traveling to the past.

This is a lesson that Paul Driscoll learns the hard way. He is overwhelmed with despair for the future of humanity and pushed to the brink of madness by the suffering and destruction that he is witnessing in his own time. The creation of a time machine seems to offer salvation both for Paul and for humanity. If Paul can identify key moments in human history that have led us down this dark path then he can potentially avert the dystopian world that he finds himself in now.

He identifies three key events that he believes are crucial to the fate of humanity. Let's focus our discussion on the assassination of Hitler. He travels to a hotel room in Berlin, 1939, from which he will have a clear shot of Hitler for the brief period during which Hitler will be addressing a crowd across the way. He picks a date two months before the start of World War II with the hope that, by assassinating Hitler, he will be able to prevent the war and thus significantly alter the course of human history.

Of course, things do not go as planned. A maid knocks on the door and distracts him, causing a delay in his plan. Moments later two SS officers bang on the door, having been tipped off by the maid of suspicious happenings. Again, Paul is distracted. The speech ends and Paul misses his chance because, as Lewis predicted, mundane events conspired to prevent his timeline altering action. But we already knew that Paul must fail. Imagine Paul is successful. He kills Hitler. World War II is averted. The world of the future becomes a better place than the world that Paul has come from. But this means that Paul will never be motivated to build and use a time machine in order to alter the past. If the world is a good place Paul will have no reason to try and save humanity.

Even assuming Paul still ends up wanting to travel back in time to change history, he will have no reason now to travel back to kill Hitler. If Hitler had died before World War II (and there had been no war) then probably very few people would even remember Hitler in Paul's time. So, there is no reason at all for Paul to identify Hitler as a person that should be killed in order to save humanity. Thus, Paul will never travel back in time to kill Hitler. So, Hitler won't be assassinated and World War II will happen just as it originally did . . .

We might well be tempted to ask why Paul doesn't just go further back in time and try again, perhaps this time trying to kill baby Hitler? But if it really is impossible to alter the past then we can expect that any attempt, no matter how well planned, will fail for some reason.

While it might not be possible to change the past, it does seem at least theoretically possible to interact with the past, as long as all of the actions that we engage in are the actions that history already includes us doing. Paul learns another hard lesson when he tries to merely escape to the past, having given up on changing it. On his final journey, he travels back to the cozy and idyllic (both in name and in actuality) town of Homeville, Indiana. He has concluded that the past is unalterable and, given his distaste for the present, he hopes to live out his days in a simpler, more peaceful (and less radioactive) era. He is careful not to do anything that he believes might change the future, which shows that he has not yet learned the lesson that the past is unchangeable. Paul will do whatever he already did in 1881. Any action he takes is the action that contributed to the future he remembers.

Paul has an apparently vast historical knowledge and he remembers that the schoolhouse will catch on fire, seriously injuring several children. He vows to do nothing to try to stop the event from occurring, but when he sees the lantern he believes will cause the fire hanging from a wagon he tries to get the owner to put the lantern out. Of course, in an ironic twist his actions spook the horse, causing it to run towards the schoolhouse. Paul causes the very event he was trying to prevent. This is not to say that the event was fated to happen and that no matter what Paul did the fire would still occur. Rather Paul had always caused the fire and it was just his foreknowledge of the fire that always leads him to accidentally start the fire. Paul did exactly what he was supposed to do, with rather tragic consequences. Defeated and resigned Paul returns to the future for the final time. He will no longer focus on the past. Rather he will look to the future, the only place where it may yet be possible to bring about change.

Because, whoever heard of a man going back in time . . . in the Twilight Zone?

The past is a constant part of our present. We value our memories and wish longingly for days gone by. We regret the folly of our youth and curse the mistakes we have made, wishing we could rewrite our own personal histories. We ponder how things would have turned out had events unfolded differently. We may someday find ourselves with the ability to travel back in time, to see historic events unfold or even to interact with our formal selves. Whether we should travel to the past if given the chance, and whether we should try to change things are important questions, but if we're correct that our actions can never alter the past they may also be entirely unnecessary questions to answer. If ever in human history a person will travel to a time before 2019, then the history of the world at this moment already includes those visits, and if we're correct, nothing that happens from this moment forward can change the inevitability of these visits, or the actions of those travelers.

If ever humanity finds itself faced with such options and temptations we may well need to look back to find the answers, and we just might find those answers in the Twilight Zone.

2
Where Is the Twilight Zone?

FRANK SCALAMBRINO

Can philosophy help us find the Twilight Zone? Yes, it can. In fact, following a brief series of ideas beginning with Descartes, moving through psychoanalysis, and arriving at the idea of "the Uncanny," the Twilight Zone can be understood as a televised expression of the philosophy of surrealism.

Just as the images constructed by Salvador Dalí, René Magritte, M.C. Escher, and René Masson, may provoke an experience of the uncanny in those who view them, so too *The Twilight Zone* is an expression of surrealist philosophy both in its emphasis on the imagination unbounded by reason and in its capacity to provoke a feeling of the uncanny in its viewers. The "Intro" to the original *Twilight Zone* series explains that "the area we call the Twilight Zone" is "the dimension of imagination."

Both as a philosophy and as a movement in the history of art, surrealism began in France. Though the art movement was profoundly influenced by the painting style known as "metaphysical art," which is of Italian origin, surrealism officially originated in Paris with the publication of André Breton's first *Surrealist Manifesto* in 1924. From its very inception the motor force of surrealist art was the desire to circumvent conscious control of the artistic process. Whatever the creative forces from which art comes, it is as if the conscious—ultimately rational—forces of the artist were understood as constraints on non-conscious forces. So, surrealist art and the philosophy of surrealism center on methods to unleash the subconscious, spiritual, or supernatural forces driving artistic creation. In regard to its overall conception and aim, the same is true about the *Twilight Zone*. For example, *The Twilight Zone* provokes us to ask philosophical questions such as: Have we already moved beyond "being human"? Does the experience of time as "linear" somehow depend on a rational worldview? Why do we privilege the interpretations and phenomena found in "waking life" over those in dreams?

There were, officially, three manifestoes of surrealism, the first two of which were written by Breton. In the first manifesto, of 1924, surrealism was defined as:

> Psychic automatism in its pure state, by which one proposes to express . . . the actual functioning of thought. Dictated by thought, in the absence of any control exercised by reason . . . exempt from any aesthetic or moral concern.

From this starting point surrealists developed their famous method of "automatic writing," especially as seen expressed in Breton's celebrated surrealist novel of 1928, *Nadja*.

In the *Twilight Zone* episode, "A World of His Own," we meet a playwright whose frantic speaking into a tape recorder produces an imaginary world in which he lives and interacts with imaginary people. Surrealists may recognize this as a form of "automatic writing." "Automatic writing" refers to a process used to circumvent conscious and rational control of the writing process. On the one hand, this surrealist method aims at accomplishing the goal Breton announced in the first manifesto of Surrealism. On the other hand, this aim becomes articulated as a place or a zone by the second *Surrealist Manifesto*, of 1930.

According to Breton, "Everything tends to make us believe that there exists a certain point of the mind in which life and death, the real and the imagined, past and future, the communicable and the incommunicable, high and low, cease to be perceived as contradictions." What's more, Breton definitively explained: "Now, search as one may one will never find any other motivating force in the activities of the Surrealists than the hope of finding and fixing this point." This point, as we'll see, is the *Twilight Zone*.

In "The Mirror," we meet a farmer who, through leading a rebellion, replaces the overthrown dictator. Later, when he looks into his mirror and reflects on himself as the new dictator, he seems to only understand himself in paranoid ways. This episode reminds us of Salvador Dalí's surrealist method, developed from 1930 to 1934, known as the "paranoiac-critical method."

On the one hand, Dalí's innovation was both consistent with Breton's automatism and applauded by Breton. Dalí famously described his approach as a: "spontaneous method of irrational knowledge based on the critical and systematic objectivity of the associations and interpretations of delirious phenomena." Recalling the surrealist desire to circumvent rationality in the interpretation of the phenomena of experience, Dalí highlighted the sense in which paranoia establishes associations across experiences and phenomena without rational constraint. On the other hand, Dalí's method indicates a moment in the history of surrealism in which surrealist philosophy immersed itself further in the theories of Freudian psychoanalysis.

Now, even though Breton credits his shift away from Dadaism—the shift which eventually established surrealism—to his reading of Sigmund Freud's *The Interpretation of Dreams*, history has shown that—as cultural critic Theodore Adorno pointed out—it was surrealism's deeper immersion into Freudian psychoanalysis which led to the death of the official surrealist movement. The point of stating this here is that whereas Breton's Surrealism was snuffed-out after becoming constrained by the limited possible "Freudian" interpretations of experience, *The Twilight Zone* was able to successfully provide a televised expression of surrealism precisely by circumventing being pigeon-holed by "Freudian" interpretations. If psychoanalysis is understood as a kind of "taking apart" of the psyche, a literal "psycho-analysis," then surrealism and psychoanalysis are quite similar. In fact, in their de-stabilizing or deconstructive modes, Surrealism and psychoanalysis are nearly indistinguishable; however, in their (re)constructive modes, the rational "science-like" character of psychoanalysis bars it from being the same as surrealism.

At the heart of the distinction between surrealism and psychoanalysis is a dispute about how to understand "the

Unconscious," or the "subconscious" forces involved in artistic creation. Speaking of this overlap of provocative de-stabilizing activity—with which *The Twilight Zone* also overlaps— French psychoanalyst Jean Laplanche characterized the essential feature of the Unconscious as "unbinding." In other words, the subconscious artistic forces may be seen as themselves de-stabilizing or deconstructing the binds which rationality places on experiences and the experience of phenomena.

On the one hand, the French scene for surrealism was set by Descartes with the beginning of modern philosophy. On the other hand, when observers witness art created by subconscious imaginative forces "unbound" by reason they may have an experience characterized as "uncanny." And so, discussing these two aspects of surrealism should contribute to a deeper understanding of the Twilight Zone and philosophy.

The Surreal and the Uncanny

Recalling one of *The Twilight Zone*'s persistent themes, Western philosophy, in light of the findings stemming from science and technology by the time of the Renaissance, was experiencing a "crisis of authority" in regard to the philosophy of Aristotle (especially his physics) and sacred scriptures (especially in regard to the Copernican system). According to the standard narrative, this created the need for a "new philosophy" with which to establish "certainty."

René Descartes is considered "the Father of Modern philosophy" because he is credited with discovering the "Archimedean Point" of certainty with his "I think, therefore I am." What this means is that though we may be able to doubt everything, when we are doubting we cannot doubt that we are doubting. Since doubting is a kind of thinking, Descartes took the fact that we may be certain that thought is happening to be a sign that we can be certain of our mind. The conclusion that we can be certain of our mind logically follows from the idea that the mind is responsible for thinking.

Descartes's use of rationality to deny that life is a kind of "dream" perfectly contextualizes surrealism. *The Twilight Zone* addresses this question in the episode "Shadow Play," where the protagonist tries to explain to everyone in the world that they are in a dream. How do we know we're not in a dream, or some kind of simulation? Descartes's answer to this question involved using rationality to arrive at the certainty of our own mind—a mind, which is "awake" because it is rational. Yet, from the certainty of one's mind comes the infamous "mind-body" problem, and by way of this problem, surrealists are able to destabilize the rational construction which may suggest that the body is not in a dream. Whereas Aristotle famously characterized human beings as "rational animals," Descartes's mind-body problem set the stage for modern philosophers to characterize human beings as animals bound (or leashed) by rationality.

According to Descartes the products of the rational mind are "clear and distinct," and the sense-perception products of the body's capacity for imagination are "obscure and confused." By calling the privileging of clarity and distinctness into question, surrealism—just like *The Twilight Zone*—may be seen as an attempt to restore liberty and primacy to the animal, otherwise bound by rationality. For the surrealists, however, the either/or distinctness between either "clear and distinct" or "obscure and confused" is itself a product of rationality. Therefore, that dimension associated with the animal body's power of imagination may be characterized as a "twilight zone." So, the "twilight zone" may be characterized as "the dimension of the imagination" seen "in the absence of any control exercised by reason" and "exempt from any aesthetic or moral concern," as described by Breton.

Neither "clear" nor "obscure," then, characterizes "the surreal," rather the surreal is more like fantasy and dream, and the experience of the surreal may be characterized as "uncanny." Consistent with the de-stabilizing philosophy of both surrealism and psychoanalysis, "uncanny" describes some experience or phenomenon which is both familiar and unfamiliar, or both strangely familiar and alien, simultaneously. A leashed animal, so to speak, is both experiencing the projections of its imagination and not experiencing them, insofar as it is experiencing them in terms of being constrained by its leash. One could imagine a dog who enjoys chasing cars; supposing that dog were placed inside an "invisible fence" attached to its "shock collar." After being constrained long enough the dog would no longer attempt to run outside the yard.

Now, if we suppose further that a car drives by that the dog would have, in its previously un-bound condition, chased after, then we can also imagine that the dog would have some experience internal to its imagination—some bodily reaction—despite maintaining its composure. Whether we say the dog has "repressed" its desire to chase cars or not, we can at least make two comments about the dog were it to be suddenly liberated from its condition.

First, the dog's un-bound relation to the stimulation of the car would include a release of energy which was otherwise bound by the "authority of the invisible fence," so to speak. Second, the dog's "new" encounter of the car as now un-bound would be uncanny for it. The un-bound experience would seem strangely familiar and yet also alien, since it had become acculturated, or indoctrinated, to the clear and distinct bounds of the invisible fence.

Notice how this links up with the deconstructive modes of both surrealism and psychoanalysis. Just as surrealism is interested in how phenomena of experience would be associated with one another in a dimension unbound by reason, so too psychoanalytic techniques of "free association" and "dream interpretation" are supposed to allow for circumventing "the censorship" coming from the "super-ego" which would otherwise bind the experience privileging "clear and distinct" interpretations of phenomena. The idea is that "reality" may actually be "surreality" for those individuals freed from the constraints of rationality. Similarly, the American television series *The Twilight Zone* can be understood philosophically as both portraying the surreal and provoking an experience of the uncanny in its viewers.

A Televised Expression of the Philosophy of Surrealism

The Twilight Zone provides us with no shortage of the "gripping images of human catastrophe" which Breton discussed in his second *Surrealist Manifesto*. Yet, it is as if surrealism is located at the closest proximity to madness, while being the greatest assurance against the anguish of being mad. This is the case insofar as being identified as "mad" depends on a position privileging the rational to determine its truth.

This is a deep aspect of *The Twilight Zone*'s fascination. Of the persistent themes of *The Twilight Zone*, it is as if "madness" is invoked in every episode without ever being an episode's theme. And, as the television show often seems to ask: how do we return to embrace a "rational" worldview of reality after entering the surreality of the Twilight Zone?

"The Shelter," is an excellent example for being so straightforward. In the episode, there is a large gathering of suburban community members at a birthday party for the local doctor. Everyone knows one another and is cordial. The doctor happens to have a fallout shelter, and suddenly an air raid defense alarm sounds. After the doctor locks himself and his family in the shelter the rest of the people at the party want in, and after he refuses, their cordiality quickly turns into aggression, rage, hostility, and racism. Just as the mob breaks into the fallout shelter an announcement is made stating that the air raid was a false alarm. The episode speaks to the imagination unbound by rationality and political correctness, while invoking an experience of the uncanny in viewers, opening a space for them to wonder about their true presence bound by rational conventionality.

Season One's "The Lonely" provides both a critical analysis of a "loving" relation to a significant other and echoes a consistent Surrealist expression regarding the female body. The year is 2046 and the story centers on a man found guilty of murder and sentenced to solitary confinement on an asteroid. His only contact with another person is during the short periods of time when a ship from Earth lands to drop off food and supplies for him to survive. The captain of the ship is sympathetic to the prisoner, believing that the murder was actually self-defense. So, during one re-supply, the ship captain secretly delivers a female robot to the prisoner. At first he rejects her as a "machine." However, later he begins to relate to what he takes to be the robot's "feelings," and the robot begins to mirror his mannerisms and sayings.

He falls in love with the robot, and one day the ship captain unexpectedly shows up and tells the prisoner he has been pardoned. The ship is there to bring him back to Earth; however, they must leave immediately, and given concerns over space and fuel, the prisoner cannot take anything with him. Suddenly the prisoner does not want to leave the prison because he loves the robot, and cannot take it with him.

As if interrogating the surreal nature of loving relations, the prisoner insists that the captain doesn't understand the robot in the way that he does. However, the ship captain shoots the robot, exposing its internal wires, and the prisoner reluctantly boards the ship attempting to assure himself that she was just a machine and her personality was a figment of his imagination. This episode produces an experience of the uncanny in its viewers by interrogating the sense in which a "love" relation depends on the imagination while simultaneously constraining it. The robot is in fact a robot, and the prisoner's love may, in fact, be true love; however, if it is real true love, then what is the surreal truth of love?

The episodes "Miniature" and "The Sixteen-Millimeter Shrine," both explore the question of to what extent we can "live" in our imagination, especially in light of the surrealist idea that doing so is always already the case and inevitable. In "Miniature," dollhouse figurines "come to life," and in "The Sixteen-Millimeter Shrine," an aging movie star refuses to perceive herself in terms of her present bodily condition, rather watching movies of herself from her youth, imagining that everything and everyone from that point in time have remained the same—herself included. This relation to a surreal dimension of imagination unbound by rationality or the perspectives and perceptions of others is also explored in "A Stop at Willoughby," which portrays an executive under significant work pressure as he gains access to a tranquil town from the 1880s through his dreams. Just as in the other cases, the episode produces an experience of the uncanny in television viewers as they recognize the manner in which the "worlds" of their unbound imagination may be preferable to the constraints of "waking life," while witnessing these characters choose to inhabit them.

3
The Short-Sightedness of Henry Bemis

ALAN PICHANICK

"Time Enough at Last" is one of the most beloved episodes of the *Twilight Zone*. Marc Scott Zicree in *The Twilight Zone Companion* said that "few can watch it and not be seduced by its simplicity and its pathos." And although its story is set almost sixty years ago, the story of Henry Bemis has even more to tell audiences today about our relationships with each other and our ambivalence towards technology, an ambivalence that results—only and ironically—in self-destruction.

The episode is so moving, at least in part, because we all share Henry Bemis's desire for time to ourselves. But who among us is not horrified by the perverse gratification of that desire—to be abandoned in a world of such extreme loneliness that we cease to even recognize ourselves? The episode puts forth a tragic choice for viewers to ponder. Do we accept our social and technological world for what it is, even with the limitations it places upon our freedom? Or should we withdraw from this world in order to achieve liberation? Part of the brilliance of the episode consists in its unwillingness to provide a solution to this problem. In *The Twilight Zone*, the discovery of the problem may result, at best, in an ultimately fearful self-knowledge.

Henry Bemis's Wish for Time

At the beginning of the episode, Henry Bemis is a man surrounded by nothing but time and other people. His only wish, however, is that time be his only companion so that he may immerse himself in his books unhindered by the demands of his boss and his wife.

We're introduced to Henry Bemis and his comically thick glasses in the opening scene of the episode. Working as a teller at a bank, Bemis counts out money for a customer. But he's far more interested in asking her whether she has read *David Copperfield*. Bemis wants to discuss the story with her but she is only concerned that he has, in his distracted state, shortchanged her *again*. Bemis politely corrects his error, but he does not even notice when she has left. He is too enthralled with the story he is trying to discuss with her. It seems that Bemis cares more about the people in his books than the people right in front of him.

When his boss calls him in to his office to reprimand him, we get Rod Serling's opening narration:

> *Witness Mr. Henry Bemis, a charter member in the fraternity of dreamers. A bookish little man whose passion is the printed page, but who is conspired against by a bank president and a wife and a world full of tongue-cluckers and the unrelenting hands of a clock. But in just a moment, Mr. Bemis will enter a world without bank presidents or wives or clocks or anything else. He'll have a world all to himself . . . without anyone.*

Serling's narration spells out both Bemis's wish and the obstacles to its fulfillment. Henry Bemis is a "dreamer" whose "passion is the printed page." Unfortunately for Henry Bemis, there are those that conspire against him. A bank president. His wife. A world full of tongue-cluckers. And most interestingly, "the unrelenting hands of a clock."

Henry Bemis is trapped in a world in which time marches on under the control of others. His wish is not only to pursue his favorite activity. He wants time to be his. But in *The Twilight Zone* such a seemingly innocent and universally human wish is shown to have terrifying consequences to those, like Henry Bemis, who are short-sighted. The short-sighted wish to have time all to himself will turn out to result in his own destruction.

The Cage of the Bank

When the Bank President calls him in to his office, this exchange takes place:

MR. CARSVILLE: You, Mr. Bemis, are a reader!

HENRY BEMIS: A reader?

MR. CARSVILLE: A reader! A reader of books, magazines, periodicals, newspapers! I see you constantly going downstairs into the vault during your lunch hour. [*Bemis tries to sit down, but Carsville slams on the desk.*]

MR. CARSVILLE: An ultimatum, Mr. Bemis! You will henceforth devote time to your job and forget reading or you'll find yourself outdoors on a park bench reading from morning to night for want of having a job! Do I make myself perfectly clear?

HENRY BEMIS: Oh, that's perfectly clear, sir, it's just that . . .

MR. CARSVILLE: [*interrupting*] "Just that" what, Bemis? Make it quick and get back to your cage!

HENRY BEMIS: [*sitting down*] It's just that my wife won't let me read at home. See, when I get home at night and try to pick up a newspaper, she yanks it out of my hand! And then after dinner, if I try to find a magazine, she hides them. Well, I got so desperate I found myself trying to read the labels on the condiment bottles on the table. Now, she won't even let me use the ketchup.

MR. CARSVILLE: [*smiling*] Unasked, I give my reaction to this: your wife is an amazingly bright woman.

Carsville is actually right, though he doesn't know it. Bemis will end up outdoors without a job, because he is reading in the vault when everyone else is destroyed by a nuclear explosion. He is also right to call Bemis's workspace a "cage." The way Bemis sees things, his job is a prison in which his time is not his own. His books are his only world in which he is not at the whim of others. None of this concerns Mr. Carsville. The bank president stands first and foremost for the efficient progress of work in the corporate world, which Bemis would slow down with his isolated, nonproductive reading. Intellectual labor, unless it makes a profit, is of no value here.

But there's an important sense in which Mr. Carsville has misunderstood Henry Bemis. Bemis's desire to read is not pure misanthropy, nor is it complete disengagement from the world. His desire to talk to his customer about *David Copperfield* is a desire for companionship. His interest in books also reveals an interest in the lives of other people. He not only reads poetry and literature, but also newspapers, magazines, and what's printed on the ketchup bottle! Henry Bemis is not a hater of human beings. It's only the people in front of him—with their shallow and vain pursuits—who disappoint him.

Unfortunately, for Henry Bemis, his home is only another prison where this holds true.

The Cage of Henry's Marriage

Henry sits in his comfy chair trying to read the newspaper only to be interrupted by his wife, screaming "HEN-RYYYYYYYY!" She then storms into the living room to snatch the newspaper from his hands and announce: "I won't tolerate a husband of mine sacrificing the art of conversation."

Time is Henry Bemis's enemy in his house, just as it is in the bank. But in the bank it is because time marches on towards a more efficient and productive future which Henry impedes. Henry's reading presents a different problem at home. His reading, apparently, is an obstacle to the demands of polite society—at least according to his wife. His time is the property of others, who expect and demand that he conform to their wishes.

The best Henry can do is respond with a submissive "Yes, dear" and attempt to smuggle a book of modern poetry into his jacket pocket to yet another insufferable dinner party. But his wife has outsmarted him this time. She has crossed out all the words in this volume, making it impossible to read and she joyfully brings this fact to Henry's attention as they get ready to leave the house. Her action is beyond cruel.

Henry's glasses, his thick comical spectacles, fall from his face to the floor as he drops the book and then gathers up the damaged text. He replaces his glasses upon his face and can only ask his wife why she has done this. She responds, "Because I am married to a fool."

Ironically and tragically, in the closing scene, foreshadowed here, Henry Bemis *will* turn out to be a fool. But it will only be after he gets his wish that his foolishness will be exposed. Henry Bemis's only wish—to be away from his boss, his wife, and the unrelenting clock—will now be granted. And the cold universe in which such a wish is granted will make Henry Bemis wish for the former cruelty of his wife.

The Despair of the Sole Survivor

Henry gets his wish at the bank the following day. Henry locks himself in the vault to eat his lunch and read by himself. The headline on his newspaper reads:

H-BOMB CAPABLE OF TOTAL DESTRUCTION

As Henry Bemis looks down at his pocket-watch, it suddenly shatters. A powerful image. Time as he has known it has now stopped. The pages of the book he has brought fly open. Another suggestive image. This perhaps is the beginning of Henry Bemis's new story. An explosion shakes the walls of the bank, knocking him unconscious.

When he comes to, his glasses barely hanging on his face, he exits the vault to discover the desolate devastation of a wasteland left by a nuclear explosion. He quickly discovers that he is the sole survivor. He searches for others and screams for his wife. It is telling that his first response to this nuclear holocaust is a horror at being alone. He does not celebrate the destruction of everyone around him, but spends almost the rest of the episode in disquieting fear. Rod Serling narrates:

> Seconds, minutes, hours. They crawl by on hands and knees for Mr. Henry Bemis, who looks for a spark in the ashes of a dead world: A telephone connected to nothingness; a neighborhood bar, a movie, a baseball diamond, a hardware store, the mailbox at what was once his house and is now rubble. They lie at his feet as battered monuments to what was but is no more. Mr. Henry Bemis on an eight-hour tour of a graveyard.

Time is now all Henry Bemis has. His wish for time away from the boss, the wife, the tongue-cluckers, even the unrelenting clock itself, has not resulted in the dream of solitude for which he yearned. It's a horrific nightmare. When he realizes that his lucky reading break in the bank vault saved him from the fate that has come to everyone else, he says, "The thing of it is . . . I'm not at all sure that I want to be alive."

After this, Bemis finds enough food to eat. A temporary relief. For his survival will be plagued by a painful loneliness. As Henry gets ready to go to sleep, he takes off his glasses and he says to himself:

> The very worst part is being alone. Is this how it's going to be? Sitting around day after day? Eating, smoking, reading the same half of a newspaper . . . over and over . . . over and over . . . [*he drifts off to sleep*]

Bemis has left his previous cages only to find himself in another. With no wife and no boss and no other people, he's now a prisoner to time's monotonous self-repetition. Now that time is all he has, everything will be the same "over and over and over and over." Such sameness terrifies him into exhaustion.

When he wakes, his hope is briefly restored by his discovery of a car, but this hope is also dashed when it won't start. He now must convince himself that his loneliness is not a reason for despair. It is instead, he reasons aloud to nobody, the very solitude he always wanted.

> This is solitude. I've never had much solitude. I have enough to occupy my mind and my time. I have enough food. And I am really very fortunate.

But it is clear that he is not persuading himself. Bemis becomes more and more panicked the longer he thinks about his new "solitude," especially when he realizes how little he has to "occupy his time." Bemis quickly begins calling "HELP!" and runs haphazardly through the wasteland as it dawns upon him that his solitude is a lonely prison, where time is his only companion.

In his running about, he stumbles upon a revolver. He is now ready to kill himself.

> "If it weren't for the loneliness. If it weren't for the sameness. If there were something to do."

The monotonous self-repetition of time is more frightening and unbearable than death itself. This is the result of Henry Bemis's wish and his lucky lunch break in the bank vault. He points the revolver at his head and sends out a final hopeful prayer in this desolate wasteland, "I know I will be forgiven for this." Is there a god in this barren world? If there is, it is a cruel one. For just as Bemis is ready to kill himself he sees the toppled sign for the PUBLIC LIBRARY.

A Prayer Answered?

As soon as Henry Bemis sees the sign for the library he drops the revolver and runs up the steps of the now decimated structure, in glee. "Books! Books! All the books I'll ever want!" he says, as he discovers volumes and volumes to read. Arranging his books into piles, Bemis is able to reassert his power over time.

> [*pointing at the various piles*] "January, February, March, April . . . This year, the next year . . ."

Time no longer threatens him with a monotonous, meaningless, repetitive sameness. Henry Bemis is finally happy. He looks lovingly at the giant clock lying on the library steps and talks with it like a newfound friend. Embracing the clock, he says:

> "And the best thing is there is time now, all the time I need, all the time I want. Time, Time, Time. There's time enough at last."

Henry Bemis has experienced all previous time as slavery. The clock of the bank sacrifices Bemis's freedom to the efficient march of corporate progress. The clock of his home sacrifices his freedom to his wife's social demands and expectations. And the clock of a lonely, lifeless world sacrifices his freedom to the meaningless repetition of a machinelike existence.

Time spent reading is the only time that allows him to engage with the world without letting the world dominate him, and to reassert his identity and humanity. The discovery of the books answers his prayers by restoring meaning, identity, and freedom to Henry Bemis. But in *The Twilight Zone,* his prayer has not been fully answered.

The Tragic Short-Sightedness of Henry Bemis

Henry Bemis spies one more book lying just below where he sits on the steps. He bends over to pick it up. As he does so, his glasses fall from his face. Bemis gropes about to find them and replaces them on his face, but he discovers they are now shattered, like his pocket-watch that shattered as a result of the explosion. Bemis cannot see. The camera reveals to us what the world looks like through Henry Bemis's eyes. Everything is a blur.

It's not just that Henry Bemis can't read his books. It's not only that Henry Bemis can't see. The possibility of any meaning—meaning that had just been restored moments ago—has been taken away from him. He cannot, in this condition, even choose to take the action of ending his own life as he could moments before discovering the library.

The problem is not that Henry Bemis is now blind. He is now, without his glasses, "in a world all to himself . . . without anyone", as Rod Serling said in his opening narration. Up until this moment Bemis's glasses connected him to whatever was left of his relation to other human beings and, as a piece of technology itself, the glasses allowed him to immerse himself in books. Books written by other people about other people. But now, Henry Bemis is finally himself by himself without a world of others and removed from the last piece of technology connecting him to it. Earlier states of crippled freedom seem like complete liberation in comparison to the prison he is now in.

What viewer cannot feel deep, overwhelming pity for Henry Bemis as he stares out and says:

"That's not fair. That's not fair at all. There was time now . . ."

Recall that this is the second time Henry Bemis's glasses have fallen from his face. The earlier moment occurred when his wife had crossed out the text in his book of modern poetry, rendering it illegible. Then he asked, "Why do you do these things?" And he received an answer (perhaps an unsatisfactory one), but an answer nonetheless: "Because I am married to a fool."

But now Henry Bemis does not even ask why this has happened. There is no one to plead his case to. He has already made his prayer and this blindness is his answer. Now without his glasses, he sees for the first time most clearly the nature of the world and his place in it. We human beings do not grasp the whole of things. We are all short-sighted when it comes to the consequences of our actions and our dependence on other human beings and our technology. Most short-sighted among us are those who think we can completely remove ourselves from such dependence. Consider Rod Serling's closing narration:

> *The best laid plans of mice and men. . . and Henry Bemis . . . the small man in the glasses who wanted nothing but time. Henry Bemis, now just a part of a smashed landscape, just a piece of the rubble, just a fragment of what man has deeded to himself. Mr. Henry Bemis . . . in the Twilight Zone.*

Both Henry Bemis and his wife are right. The universe is not fair and he is a fool. But not because he loved books. His foolishness consists in a misanthropic desire for a timeless world to himself.

It turns out that this fantasy is only possible if he excepts himself from his position within the technological system. It's only because Henry forgets that his very vision is dependent on society that he can reject society. But he does so only at his own peril. In achieving his wish he himself becomes "a fragment of what man has deeded to himself."

Henry Bemis's fate certainly prompts us to question how much reliance we should or can place on technology in our information age if we hope to forestall becoming such fragmented versions of ourselves. Yet at the same time it leaves us uncomfortably uncertain about whether we should or can reject the technological system and world of others in which we are embedded as human beings.

Many viewers have commented about the fate of Henry Bemis (perhaps half-jokingly) that it made them always carry around a second pair of glasses. But a serious problem remains here. Henry Bemis's desire for freedom is one we should and do recognize. Can we satisfy that desire with yet another technological solution? The episode does not give us an answer, but it does frighten us with the horrifying choice: either we accept that time is not ours or time may end up being our only companion. It seems therefore that the solution for us is not a technological one, but a philosophical one. It requires not another pair of glasses but a new kind, a kind of glasses that foster clear vision of our possibilities, limits, and dependence on one another. Only with such glasses can we possibly prevent—if we can—the calamity that befalls the short-sighted Henry Bemis.

4
Faces from Another Dimension

ALEXANDER E. HOOKE

> The being that presents himself in the face comes from a dimension of height, a dimension of transcendence whereby he can present himself as a stranger without opposing me as obstacle or enemy.
> —EMMANUEL LEVINAS, *Totality and Infinity*, p. 215

Viewers do not meet a face for almost the entire episode of "The Eye of the Beholder." We hear voices and sounds of an operating room. We see backs or shadows of doctors and nurses, with recognizable human heads focused on a patient.

The patient's face is also hidden, wrapped by layers of bandages. Her gestures and voice indicate both hope and fear. For this is her eleventh and last operation allowed by the state in order to change a mistake made by nature. The patient was born with a deformed face. And if this fails, she will be exiled to a place with other humans who are the unfortunate victims of nature's mistakes.

At last the bandages are slowly unwrapped. Viewers, doctors, nurses, and the patient anxiously await the result. The patient looks into the mirror and shrieks—another failure! But for viewers this is impossible. By any measure the patient is beautiful—how can she be shrieking when seeing these results? Then the camera turns to her medical attendants. They have piglike faces, but so distorted and hideous that it is an insult to pigs to describe their faces in this way. And yet, in their world such faces must resemble the standard and reflect the sense of normality. The concluding twist is disturbing and unforgettable to anyone who sees this episode for the first time.

It is not just the twist of juxtaposition between the patient's lovely look and the scrunched depictions of her well-intentioned medical attendants. What is also unforgettable is our response to the characters' own disturbed faces in *The Twilight Zone*. When they close an episode with the look of dread, despair, mockery, or hope, we viewers respond with a smirk, smile, laughter, or a sense of human absurdity.

We are not the woman horrified by her face and imminent exile. We are not the medical staff staring in dismay because they are unable to correct this deformity of nature. As viewers, and as human beings in everyday life, our attention to other faces is often mundane and matter of fact. But there are times when another's face captures our imaginations and sparks our thoughts. These times can be found in some of the most memorable episodes of *The Twilight Zone*.

The Face in Philosophy

The status and significance of the face has drawn considerable philosophical discussion. Søren Kierkegaard pondered the possible anxiety of the knight of faith, such as Abraham's look while preparing to sacrifice his son Isaac due to a divine command. Jean-Paul Sartre contemplated the existential gaze or look humans exchanged with one another—from waiters and rebels to seducers and antisemites—insofar as their authenticity or freedom was in question. Simone de Beauvoir extended this gaze to the faces of those who are elderly or relegated to the second sex in order to uncover fundamental attitudes of modern culture.

Probably the most extensive focus over the past thirty years on the significant and varied existential responses to the face has appeared in the writings of American philosopher Alphonso Lingis. The chief English translator of Levinas, whose analysis of the face was an undeniable influence, Lingis's own works incorporate meditations on as-if-you-are-there descriptions of other individuals. His writings often begin with a direct photo of other human beings. Their faces emerge from all parts of the planets. Their faces reveal stories of passions, ideals, suffering, joy, absurdity, and courage. They convey and incite thoughts about truth, beauty and goodness. Through photographs and written words, Lingis emphasizes our response to these faces as a key philosophical moment.

Through television, *The Twilight Zone*'s creator Rod Serling extends these responses to still further surprising and disturbing situations. Marc Scott Zicree's *The Twilight Zone Companion* is especially helpful here, as he often includes snapshots of the varied faces in the episodes. This allows us a chance to look at them more carefully, which an initial TV viewing usually precludes. Serling's range of faces are also haunting. The other dimensions present faces of aliens who want to eat us, robots that seduce us, grim reapers who befriend us, casino machines that beckon us. We see more than simply a panorama of faces as if strolling through a museum of portraits or a neighbor's photos from a recent trip. We are captivated by our unexpected responses to fantastic or perplexing situations that other humans are confronting. In the words of its creator Rod Serling, "*The Twilight Zone* is about people—about human beings involved in extraordinary circumstances, in strange problems of their own or of fate's making" (*Twilight Zone Companion*, p. 96).

The face immediately comprises vivid and memorable aspects of the physical: nose, eyes, mouth, hair, jaw, as well as the joyful smile or the saddened frown. It also presents a distinct experience, one in which we are welcomed or contested and begin to learn some of the mysteries of another. To face someone or face up to the facts implies that "face" initiates an active and uncertain moment. Paramount for Lingis is how the question of trust arises when we first meet a strange face.

Most of the time we look at one another as interchangeable or anonymous figures. To really encounter another face is to prepare ourselves to trust the unknown—possible lover or friend, potential partner or collaborator. For Lingis this dimension is embodied by the face-to-face encounter. *The Twilight Zone* illuminates faces that at first resemble those in this dimension, but as we soon discover they are from another dimension, one that often teaches a harsh lesson about trust.

Duped by the Faces of Death and Satan

How do we portray death, Satan, aliens, and monsters? Which sensations warn us that evil and its cousins are lurking about?

The horned serpent, with long tail and little demons dancing on his shoulder, dwelling in the raging fires of Hell, has long been an enduring image of the Devil. Berndt Lotke, in his depictions of the dance of death, shows skeletons prancing around and mocking royalty and the devout. In his histories of death that depict the manifestations of the Devil, Philippe Aries describes horrific images, such as those found on gravestones, church murals, or the paintings of Hieronymus Bosch. From these accounts we witness serpents and monsters who feast on the flesh and violate the bodies of human beings.

In this light consider how *The Twilight Zone* ingeniously masks the figures who rank among the greatest human nemeses. Serling presents the faces of Robert Redford, Sebastian Cabot, Jonathan Winters, and Anne Francis, among many notable actors. From other television programs or movies we have already learned to trust their welcome faces, a trust *The Twilight Zone* mocks and undermines. We discover that the young and handsome Redford is the face of death, the avuncular Sabot's humor betrays the face of Satan, Winter's witty and charming look conceals devilish mischief, and Francis's sullen beauty is actually the face of a witch.

Some case studies. "Nothing in the Dark" introduces an aging Wanda Dunn. Her entire neighborhood has been abandoned. She's the only tenant left, and refuses to open her front door out of fear of the Grim Reaper. In the wintry snow, she hears groaning outside the front door. It doesn't go away and she can't help but open the door to make the noise stop. Instead, she finds a young, vulnerable, and attractive man (Robert Redford) who seems to be gasping his last breaths. He pleads for her to let him escape the bitter cold. She finally relents.

A contractor soon arrives, ready to demolish the woman's tenement with the rest of the abandoned abodes. This is like nature, his analogy contends, where the old trees fall in order to make way for the new trees. At first the old woman despises the contractor as the satanic destroyer. But no, she turns to the young man she saved from the fatal freeze. Surely he is strong and clever enough to save her. Then she realizes her mistake—his handsome features turn into the face of death.

"A Nice Place to Visit" presents an array of appealing and dubious faces. First is the culprit of the episode, a petty thief named Rocky who was shot to death while attempting to escape the police. The story-line is fairly basic in *Twilight Zone* terms. A dead person obtains an afterlife, albeit unsure where. He is introduced to Pip, an avuncular, chubby, smiling and gentle gray-bearded man (played by the endearing Sebastian Cabot.). Who could not trust this guy? Pip will be Rocky's guide to satisfying his post-worldly desires. Rocky wants the same as he wanted on earth without the painful side-effects.

So Pip grants Rocky's every wish. He wins every game at the casino, captures the fancy of every woman he meets and draws the envy of his compatriots. Heaven on earth, Rocky concludes. Then he realizes how boring it is to have every desire met. Victories are guaranteed rather than won by skill or smarts. The beauties soon stir no more passion than sitting next to mannequins. If this is heaven, Rocky concludes, perhaps he might take a chance on the other place. The rejoinder from Pip is abrupt and strangely bemused. "This is the other place!" Pip then bursts with a hearty laugh, and the moment we viewers get it we laugh too. Thus the insidious power of *The Twilight Zone*: it has us laughing with the Devil.

"Jess-Belle" echoes the traditional folk or fairy tale. Serling's opening introduction captures a tradition of story telling that keeps the audience in suspense. It is tantalizing and haunting at the same time. Serling begins, "The Twilight Zone has existed in many lands, in many times. It has its roots in history, in something that happened a long, long ago and got told about and handed from generation of folk to the other." If he were the Brothers Grimm, this could just as well have been "Once upon a time in a faraway land, there lived . . ."

The faraway land here is a remote valley in the Blue Ridge Mountains. A young man named Billy-Ben falls in love with a farmer's daughter and wants to marry her. Jess-Belle has other ideas and seeks Billy-Ben's amorous attention. She enlists the help of an old lady, Granny Hart, rumored to be a witch, for a magical love potion to turn Billy-Ben's focus to her. It works. Alas, Jess-Belle winds up selling her soul to the old lady and becomes a witch herself. She now wants to die, no matter who loves whom. Granny's consoling words are striking, "Why, you're looking at it all wrong. Be a witch. Take a witch's pleasure. Take the man you bargained for—*give him witch's love!*"

Love thy neighbor as thyself, encourages the Bible and most sacred texts. Careful, cautions the Twilight Zone. We often love the neighbor who, it turns out, is the face of the Grim Reaper or the Devil.

Proof of Trust

Trust is a bond that attaches to a singular individual. We trust someone who affirms something though we do not see or cannot understand the evidence or the proof this person may have: we trust the person.

—ALPHONSO LINGIS, *The First Person Singular*, p. 77

Many of us are convinced of our ability to accurately read another's face. Given Skype, Facebook, PhotoShop, Date Lab, among so many other sites of social media, the tradition of the face-to-face interview should be regarded as an outdated ritual and waste of time, money, and energy. It is not, since the live interview remains an essential part of recruiting, hiring and selecting other individuals to join us at work, play or romance.

Lingis's epigraph evokes moments when we trust another without any reassurance from rational investigation. Trust can be a leap into the unknown. But many people insist there is a correlation between knowing someone and trusting someone. Only after critical thinking and emotional deliberation of another's face do we decide to trust. As *Homo sapiens,* we insist on proof so that we can wisely choose and calmly address our interests and emotions.

Enter the Kanamits. They arrive from a distant planet in a saucer-like space ship. As they begin descending, the earthlings fear an invasion. Everyone is ordered to seek shelter while the military is alerted for immediate preparation to strike the aliens before they strike us. A war seems inevitable.

As presented in the episode "To Serve Man," the Kanamits emerge from their vehicle with simple clothing, gentle eyes, a sheepish grin, quite human-like except for their huge foreheads that make them eight or nine feet tall. They communicate via mental telepathy, but can emulate the human voice when meeting their hosts. The one who approaches the Earthlings is quite gentle, soft-spoken, assuring his hosts that he means no harm.

To the contrary, these aliens want to provide for their hosts: end their wars, prevent famines, and resolve human disputes amicably. After all the promises of Plato, holy messiahs, Karl Marx, or romantic naturalists, these Earthlings are finally experiencing the true taste of utopia. No need for police or farmers. Now neighbors greet each other cheerfully and everyone can eat as much tasty food as they desire. They are tranquil, laughing and living high off the hog.

The Earthlings are soon invited to the Kanamits' planet. Though at first suspicious, they now anticipate the latest benevolence from their new-found alien friends. So excited for an even more pleasurable utopia, long lines begin forming at the space ship to whisk insatiable Earthlings to the other planet. Clearly, most of us would count this as proof of trust.

Two scientists and linguists remain suspicious. They happen upon a Kanamit book, but find it nearly impossible to translate. After many hours of hard work, at last they believe the book's title is *To Serve Man*. The male scientist is satisfied and heads for the space ship to join the others eager to depart. The female scientist stays focused and finally learns the book's contents. She runs to the ship's stairway and shouts to her colleague: "*To Serve Man* is a cookbook!" Too late. The Kanamits are already pushing him into their flying saucer. Soon he will be their dinner.

A second twist on proof of trust appears in the initial season's first episode, "The Lonely." Corry is condemned to another planet for fifty years for murder. Serling asks us to "witness if you will a man's mind and body, shriveling in the sun, a man dying of loneliness." He is left a package by a crew that visits him twice a year, only long enough to play a game or two of checkers. He reads the directions and assembles a figure that looks like and talks like a woman, named Alicia. She (it?) seems gentle and caring, trying to engage Corry's attention while ending his loneliness. He loudly objects that he will have none of this trickery with a mere robot. Then Alicia sheds a tear. For me, this moment changes everything.

Suddenly they become the proverbial "two peas in pod." They take walks, talk about this and that, play games and enjoy silent sunsets together. Distrust is replaced by trust. If we were to apply the Turing test (humans trying to distinguish human from artificial intelligence), it is clear that Corry and Alicia are in love, regardless of the organs or hardware that lies beneath their surfaces. Soon Corry learns that he is pardoned for a crime he knew he did not commit. He can return to Earth, but the space ship is not big enough to carry Alicia. If you were Corry, what would you decide?

(Parenthetical aside. Here I do not want to divulge the ending. Watch this episode and discover the conclusion on your own. Consider Corry's options. I showed this to my students and they were as startled by the ending as I was when first seeing it. In writing about these episodes, I—and all my fellow contributors to this project—have the luxury of revisiting them and experiencing them differently than the first time. Whether it is a song, poem, movie, novel, or TV show, the first encounter can be so surprising and intense that later viewings can never match it. Yet to revisit them is to re-experience and rethink them. Somehow, some works, such as "To Serve Man" and "The Lonely", are among those that offer fresh insight even from a fourth or fifth encounter.)

Here *The Twilight Zone* is perhaps most prophetic. "The Lonely" was first broadcast in November 1959. Today there are serious and extensive debates about the future relationships between robots (machines with artificial intelligence that physically resemble human beings) and ourselves. A recent book, *Robot Sex,* is a collection of articles by scholars and researchers discussing whether human-like robots actually can express emotions, fall in love, be physically or sexually violated, have rights such as those articulated in the Bill of Rights. They address whether a robot could have more intrinsic value than a thug or terrorist, or be a companion to elderly residents in nursing homes or patients recovering in a hospital.

Rod Serling might be credited as one of the first to explore this theme in a variety of ways that encompass ordinary human life. "The Mighty Casey" presents a robot baseball pitcher who overwhelms all the batters with strikeouts and weak fly balls. Then someone tries giving Casey a heart, and suddenly he throws lollipops so the batters can crush the ball. "The Elegy" plays on the illusions of dealing with people unsure whether they are encountering real or robotic humans.

"The Fever" highlights the smarts of a slot machine. Franklin and his wife are in Las Vegas for their wedding anniversary vacation. Franklin is miserable from the start, particularly disgusted with all the lights and sounds of these money-grabbing machines. In a moment of weakness, he drops a coin into the slot. He wins a jackpot. Immediately he ignores his wife and is fixed in front of the machine for hours. He loses all his money. He goes to bed, but the machine outsmarts him. Sleeping next to his wife, all he can hear is the machine calling him, "Franklin. Franklin. I miss you." In Serling's narration, this one-armed bandit is a "monster with a will of its own."

Looking for a proof of trust? Don't look into The Twilight Zone. It admonishes us that a proof of trust is nearly impossible to ascertain, even in our own dimension. Serling's radical challenge endures—what's the difference between us and our creations?

The Most Truthful Face—of Love, Trust, and Courage

Trust means seeing what exceeds the possibility of seeing, what is intolerable to see, what exceeds the possibility of thinking.

—ALPHONSO LINGIS, *Trust*, p. 199

A couple married for some fifty years are recognizing the mortal limits in one another. John and Marie Holt have been so happy together for so long. She is getting weaker and more tired while his physical ailments continue to provide increasing pain. They wonder if they can be granted still more joyful times on this planet. Could they be granted that curious and relentless human desire—a rebirth or return to their blissful youth?

The couple meets a salesman from the New Life Corporation. Like a car dealer guaranteeing the durability of a car, the salesman promises John and Marie 112 more years on Earth if they purchase this latest invention. He shows them different models that promise a new beginning. As if taking a spin in a prospective car, the couple can try out their new bodies and, if dissatisfied, return to their own bodies within the week.

Here is a decision or dilemma to be addressed in the episode titled called "The Trade-Ins." The procedure for both costs $10,000, yet they have only $5,000. Marie persuades John to go first. When he returns as a twenty-five-year-old man he can work and save enough money for Marie to also have the procedure. At least, that's the plan.

Johns insists they go together, so he looks for a quick $5,000 at a poker game. The neophyte John loses badly to a circle of regular players. Finally, in five-card stud, John gets three kings, an excellent hand. He goes all in. But another player has three aces. John declares his hand. *Twilight Zone* viewers see the other player's three aces. Poker players are generally a heartless bunch. Surely, we tell ourselves, John goes home having lost all his savings. Not here. All we see is the player folding his three aces and telling John he has won.

Still having his $5,000, John promptly gets the procedure because, according to the salesman, "this special offer" will soon expire. An anxious Marie waits in the lobby. She gets brief updates from one of the medical people; otherwise, she's quite alone. Then John returns as a bustling twenty-five-year-old handsome stud. Offering some cheerful words about how energetic he feels and all the pain is gone, the enthusiasm falls flat. They quickly but silently stare into each other's eyes. We see his vibrant and shiny face, we recognize her wrinkles and now sorrowful eyes. To borrow from the Lingis epigraph above, what they now see in one another is alien, intolerable, and beyond their own possibilities of thought. Their faces recognize without speaking a word that this is not truly "them." John immediately returns to the doctors and is transformed back to his previous self.

The scene closes with John and Marie walking together into the horizon accompanied by Serling's sardonic yet heartfelt final remarks. He cites a passage from Kahlil Gibran about how "love gives not but itself and takes not from itself, love possesses not nor would it be possessed, for love is sufficient unto love.' Not a lesson, just a reminder, from all the sentimentalists in the Twilight Zone."

Postscript

Marc Scott Zicree, thoroughly familiar with Serling's wit, cynicism, and sense of human absurdity, sees "The Trade-Ins" as a "story about love and courage." In more ways than one. Unknown to viewers, the lead male actor playing the aging husband, Joseph Schildkraut, was undergoing his own pain during the filming of this episode. His wife was very sick and died in the middle of production. Upon the sad news, Schildkraut insisted they finish the production. According to the director, Schildkraut's courage and love was remarkable. He played his role impeccably, but after a particular scene, "he was in real tears, off-screen."

The most truthful face: off screen, or on screen—but only in the Twilight Zone.

Second Dimension

Beyond the Boundaries of You and Me

5
True Love or Artificial Love?

CHARLES KLAYMAN

Can loving a robot be true love? At first glance, the question seems simple enough, but it might actually be a spark that ignites even more questions.

Is there a difference between love and true love? What exactly is love—or true love, for that matter? What sort of things can be one's true love? We could ask someone who claims they have true love for a robot and examine that relationship, but I doubt we could find such a person in our present world. Fortunately, we can find such a person who will function as our case study and that person can be found perhaps only in a dimension of things and ideas, in the *Twilight Zone*.

Our Case Study

In the episode "The Lonely" (1959), convicted felon James Corry is serving his sentence alone on a desolate, desert asteroid. Already into his fourth year of a fifty-year sentence, Corry plagued by silence and isolation is racked by loneliness almost to the point of questioning reality. However, he does receive visitors four times a year; the supply ship and its commander, Captain Allenby who is sympathetic to Corry's plight. Besides supplies and news, Allenby brings items like books and mechanical parts to tinker with, to help Corry pass the time and ease his isolation. With no word of a pardon, Allenby secretly brings Corry an entirely different item, a robot.

The robot has the physical appearance of a human woman including flesh, hair, and breath. "To all intent and purpose this"—the robot named Alicia—"is a woman. Physiologically and psychologically she is a human being with a set of emotions, a memory track, the ability to reason, to think, and to speak" ("The Lonely"). Corry at first rejects Alicia, seeing her as a farce until tears stream down her face and she claims "I can feel loneliness, too" ("The Lonely"). It seemed Corry was fascinated with Alicia's humanlike functionality. Yet over time he no longer feels lonely and although he is fully aware of Alicia's nature, he claims "I love Alicia. Nothing else matters" ("The Lonely"). At the end, Corry receives a pardon but cannot take Alicia back to Earth; there is no room on the ship and the departure time is quickly approaching. Despite Corry's passionate protestations that Alicia is a woman, Allenby shoots her, which not only exposes Alicia's innards of wires and circuits, but also ends her existence and resolves the conflict.

Was Corry's love for Alicia true love? If it was, then it was a tragic affair. If it wasn't, then what was it? To investigate this matter, an analysis of love is required in order to articulate what "true love" is. Ultimately, if I'm correct, then Corry's love was not true love but something else entirely.

Qualities of Love

Figuring out what love is might be a daunting task since love comes in a variety of forms. Luckily for us in his book *The Four Loves,* philosopher C.S. Lewis (1898–1963) classified four general types of love, which are *charity, affection, friendship*, and *Eros* or romantic love. Before delving into each type, it is important to point out that all types of love have common qualities in one degree or another. Those qualities are *gift-love*, which is an offering to the beloved; *need-love*, which is needing something from the beloved; and *appreciative-love*. These qualities may manifest differently for different types of love.

Consider a song you might love. Gift-love manifests when the song comes on the radio and you *give* it your attention. In fact, you might give it so much attention that you memorize the lyrics. Yet, you may *need* it so much that you purchase a recording of it or there might be a time when you have an urge to listen it. It goes without saying that you *appreciate* the song, that you judge it to be a very good song.

Now consider a mother and her son. She does the laundry and cleans the home not because she finds those chores exhilarating or fears that dirty clothes and a dirty home would give her a bad image, nor does she expect anything in return like payment. Instead, her motivation comes from her love for her son; it is her love that compels her to do those chores in order to *give* her son clean clothes and a clean home. While she may seem domineering or nosy when she asks where he is going for the night, it is her love that prompts her *need* to know so she may ascertain his safety or more likely, to ease her conscience since she does not want to lose him.

However, the qualities of love are not without their pitfalls. For gift-love, we might give too much, which might not only leave us exhausted but may also motivate us to give up our very own lives. For need-love, the need might be so extreme that it develops into a poisonous, selfish obsession. Finally, for appreciative-love, the love may be so strong that it distorts our perception to the point we believe our beloved can do no wrong.

Types of Love

If the three qualities of love are evident in Corry's relationship with Alicia, then it shows that he loved her but it does not indicate the type of love nor does it tell us if it was *true love*.

One form of love, *charity,* is fundamentally an expansion of gift-love. For Lewis, charity or rather "Divine Gift-love in the man enables him to love what is naturally lovable; lepers, criminals, enemies, morons, the sulky, the superior and the sneering" (*The Four Loves*, p. 177). While Lewis further explained charity by referring to the Christian God, such an elaboration is not necessary for our purposes. It is enough to say that charity is a general form of love where the beloved is not a particular person, but rather it is the whole of humanity, which is appreciated or valued as very good. Gift-love may manifest as a need to do, say, volunteer work or to contribute to a charity for the betterment of humanity. Need-love may manifest as a need to serve the general populace in order to identify oneself as a humanitarian, as having a kinship with the rest of humanity.

The second type, *affection*, has familiarity or accustomedness as its basis. The beloved might be a jacket often worn or a restaurant visited frequently. However, "Change is a threat to Affection" (p. 70). If my favorite restaurant changed its menu, I might be upset or confused because I grew so accustomed or habituated to the previous menu that I expected to see the same items. Gift-love may manifest as a need to contribute to the maintenance of the routine or the familiarity. If my favorite jacket is torn and unwearable, I may give it my attention and mend it. Need-love may manifest as the need to keep the routine. Even if my jacket is no longer wearable, I may claim that I need it and refuse to throw it away.

The next type, *friendship,* is based on a common view, belief, or interest. Yet it is important to note that for Lewis, there is a distinction between friendship and companionship. On the one hand, friendship is based on a shared way of seeing and caring about the same truth (p. 99). On the other, companionship is based on the instinct to co-operate. All friends are necessarily companions, but not all companions are necessarily friends. Nevertheless, companions can become friends. Companionship is not a type of love, but it has the potential to become a type of love that is friendship. Gift-love may manifest as the need to give moral support or aid. Need-love may manifest as the need to have one's way of seeing the world validated.

The last type, *Eros* or romantic love, is primarily mental. That is to say, romantic love is the state of being in love and not based upon sexual desire or per Lewis's terminology, *Venus* that is the same sort of sexual desire experienced by animals (p. 131). I am not saying that *Eros* and *Venus* are not connected, but rather *Eros* does not develop from *Venus*. Romantic love starts from a certain mental state or preoccupation where the important aspect of the beloved is not their gender but their unique self or rather the "real them" (p. 33). In other words, romantic love develops from a fascination with a specific, irreplaceable individual person or self. While "one of the first things *Eros* does is to obliterate the distinction between giving and receiving," the qualities still manifest (p. 137). Gift-love may manifest as giving affection, support, or even one's own life to the beloved. Need-love might manifest as a need simply to be in the beloved's presence.

The categories Lewis provided are broad ones that are not mutually exclusive. It is possible—and it is often the case—that the object of one type of love is the same object of another type of love. Additionally, one type of love may cease and become another type of love. Affection may turn into friendship, and friendship may turn into *Eros*.

True Love

What is meant by "true love?" If it means "to love truly" or "truly love," then that implies a love that is genuine. While a person might claim they truly love their beloved, the claim alone is not enough to justify that their love is genuine, that they are sincere and not making an empty claim. If a person's own testimony is not enough to convince us of their sincerity, then perhaps the *pragmatic maxim* may be instrumental. Developed by the American philosopher Charles Sanders Peirce (1839–1914), the maxim is a way to think about the meaning of concepts. In his essay "How to Make Our Ideas Clear," Peirce advised:

> Consider what effects, which might conceivably have practical bearings, we conceive the object of our conception to have. Then, our conception of these effects is the whole of our conception of the object. (p. 132)

If someone claims that they "truly love," we only need to consider their claim and the practical effects of "truly loving," which is to say how it manifests in the world. The meaning of a concept is the assemblage of its practical effects. For example, if I claim "I truly love the song 'This Old Man'," but then I am indifferent or ignore it entirely when it comes on the radio or refuse to have a recording of it, then my claim turned out to be meaningless. If I truly love that song, I may sing it in the shower or download it as my ringtone. The collection of practical effects—singing it in the shower and having it as my ringtone—is the meaning of "truly loving a song." In other words, to truly love a song means singing it in the shower, having it as a ringtone, and so forth.

Yet does "true love" mean "to love truly?" On the one hand, it seems appropriate to say "I truly love 'This Old Man,'" but on the other it does not seem appropriate to say "My true love is 'This Old Man.'" So, "true love" is not equivalent to "truly love." However, since "true love" is true, it requires sincerity; sincerity is a necessary element of true love, but it is not sufficient. If "true love" was insincere, then it would be false love and "true love" that is false is not love at all.

It seems inappropriate to say "My true love is 'This Old Man'" because the relationship is nonreciprocal, which is to say only one party exhibits the three qualities. While I exhibit gift-love, need-love, and appreciative-love, the song cannot reciprocate in the same manner. Yet, it might be argued that the song does provide gift-love in the form of music and need-love since it needs to be listened to in order to be acknowledged as a song. But that assumes the song is able to love and is motivated by love. To say the song provides gift-love and need-love is to personify it and clearly the song is not a person who willfully provides the qualities of love.

I am not saying we will ourselves to love but rather, while love might be a force that compels us, we may resist it or willfully choose how it will manifest in the world and many objects of affection, like a song, cannot do that. Since a song is an object of affection, true love does not fall within that category. I am not saying that true love and affection cannot go hand-in-hand but rather true love is not necessarily affection.

Like many objects of affection, the beloved of charity cannot reciprocate either because the beloved is a broad general category. On the one hand, if charity required reciprocation, then the whole of humanity would reciprocate to the individual who contributed to charity. On the other, some objects of charity may reciprocate but it is not a requirement. Since charity is an extension of gift-love, the primary attribute is giving and not receiving. Even if some objects of charity reciprocated, what is reciprocated is charity that is love directed to humanity in general and not to any specific person.

Apparently true love requires a specific person who can willfully reciprocate the qualities of love. If that's the case, then friendship and *Eros* are best candidates for true love. Both types of love require reciprocity, which comes from a particular individual and not a group of persons. Yet in the realm of friendship, "true love" does seem appropriate. If friendship has a form of true love, it would likely manifest as "best friends forever." However, friends stand side by side whereas romantic lovers stand face to face (*The Four Loves*, p. 91). The point of *Eros* is to unite with the beloved, so that two lovers become a single unit or rather "an item." In order to form this union, the romantic lover requires only one unique irreplaceable person; no one else will do. Only with this unique individual can a romantic union be forged until the distinction between two lovers is blurred and this is especially so since *Eros* obliterates the distinction between giving and receiving. "True love" falls within the realm of *Eros* where there is no reciprocity since the union goes beyond reciprocity.

Did Corry Love Alicia?

If Corry loved Alicia, it seems likely it was either affection or friendship. It could not be charity since charity is directed at a general group rather than an individual. Corry might have had affection for Alicia since she has been with him for eleven months and became part of his life, "an integral part." Corry could have grown accustomed to Alicia over the months. However, Corry confessed "Alicia is simply an extension of me. . . The things that she has learned to love are those things that I've loved." If so, then Corry and Alicia shared the same interests and likes, which is characteristic of friendship. Regardless if it was affection or friendship, it was nonetheless a "very strange and bizarre relationship" ("The Lonely").

But was it true love or even *Eros*? It might be objected that it cannot be since Alicia was a machine and not human. Yet declaring that humanity is a requirement amounts to a form of prejudice. True love may exist between Martians or even between a human and a Martian. Regulating true love only for humans might amount to a prejudice similar to what philosopher Peter Singer called *speciesism*, which is the bias against other species ("All Animals Are Equal," p. 122).

The underlying issue is whether Alicia was a *person,* something that has moral rights, such as the right to life. What does something need in order to be a person? Does it need a mind, a soul, or the ability to communicate? Pinpointing the precise characteristics necessary for personhood is debatable. In fact, there is no need to determine whether Alicia was person nor is there a need argue along the lines "even *if* she was a person." We only need to determine if there were any practical effects that resembled those of true love. The issue becomes more problematic because while we have privileged knowledge about Corry, we are privy to his thoughts, we do not have that privilege with Alicia. Our inquiry is restricted to whether Corry's love exhibited any of the three qualities.

Corry did not express gift-love. While he taught her the constellations, we have no evidence that he gave anything to Alicia; however, we do not have any evidence that he did not give her anything. When he discovered that Alicia would not accompany him on his return to Earth, Corry did not sacrifice his place on the ship for her nor did he consider leaving and then making a return trip to get her. Leaving the asteroid seemed to be more important than being with Alicia.

Corry did not express need-love for Alicia. His need for Alicia might have been motivated not by love but by loneliness. At the end of the episode, it seemed he needed Alicia but that need might have arose from affection and not *Eros*. Corry was so used to having Alicia around that he assumed Alicia would have passage on the ship. It seems that his need for Alicia was prompted by an obligation as if he owed her his life since Corry claimed "Without her I'd have been finished. I'd have given up." While Corry did not express need-love, it is fair to say that he expressed appreciative-love insofar as he appreciated Alicia: because of her Corry was "not lonely any longer. Each day can now be lived with" ("The Lonely").

It Wasn't Love, So What Was It?

Corry was plagued by loneliness until Alicia's arrival so it seems that fending off his loneliness was her primary purpose, especially since they both knew she was a robot. Allenby brought her to the asteroid to keep Corry company.

Allenby acknowledged that Alicia might be an illusion or perhaps salvation, likely to save Corry from loneliness. Yet if Alicia was brought to save Corry from loneliness, then she was brought as his companion and companionship originates from the instinct to co-operate. Prior to Alicia's arrival, Corry's instinct to co-operate was deadened by his loneliness and the desolation of his environment, yet probably triggered when he saw Alicia cry and claim that she can feel loneliness too.

Corry seemed to affirm that Alicia was an illusion or a lie. While comparing her to a car he had put together, "that heap doesn't mock me like you do. It doesn't look at me with make-believe eyes and talk to me with a make-believe voice." Yet we already know that previously Corry wondered what he could believe in, "what is left that I can believe in? The desert and the wind? The silence? Or myself—can I believe in myself anymore?" In the presence of a make-believe or fictional person, instead of believing Alicia was an actual person, Corry became fictional as well. Philosopher Kendall Walton, explained why we react emotionally to something we know to be fictional, stated "Rather than fooling ourselves into thinking fictions are real, we become fictional. So we end up on the 'same level' with fictions" ("Fearing Fictions," p. 23).

Much like a movie-goer who experiences fear while watching a movie she already knows is fictional, Corry reacted emotionally as if Alicia were a person and not a machine that was an extension of himself. Corry acted or role-played a person who believed Alicia was an actual person. Perhaps it was unintentional, yet it provided Corry with something to believe in that was real, although it was only an illusion that vanished when Allenby shot Alicia and announced "All behind you. Like a bad dream. A nightmare" ("The Lonely"). Corry had make-believed he was another Corry stranded on a desolate asteroid who believed Alicia was an actual person.

Can loving a robot be true love? It can if it exhibits the practical effects of true love; if it manifests as true love. However in our case study, Corry did not display true love for Alicia. It can be argued he displayed affection and friendship towards her yet whether she reciprocated it is unknown

since we were not privy to her thoughts and then again, we
don't even know if she even had any thoughts in the first
place. To answer the question of reciprocity, whether a robot's
love for a human can be true love, is a topic for another investigation.

6
In a Mirror Is Our Image

JOHN V. KARAVITIS

Beep beep beep beep! It's Monday morning, and the alarm clock did that thing that it always does. That thing that it does all too well. And you can't blame it, not really, of course, since you told it to make that electrifying *beep beep beep beep!* that shocked you out of your restless slumber. Your car, your cell phone, your computer at work, they all have their uses, too; and you rely on all of them just as much to get through the day, with nary a passing thought.

Until they do something that they weren't supposed to do, that is. Something that made you stop and take notice of them and *their* place in *your* world. Perhaps they froze and had to be restarted. Perhaps they crashed because their designers failed to foresee a specific situation that they would be asked to perform in. Or perhaps they made a mistake because *you* misunderstood exactly what *they* were capable of doing for you.

Now imagine your world with these same things that you've been relying on, only they don't just react when you tell them to do something. Instead, they now *know* what they're expected to do; and, if they don't, they'll just ask you up front. You know. *Talk* to you. And maybe you'll find yourself interacting with them so often that you start seeing them as an extension of yourself. Like a close, personal friend that you can always rely on to listen to you when you're down. Maybe they become so much a part of your daily routine that you've taken to thinking of each of them *as a person*. With a name that *you* gave them.

A lot of what we've taken for granted for so long in science fiction is rapidly turning into science fact. This includes advances in artificial intelligence and materials science which are being applied to objects that we deal with in our daily lives. Present-day examples would be intelligent personal digital assistants; self-driving cars; and artificial intelligence programs that can consistently outperform human players in games like chess and go, or even write news articles and fiction novels from scratch. Any job that a person can do that is repetitive, or requires very little original thinking, will eventually be taken over by some form of artificial creation. People have even started talking about sex robots! And one day, we'll surely see androids indistinguishable in appearance and behavior from flesh and blood human beings.

What then? What moral duties would we owe these sentient, intelligent, and self-aware artificial creations? If an android is indistinguishable from a human being in its appearance and acts autonomously, would it have a valid claim to being our moral equal? Could you ever be truly in love with one, or it with you? Or would our moral duties to these artificial creations be no greater than those we currently acknowledge as owed to dogs and other seemingly intelligent and social animals?

Whether any moral duties are due to artificial creations requires us to first look at both how closely they resemble us and the effects they have on our lives. This implies that there is a spectrum of artificial creations, from the very simple to the very complex. We can consider four points on this spectrum:

1. **an artificial creation with limited capabilities and a narrow, specific function**

2. **an artificial creation with some human-like behaviors and characteristics**

3. **an intelligent, self-aware, autonomous android, indistinguishable from a human being**

and

4. **a human being whose entire body is now made up of synthetic replacement parts.**

Thirteen episodes in the original *The Twilight Zone* (1959–1964) television series cover these four points. People who are merely augmented in some way (such as cyborgs), but who still possess at least a flesh and blood brain, would still be considered human beings. Our moral duties to them would be covered by existing ethical theories.

I'm a Man! And That Makes Me Better!

Artificial creations like sophisticated computer systems or simple robots may not be viewed as anything more than just complex machines. Nevertheless, they can have a dramatic impact on the people around them. In "The Brain Center at Whipple's," all is not well at Whipple's Mfg. Co. At least, not for its former employees. Owner Wallace V. Whipple has installed the "X109B14 modified transistorized machine," which now undertakes all the functions that had previously required flesh and blood workers.

Although chief engineer and plant manager Walter Hanley see this as "a lot of men out of work," Whipple sees it as "progress"—until he too is out of a job! The X109B14 doesn't appear to be much more than a sophisticated computer system that can schedule workflow and use other, simpler machines to create products. In "Steel," boxing matches are no longer between men. Boxing is considered too violent a sport for men to risk their lives in, so robots are used in their place by law. These robots (incorrectly referred to as "androids") are merely physical automatons. They are not capable of doing anything more than performing as a boxer in a boxing ring. Outside of the boxing ring, they are turned off. An owner of one of these robots, "Steel" Kelly, himself a former boxer, needs money to repair his robot, "Battling Maxo." To earn this money, he decides to take its place in a boxing match!

In "The Old Man in the Cave," a small community in a post-apocalyptic America depends on an old man in a cave to tell them where to plant crops and whether food from before the war may be contaminated. It turns out that the "old man" is nothing more than a sophisticated computer system. Feeling that they have been deceived, and thus somehow cheated by it, the community needs almost no prodding to destroy it in an orgy of violence.

Here, we see artificial creations that, although nothing more than sophisticated, highly advanced, specialized machines, nevertheless, in some way, shape or form, take the place of people. In their own way, these artificial creations draw deep emotional responses from the people who use them. Plant foreman Dickerson vents his anger at plant manager Hanley over being replaced by a computer. "Ever notice how it looks like it had a face? An ugly face. A miserable, ugly face. It's not a machine, it's an enemy, it's an opponent. I swear we've got to *hate* a thing like this."

Steel Kelly is obsessed with his robot. He seems to look at it as though it were alive—or perhaps, unconsciously, as his proxy in the boxing ring. "Yeah, you're gonna do okay, boy. You're gonna do okay." The community that destroyed the computer in the cave thought of nothing but the hardships that they had endured, and not that the "old man" had kept them alive for a decade. Even when it's clear that the artificial creation is not a person, if it has an impact on people's lives, they will anthropomorphize it and react emotionally to it.

Traveling the Uncanny Valley

When an artificial creation exhibits human-like characteristics or form, it's likely that it is intended as a replacement for human beings, and not just for the function that the person provided. However, the replacement is still clearly not human. In "The Might Casey," a robot baseball pitcher named Casey performs perfectly on the mound. "He pitches like nothing human," says the Zephyrs' catcher.

All is well until Casey gets "beaned" by a baseball and is taken to a hospital, where it's discovered that he is not a man! Baseball rules require that a team be composed of nine *men*. To circumvent this rule, Casey is given a heart, albeit a mechanical one. In a sense, "he" continues to work perfectly—except that now he doesn't have the heart to strike out any batters! In "A Thing About Machines," Bartlett Finchley, a writer for gourmet magazines, hates the machines that are in his house: clock, radio, television, typewriter, electric razor. "I have never been able to operate machines," he says. To him they are "A collection of Frankenstein monsters, whose whole purpose is to destroy me." He frequently vents his anger at them and breaks them.

However, the machines hate him in turn, and they tell him so. His car eventually chases him into a swimming pool, where he drowns. In "From Agnes with Love," Agnes, a Mark 502-741 computer, is a sophisticated artificial intelligence. "She" falls in love with James Elwood, one of the programmers, and sabotages his love life prospects with a co-worker in order to have him for "herself." In "Uncle Simon," an inventor dies, only to be replaced, in spirit if not in deed, by his last invention: a robot that eventually comes to exhibit all of his mannerisms. Although it's clearly a robot, its mannerisms are such that the inventor's surviving niece comes to feel as though her uncle were still alive.

When artificial creations look like or behave like human beings, people will interact with them as if they were real people. However, unless they're completely like real people in appearance and behavior, if there is something even just a little bit off, there is a feeling of unease when interacting with them. This is referred to as the "uncanny valley." The object you interact with seems as though it should be a real person, but you know it's not. It's unsettling, and you just don't know how to react to it.

When it's discovered that Casey is not a man, no one quite knows what to do with him. Bartlett Finchley becomes enraged and defiant. "I will not be intimidated by machines!" Programmer James Elwood has a hysterical breakdown when he learns that his failure to woo his co-worker Millie is the result of Agnes's desire to have him all to herself. "You're just a machine! You can't love *or* hate!" he screams at her. Barbara Polk, having been browbeaten by her Uncle Simon for twenty-five years, and now trapped with a mechanical version of him that will outlive her, is apathetic and listless. The robot's mannerisms are exactly like her uncle's, and it's *her* mannerisms that are now robotic!

Fearfully and Wonderfully Made

Five *Twilight Zone* episodes have artificial creations—androids—that are so humanlike it seems impossible to tell the difference. In "The Lonely," James A. Corry, a prisoner incarcerated on an asteroid, is given a female android—"Alicia"—as a companion. She looks exactly like a female human being; and she behaves like one, albeit in a somewhat wooden and stilted fashion. The instructions that came with her are clear: "To all intents and purpose, this creature *is* a woman."

Corry eventually comes to treat her like a real woman and a companion, and eventually appears to fall in love with her. Later, when Corry is pardoned, and the supply ship comes to retrieve him and bring him back to Earth, he's told that he can't take Alicia with him. To convince him to leave her behind, the captain of the supply ship shoots her in the face, terminating her.

In "I Sing the Body Electric," three children whose mother died are given an android grandmother to raise them. At first, Anne, the eldest child, rejects her; but, in due course, they all come to accept her. When the children are ready to leave home for college, the father tells Grandma "You've been good to us. And for us." We then learn that, with the children all grown up and off to college, their "grandmother" will most likely go back to the factory and be disassembled, perhaps one day to be repurposed for another family.

In "A World of His Own," Gregory West, a playwright, has the ability to create "people" just by describing them in his desktop Dictaphone machine, a form of audio recording device. (Although perhaps more fantasy than traditional science fiction, I have included this episode because it has the general feel of creating an artificial person, just as if one were creating an android.) Should he take the Dictaphone tape that describes a particular creation and throw it into the fire, that creation will vanish.

When his wife Victoria comes home early one day, she sees him with a beautiful blonde—Mary, his latest creation. He destroys Mary before his wife can come into his study to confront them. When he finally reveals where the woman came from, his wife refuses to believe him. When he reveals to her that she too is a creation, she still refuses to believe him. She takes the Dictaphone tape that allegedly holds her description, and she throws it into the fireplace. When her tape is burned up, Victoria West vanishes. Gregory West then goes back to his Dictaphone and creates a brand new wife—Mrs. *Mary* West!

In "The Lateness of the Hour," an elderly couple, Mrs. and Dr. Loren, live with their daughter in a house run and maintained by their android servants. The daughter feels confined living under such circumstances. "Everything built to perfection . . . Everything designed for a perfect life." She demands that the androids be dismantled. The father complies; however, the daughter then wants to "live like normal people: give parties, take trips . . ." She even wants to give her parents grandchildren. She then learns that she too is an android, after which she is reprogrammed as the Lorens's maid.

In "In His Image" (S4E1), Walter Ryder Jr., an inventor, creates an android duplicate of himself, "Alan Talbot." Unfortunately, it is defective and dangerous. It runs away before it can be terminated. Shortly after returning to the place of its creation, it is destroyed by his inventor, who then assumes *its* identity and life.

When an artificial creation is so humanlike that it is indistinguishable from a human being, people treat it as one, even when they know it is a machine. What's curious is that, in all of the episodes where the android is indistinguishable from a human being, the creation is eventually terminated.

My Warranty's Expired! Woo Hoo! Time to Upgrade!

In our search for what moral duties we would owe to artificial creations, we began with sophisticated machines that were neither conscious nor self-aware. Regardless, they had an impact on the lives of the people around them. We then looked at artificial creations that had human-like behavior or appearance—but these were only sophisticated robots or complex computers. These artificial creations had an even greater impact on the lives of the people around them. However, not being clearly human, the people around them were never truly at ease.

When we looked at androids that were indistinguishable from human beings, we saw people interacting with them just as though they were real people. Curiously, every such episode ended with the artificial creation eventually being either destroyed or disassembled.

Do humans owe moral duties to their artificial creations? In "The Trade-Ins," an elderly couple, Marie and John Holt, want to transfer their minds into new, younger bodies. They go to the New Life Corporation, which shows them the models available. The salesperson tells them, "The process is quick and painless." The transfer of your mind into a new body occurs by transferring your "memory bank, personality, continuity." The transformation can be reversed within a week if the recipient is dissatisfied. Because of the great physical pain he's in, John is encouraged by Marie to go through with it, even though they can only afford the procedure for one of them. The procedure is successful; and John is now young again, and free of physical pain. But when he sees that his still elderly wife and he now have nothing in common, he decides to return to his old body.

This episode is the most important one in trying to get a handle on the moral duties people would have toward artificial creations. The answer depends on whether artificial creations can be considered to be people. It's *personhood* that ultimately determines whether we treat something as a *moral agent*. A moral agent understands right from wrong, in some sense, and is expected to take responsibility for his actions. If something lacks personhood, either because it's not a person or, if a person, then in a vegetative state, then it is no longer a moral agent, but rather a *moral patient*. Moral agents can behave morally or immorally, but moral patients are unable to do so. Being moral agents, people *might* have some moral duties toward artificial creations that lack personhood; but we would not consider them to be "just like us."

This isn't new ethical territory. We've faced the same moral questions with how we've treated animals. Aristotle (384 B.C.E.–322 B.C.E.) saw animals as property. They had no rights. Their owner could do with them as he pleased. German philosopher Immanuel Kant (1724–1804) however felt that how we treat animals eventually influences how we treat other people. In order to maintain our humanity, animals should be treated with some care, as a matter of due course.

Contemporary philosophers Peter Singer and Tom Regan have held that the differences between animals and human beings are simply differences in degree, and not differences in kind. Granted, animals are incapable of being moral agents. Rather, we should look at them as moral patients, and acknowledge that we have a duty of care toward them. In actual practice, the more that animals have exhibited characteristics of what we see as personhood (such as intelligence and social behaviors), the more we've found ourselves treating them with respect. Perhaps the same general idea could be applied to artificial creations.

Android Owner's Manual

I've taken those *Twilight Zone* episodes that deal with sophisticated computers, robots, and androids, and I've placed their artificial creations on a moral spectrum from least human-like to indistinguishable from human. At every point on this moral spectrum, we've seen that artificial creations have an impact on our lives. Simple machines, if they affect us enough, will be anthropomorphized. We may even find ourselves venting our anger at them and destroying them. But the closer they come to looking and behaving like human beings, the deeper and more complex our interactions and relations with them become.

If you look closely, you'll come to realize that, curiously, androids in *The Twilight Zone* are created specifically to fulfill basic human emotional needs. In "The Lonely," Corry at first refuses to leave his asteroid prison without Alicia. "She's not a robot. She's a woman." In "I Sing the Body Electric," the children accept the grandmother because she takes the place of their dead mother. "This machine can love."

In "A World of His Own," Gregory West wants a woman who will cater to his needs, and not have to worry about hers. His artificial creations are "fictional characters come alive . . . They come alive so vividly." In "The Lateness of the Hour," Dr. Loren and his wife want a child who will share the rest of their lives with them. He tries to explain his creations to his daughter. "They have minds and wills. They have memory tracks, you see?" Given the revelation that Jana too is an android, Mrs. Loren panics that she will lose her daughter. "It doesn't matter what you are, or how you got here. You're our daughter!"

In "In His Image," Walter had a childhood dream. "I longed for one thing . . . A perfect artificial man . . . A duplicate of a human being. I wanted a perfect creation." Walter's dream is a quest to compensate for his perceived shortcomings. "That was my dream. A perfect version of myself." But every version of Alan to date has turned out to be defective. "Factory rejects . . . Not perfect."

In each of these cases, where there is an android which is indistinguishable from a flesh and blood human being, an emotional need—some form of love—is being fulfilled. We see in these episodes a need for companionship, for a caring and attentive parent, for a permissive spouse, for an adoring child, and for a version of oneself that one can respect.

But the most curious aspect is that in every episode that has an android, each and every one ends up being either destroyed or disassembled. Alicia was killed because she couldn't have been taken aboard the supply ship back to Earth—and not just because of the fifteen-pound weight limit. Grandma had "outlived" her usefulness. When someone becomes either too willful or rebellious, say a wife (Mrs. Victoria West) or a daughter (Jana Loren), they are replaced or repurposed. After Alan Talbot became unpredictable and homicidal, he was destroyed.

In "The Trade-Ins," we would probably still consider the recipients of brand new synthetic human bodies as persons, even though it's just "memory bank, personality, continuity" of a person that gets transferred into the new body. English philosopher John Locke (1632–1704) claimed that it's the continuity of existence and one's memories that constitutes a person's identity. Wouldn't the Holts have retained that even after having been transferred to new bodies? In that case, there would be no reason to deny personhood to an android created from scratch! Both would look like and behave just like a human being—like moral agents. Both would be *persons. Given this, the androids that were destroyed or disassembled were in fact murdered!*

If we'd have no qualms about creating androids to satisfy our needs, especially our need for love, and then disposing of them when they no longer did so, what does that say about us? This revelation may be *The Twilight Zone*'s unconscious, unstated definition of evil. *Evil is treating other people like disposable objects.*

What will we do, then, when we find ourselves in a world like that of "The Trade-Ins"? When we can replace at first one failing body part, and then another, and then another, until there's nothing original left? When a flesh and blood human being becomes a completely synthetic—an artificial—creation, what then? Won't we then be just like androids created from scratch? And will we then still hold that we will have moral duties to each other?

The Twilight Zone provides us with a mirror that we can look into and see ourselves. Hopefully, in days to come, we'll remain comfortable with what looks back at us.

7
Loss of Memory, Loss of Me?

CHRIS LAY

In his opening narration for "Person or Persons Unknown," unflappable host Rod Serling remarks that the episode's protagonist, David Gurney, is "like most people" in that he "has never really thought about the matter of his identity."

However, philosophers aren't like most people, and identity is something they tend to think about a lot. So does *The Twilight Zone*. What constitutes identity can be tricky, but here we'll keep it simple: identity is what individuates me from others, or what makes something me rather than someone else.

Generally, something is thought to be one and the same thing as me if it *looks exactly like me*. The problem is that the kind of identity "looking like" captures is *qualitative identity*, and that's not what we mean when we ask "What makes something me and not someone else?" If we think about the episode "Living Doll" for a minute, we can imagine two Talky Tina dolls that share every physical feature—the same innocent eyes, the same pigtails, and the same menacing voice. It's clear, though, that these are two *numerically* different dolls. There are *two* Talky Tina dolls, not one. So, when we ask "What makes something me and not someone else?", what we're worried about is this second, numerical sense of identity.

We Are Our Memories

In philosophy, one classic view of what makes something numerically identical with me comes from John Locke. In *An*

Essay Concerning Human Understanding (1748), Locke argues that memory is part of what unites our awareness of multiple, disparate experiences into a single consciousness. I am one and the same person as long as I am continually conscious and able to remember my past experiences.

Now, we obviously aren't continually conscious all the time; unless we're Edward Hall from "Perchance to Dream," who refuses to go to sleep out of fear of being killed in his dreams, you're probably going to need to sleep sometime. So, memory is what links periods of consciousness that get interrupted. I am the person who did something—say, who traveled back in time while visiting a gentleman's social club to try and stop Lincoln's assassination, as depicted in "Back There"—just because I am conscious of doing that very thing. For Locke, this lets us get it right when we try to assign blame and responsibility. Actions can be attributed to me insofar as I am conscious of doing them, and the way I am conscious of past actions is by *remembering* doing them.

Becoming Who You Are by Remembering It

Locke's theory is certainly active in "The After Hours," an episode which demonstrates that, absent certain formative memories, we are not who we think ourselves to be. Marsha White is a woman who has increasingly unsettling experiences while shopping in a department store for a golden thimble to give to her mother. Marsha discovers that the store's mannequins are alive and each take turns venturing out into the world outside of the store for one month out of the year. What's more, Marsha is actually one of these mannequins who just forgot her obligation to return to the store and let the next mannequin in line have a turn at living like a human person. Her apparent personal history, including the desire to buy a gift for her mother, is completely confabulated.

Here, *The Twilight Zone* advances the idea that Marsha was not one and the same with the mannequin-person at the end of the episode until she *remembered* her earlier mannequin experiences. Just before her memories return, Marsha's fellow mannequins surround her in a creepy scene whispering things like "Do you remember?" and "Remember who you are!" She then adopts the eerie stillness characteristic to mannequins and sullenly resigns herself to an unfulfilling life modeling clothes in the department store. In the Lockean sense, it is Marsha's memory *that* she is a mannequin that ties the thing returning from its thirty days away from the store to the thing who took her first steps outside thirty days prior. They are one and the same only because—and only *when*—Marsha remembers those earlier experiences and thereby endorses them as *hers*.

Loss of Memory or End of the World?

We now circle back around to "Person or Persons Unknown," where the connections between memory and identity are a bit more complicated. In this episode, a hungover David Gurney wakes up to find that no one knows who he is. The woman he claims is "his" wife doesn't recognize him, there's another man handling his accounts at "his" bank job, and all documentary evidence that he is David Gurney has simply vanished—like his phone book listing, or a supposed photo of David and his wife that instead depicts the protagonist standing in the park alone.

The man calling himself David Gurney certainly has memories; the trouble is that reality just doesn't match up with them. Locke is clear that I can't be the person who did something if I'm not conscious of doing it. But what about someone who remembers things that evidently never happened? Someone like Locke would likely affirm that such a person wasn't remembering but was imagining something wholesale. We would not, for instance, say of a woman who declares that she is actually the living doll Talky Tina that she properly *remembers* murdering Erich Streator by tripping him down a stairwell. Rather, we would probably say that she is suffering from some kind of delusion.

It is commonly thought that memories have to be factive—that is, for something to be a memory, it must correspond to something that actually happened. The man calling himself David Gurney doesn't really remember a life before his hangover because the real world reveals that no such life *in fact occurred*. This is why Serling's opening narration is explicit about what is happening to the protagonist: he is a man "who just lost his most valuable possession"—his identity. There are no factive memories connecting "David Gurney" to someone who actually acted in the world.

The end of the episode plays with this idea even more. David again wakes up in his bed, whereupon his wife consoles him and he concludes his ordeal was just a bizarre dream. Then comes the twist: David's wife washes off her sleep mask and he finds himself in the opposite position to the position he was in at the top of the episode. Now David does not recognize his wife!

Although the episode ends here, many other features of David's life are presumably also just a bit off. Perhaps his bartender insists that David's preferred drink is gin instead of whiskey, or maybe David holds a different position at the same bank. Though the differences here are less sweeping than having *no one* recognize him, David's memories at the end of the episode still lack factivity. That is, they are closer to delusions than memories. So, again, David does not remember actions that someone actually did and so cannot be the person who did them. Whoever the man at the end of the episode is, he is not the person who is married to *this* woman in his bed, as he does not remember marrying *her*.

The Lockean view recommends the same answer for both the situation where no one remembers David and where David imagines his wife differently—identity is lost in both cases because the appropriate memories aren't there. So, when Serling ponders in his closing narration "Simple loss of memory, or the end of the world?", we can see that Locke's view makes it clear which has happened. Without the appropriate memories, the person who previously had those memories has ceased to exist. Instead, we have in his place someone like David Gurney, who is an entirely new person because his memories don't link up with actual actions in the world that he could hypothetically be conscious of having performed.

Identity without Memory?

It might seem as if the factivity condition introduces a problem for the Lockean view. Couldn't "fake" memories be just as constitutive of identity as the real thing? We definitely don't want our theory of identity to let a woman's delusion that she is Talky Tina make her Talky Tina. At the same time, though, it seems plausible that there could be cases when apparent memories are just about as good as ordinary, factive ones. To see this, let's look at "The Lateness of the Hour," from Season Two.

"The Lateness of the Hour" centers around a young woman named Jana Loren who is cloistered away in her parents' opulent home and forbidden from leaving, as they insist that the family compound has everything Jana could possibly desire. Ostensibly, these desires are fulfilled by the human-like automatons her inventor father built to keep up the house. Nonetheless, Jana is highly dissatisfied with her isolated and highly regimented life and begins asking questions about suspicious family photographs that fail to match up with her actual childhood memories. Jana guesses the truth: she is an automaton, just like the house staff, only designed to be the Lorens's child rather than a butler, maid, or handyperson.

At first, we might follow Jana and contend that she—and by extension the rest of her father's robot servants—is not a person but just a "thing." This is not what the episode implies, however. Dr. Loren calls the automatons "creatures" and assures Jana they are very much alive, just like him and his very human wife. Although Jana denies this, calling the staff "walking record players" and lamenting the fact that she, as an automaton, can't feel pain nor love, this seems at odds with the way the episode presents both Jana and the staff. Jana certainly *appears* to feel. For most of the episode, she is shown to be both miserable and anxious about being locked away; even as she declares herself unable to emote, she breaks down into a fit of tears.

Earlier, Dr. Loren explains that *all* of the staff have "memory tracks" installed—detailed apparent memories that correspond to their roles in the house. For instance, the maid Nelda can recall not only a thorough account of her childhood, but also "memories" related to her skill as a maid. She asserts to Dr. Loren that she comes more highly recommended than any other such maid in the country.

So, *The Twilight Zone* at least wants to challenge our initial gut-reaction that these are *mere* machines by presenting them all as highly cognitively sophisticated and every bit as emotive as what turn out to be the plain old human characters, Dr. Loren and his wife. This is what's so shocking when we learn that Jana—the most human-seeming character in the episode—is also an automaton. Further, the automatons' apparent memories are given by Dr. Loren as a key part of what makes them what they are—from Jana to Nelda the maid.

The Lockean view that we've been considering here would deny that any of these characters have identities as persons, though. It's just a non-issue, as none of them have factive memories. Their memories aren't really memories at all because they don't correspond to anything that actually happened—Dr. Loren says almost exactly as much. All the same, "The Lateness of the Hour" gives us good reason to doubt the Lockean view, as it definitely *seems* as if Jana and the other automatons have distinct identities formed on their apparent (but not actual) memories. There's a gut punch of a second twist at the end in which we see Jana reprogrammed to act as the maid and give Mrs. Loren her five-times daily massages. Mrs. Loren even refers to the reprogrammed automaton as Nelda, not Jana—and "Jana" responds in the affirmative! We are meant to feel like she is no longer really Jana because she behaves like Nelda (and not Jana).

We're More than the Sum of Our Memories

"The Lateness of the Hour" suggests that the Lockean memory view isn't enough to explain and individuate who we are from others. We can turn to a more contemporary identity theory to get a better, more inclusive answer. In *Reasons and Persons*, Derek Parfit (1942–2017) proffers a more involved account of personal identity. For Parfit, we distinguish between persons by a full suite of mental features, not just memories. So, it isn't only memories that let us know if something is Jana or not. This is a good thing, as Jana doesn't actually *have* memories! Her apparent memories, though, are surely other kinds of mental states—probably something closer to beliefs. We can say that Jana *believes* that she was once a six-year-old, even if she never was (and so doesn't properly *remember* being a six-year-old).

According to Parfit's theory, someone at a later time is me if there is an unbroken, overlapping chain of connections between mental states that links the two of us. An example will help. This one is due to Thomas Reid (1710–1796), who was a contemporary of Locke's and used it to argue against Locke's memory theory, but I've given it a *Twilight Zone* appropriate flavor. Consider a young boy who steals an innocuous-looking magic bottle from an antique shop and is punished for it ("The Man in the Bottle"). Years later, the now young adult is on a passenger airplane and spots a gremlin on the wing ("Nightmare at 20,000 Feet"). The adult passenger remembers being punished as a boy. Then, late in life, the adult passenger is an old man who survives a nuclear blast, only to break his glasses just before he can sit down to read a beloved volume ("Time Enough at Last"). The old man remembers the gremlin but not the magic bottle.

According to Locke's more straightforward memory theory, the old man is not the same person as the boy who stole the bottle—he doesn't remember the episode and so cannot be the person who participated in it. For Parfit, though, the boy and the old man *are* one and the same person. The boy is connected by memory (among other mental states) to the adult passenger, who is connected by memory (among other mental states) to the old man. So, despite the fact that the old man and the boy aren't directly connected by memory, there is an uninterrupted chain of mental state connections leading from boy to adult to old man. Parfit calls this psychological continuity, and it involves a person's total psychology, not just memories: beliefs, desires, intentions, character traits, and more.

We can now look back at Jana's situation differently. If her "memories" are really beliefs about herself instead, she is Jana as long as she has these beliefs or there is otherwise an unbroken chain of such mental states throughout her life. This continuous chain is severed when she is reprogrammed to be Nelda the maid. There are *no* more connections between her old beliefs about herself, her desires to leave the monotony of the mansion, and so on, and the person currently massaging Mrs. Loren's shoulders. In losing these mental features, Jana's identity is also lost—she has ceased to be.

According to Parfit's view, we also get a new take on both Marsha White and David Gurney. Both cases seemed to represent deluded individuals. Marsha didn't remember that her mother wanted a golden thimble, and David didn't remember his wife, job, and bartender—these were imagined events and people that had no grounding in the real world (or, in David's case, the people were real but their roles in his life were imagined). But Parfit's view of identity lets us count these delusional beliefs as constitutive of what distinguishes us from others without conceding that we are who we delude ourselves into thinking we are. No amount of delusional belief will make a person Talky Tina. Yet, we must count these beliefs as part of a whole network of mental states that make this delusional person a uniquely individuated person—her and not someone else.

Number 12 Looks Just Like You. . . but Isn't

"Number 12 Looks Just Like You," from Season Five, gives us the cleanest case of how *The Twilight Zone* endorses Parfit's whole psychological view of identity, as well as how the pure memory view is deficient. In an intellectually oppressive future society, everyone in late adolescence undergoes a procedure called "The Transformation" wherein they are surgically altered to match the appearance of one of a small number of quite beautiful models.

As we see with a young woman named Marilyn Cuberle, The Transformation also alters the subject's mental states—beliefs, desires, and memories. The post-Transformation person in Marilyn's case seems to have *none* of Marilyn's prior beliefs, desires, and feelings. Before the Transformation, Marilyn is bookish and extremely concerned about maintaining her individuality. Her greatest fear is that she will be forced to undergo the Transformation and that it will strip her of her uniqueness, replacing her strong desire to read and learn with a shallow obsession with her looks. Post-Transformation, she is more than accepting of conformity, shouting gleefully to her friend, Val—both Transformed into matching Number 8 models—that the "best part is that I look just like you!"

Presumably, the post-Transformation person also prioritizes vanity and physical attractiveness over Marilyn's intellectual pursuits. This kind of happy stupor is seemingly shared by all post-Transformation persons now. Just before her surgery, Marilyn tries to convey to Val *why* she is so horrified by the loss of autonomy in Transformation and why she loved her "radical" father's intellectual virtue so much. Yet, Val is deaf to any sentiment this might evoke, saying that she feels only that "Life is pretty, life is fun. I am all and all is one." It's clear that the Transformation utterly changes the mental features of the subject.

We can see in Marilyn's case—and all post-Transformation persons, really—why Lockean memory theory is inadequate for determining identity. Post-Transformation persons are still connected to their pre-Transformation counterparts in one important way, even if all other mental states are changed. All post-Transformation subjects seem to fully remember everything pre-Transformation. By Locke's lights, the pre and post-Transformation subjects would have to be the same person, as the post-Transformation person is fully conscious through memory of *being* the pre-Transformation person.

But "Number 12 Looks Just Like You" sharply tells us this is wrong. The person who emerges from Marilyn's Transformation may have her memories, but she stands in a completely different relation to them than Marilyn did. For one, memories of her father no longer move her to tears or inspire her to stand against the state's attempts to impose physical conformity. And this is because the rest of her network of mental features have changed completely, swapped out for new mental states. The post-Transformation person has Marilyn's memories, but not her desire to read Dostoyevsky, her belief that the Transformation is a vile and invasive process, or personality traits like her withdrawn shyness.

With this episode, *The Twilight Zone* shows us that Parfit gets it right: the post-Transformation person is highly psychologically discontinuous with Marilyn, regardless of any factive memories she might have. Connections between her mental states and Marilyn's have been mostly (and quite abruptly) severed. It is most telling that in his closing narration, Serling does not refer to the post-Transformation person as Marilyn, but just as "a young girl in love with her-self" (certainly not a description that would befit Marilyn!). Serling doesn't call her "Marilyn" because Marilyn did not survive her surgery.

Now, we can finally see what we've gotten from this survey of a handful of episodes: a distinct picture of what makes something me and not someone else in *The Twilight Zone*. There are other episodes which support the view that our mental states uniquely individuate us from others: you can check out "The Four of Us Are Dying," "Mirror Image," "Nightmare as a Child," "In His Image," and "The Masks."

Memory is important to identity, as seen in "The After Hours" and "Person or Persons Unknown," but our memories are not all we are. Beliefs, desires, and a slew of other types of mental state can do the work of individuating us from others, even in the absence of bona fide memories—like Jana in "The Lateness of the Hour." Sometimes, as in "Number 12 Looks Just Like You," something isn't me even if it has *all* of my memories. It seems that if we lose enough mental states, we disappear altogether—literally replaced by someone else with new beliefs, desires, and memories.

So, next time you forget a friend's birthday, suddenly change your mind about what you want to order at a restaurant, or behave in a way that you might call "out of character," stop and have a good long thought; *you* just might not survive these and other psychological changes, in *The Twilight Zone*.

8
What Are You Hearing?

REBA A. WISSNER

What do Edward Hall, Adam Grant, Liz Powell, Gart Williams, and Norma Smith have in common? Their situations are determined by a dream—and sometimes their imagination. They also have another thing in common: they are the protagonists of *Twilight Zone* episodes where the musical score expresses dreaming and imagining.

Plato called the music of certain instruments "mimetic," meaning that they represented something. However he points out that while music can only be mimetic if it contains words, music itself functions as a series of signs.

In *The Sophist*, Plato characterizes music as something man-made and therefore (in his way of looking at things) unreal. He says that sounds are both real and not real in that they are manufactured, representative, and combined to create image-evoking signs. Images, according to Plato in *The Laws*, are akin to imitations whose only function is to create mental pictures for the listener.

Aristotle maintains that music, with or without words, forms images of character. He writes that melodies and rhythms can represent emotions and things. He even ascribes certain musical modes (ancient Greek scales) and rhythms to emotive and healing properties, which the Greeks called *ethos*. Music, says Aristotle, has the power to change minds, influence moral character, and cloud interpretations. Aristotle wonders why music is the only art that can do this without words.

The music of *The Twilight Zone* uses specific musical and recording techniques such as reverberation, repeated melodies, and unconventional and electronic instruments, to feature sounds unique to stories about dreaming and imagination, establishing these states for the viewer. *The Twilight Zone*'s music can reveal dream and imagination states on an entirely new level, telling us things we could never get from the visuals and images alone. The music enables us to answer some fundamental philosophical questions about dreams and imagination such as whether or not we're really ourselves when dreaming or imagining, or whether we can be sure we're sometimes in a state of reality and not always dreaming or imagining.

I Had This Dream . . .

Music has the power to mimic states of being—and dreaming is no exception. Think of the cliché movie and television flashback or dream scenes that contain ascending and descending harp music as foggy corners frame the screen, serving as the transition between current events and the past, or dreams and reality. In the 1950s and 1960s, this was also done through unconventional instruments, especially electronic instruments.

In the *Twilight Zone* episodes, "Perchance to Dream" and "A Stop at Willoughby" the music actually tells us what's happening. These episodes concern characters who are either dead or who have a dream that foreshadows their death. In both episodes, the representation of the character's dream, in contrast with reality, is achieved through the alternation of electronic and acoustic instruments in the former or new music and folk songs in the latter.

In "Perchance to Dream," Edward Hall has a vivid imagination and a weak heart. He has a dream that keeps resuming each time he falls asleep; he dreams in chapters. He goes to see a psychiatrist, Dr. Eliot Rathmann on the recommendation of his doctor because he cannot fall asleep—if he does, he will die. The dream concerns an amusement park and Maya the Cat Girl, who Edward is convinced is trying to kill him. Several melodies recur throughout the episode.

This episode features a Hammond organ, giving it a sense of eeriness and unreality, especially in the amusement park scenes, setting off the dream scenes from the reality scenes. Reverberation and echo effects are employed to reveal that we're in a waking reality, especially in the carnival scenes, which don't carry over into Dr. Rathmann's office—but the music *does*; it tells us exactly what we need to know even when we don't know that we need to know it.

The violin is electronically manipulated by using reverberation, echo effects, and other techniques to make it sound like a Theremin, an instrument typically used in old horror movies to represent aliens or monsters. A Hammond organ, complete with reverberation and echo, plays a repeated note five times, illustrating Edward's entrapment in his dream. We first hear this repetition at the opening of the episode when we see him outside of the building and it recurs frequently within Dr. Rathmann's office, beginning when we see Edward lying on the couch.

As he looks as if he's going to fall asleep, we hear the Theremin-sounding violin, playing a recurring melody on different pitch levels, showing that he's entering into some sort of dream world. We hear this whenever Edward talks about sleep and imagination. As Edward jumps off the couch, the end of the violin melody amplifies the Hammond organ reverberations, which stops suddenly as he jolts awake. A solo French horn plays Edward's "awake" music, a six-note melody that rises then falls. Thus, the amplified and electronic instruments, which all play five-note passages indicate the dream and imagination worlds and the acoustic six-note passages indicate reality.

As Edward talks about his childhood imagination, we hear repeated Hammond organ and piano melodies with reverberation—one note repeated eight times, accompanied by a descending half-step motive in the contrabass clarinet and strings. The number of times that the note repeats differentiates it from the dream motif. We also hear this music in the car flashback scene on the canyon, and the screen's foggy corners remind us that this is not happening in real time, but there is a new Theremin-like violin melody as we see Edward crash.

When Edward recounts the amusement park dream, we hear a distorted calliope waltz as the camera pans every which way. Could the music indicate something sinister or is it just representative of its unreal state? It's actually both here. The distorted calliope waltz, which we see in other episodes of the series, represents not only a misremembering of the past but also the fact that the carnival itself is a façade.

Edward even describes the amusement park as a place you only see in nightmares, noting that everything was twisted out of shape, but states that it was very real—at least it seemed that way. The second calliope waltz sounds a bit lopsided and out of tune, again representative of being unreal. As he walks over to Maya, we hear a third waltz, which becomes even faster and more frantic, showing that although he appears to have the situation under control, he really doesn't.

When we first see Maya, she dances to a drum beat that is comprised of—you guessed it—eight notes, which are syncopated, again, a bit off-kilter. When Maya talks to Edward alone, we have the Theremin-like violin and the Hammond organ reverberations, which intensify as Edward tells Maya that it's all a dream; he's home in bed asleep and that she's a part of that dream.

The piano reverberations return and become louder after she begs him to take her into the fun house and he replies, "How can I argue with a dream?" She tries to convince him that he can do everything in his dream he can't do when he's awake and we hear the repeated five-note Theremin-like violin melody return but with the descending half-step melody that we first heard in the contrabass clarinet in the violin on different pitch levels, becoming increasingly faster.

At the end of the episode, as Edward attempts to leave the office, he notices that Dr. Rathmann's secretary, Miss Thomas, *is* Maya. Frightened, he jumps out of the window. When he sees the Maya lookalike, we hear the piano reverberation melody even before we see who he's looking at. His dream is now his reality.

We then see Edward lying on the couch and Dr. Rathmann calls Miss Thomas into the office. None of the events ever happened: Edward lay on the couch when he first entered the office without saying a word, fell asleep, and had a heart attack, which killed him. We once again hear the "awake" French horn melody as they converse over his body; we're back in reality.

"A Stop at Willoughby" concerns business executive Gart Williams, who is growing tired not only of his job and the "push push" by his boss Mr. Misrell but also of pretending to be someone that he is not. In his exhaustion, he has a recurring dream during his commute home about a peaceful, small town called Willoughby in 1888 and meets a conductor who walks through his train announcing that this stop is Willoughby. Gart awakens and the conductor of his real 1960 train tells him that he doesn't know of any stop called Willoughby—at least on that line. Gart tells his wife Janie about Willoughby, even admitting that it's a town that he manufactured in a dream.

After more stress at work and several more of these dreams, he vows that next time he will get off at Willoughby. Unbeknownst to him, getting off the train means his own suicide. Gart gets off the train and meets the townspeople, vowing to go fishing the next day with the young boys who walk by. Unironically, we hear the town band playing "Beautiful Dreamer." We then see the light of the conductor's flashlight and Gart's body lying in the snow. He screamed and jumped off the train—from a heart attack, they speculate—and his body is picked up by Willoughby and Sons Funeral Home.

There are three distinct types of cues in "A Stop at Willoughby": the Willoughby Theme, the non-Willoughby cues, and folksongs. The music that features the Willoughby Theme are non-diegetic—meaning that only we the viewers can hear them, not the characters in the story. Anytime Gart either dreams of Willoughby or talks about it, the theme plays. We also hear it when an image of the funeral home sign is overlaid with an image of the town at the end.

The folksongs, which are diegetic, meaning that Gart can hear them as well as the viewers, convey serenity with their overarching tonality and simplicity, representing the simple life that Willoughby characterizes. Each time Gart begins to fall asleep, we have a whole-tone ascending flute melody that segues into the Willoughby theme. Historically, whole-tone melodies have been used in movies and television shows during dream scenes.

Unlike the other harsh-sounding episode cues, the Willoughby music is slow, lilting, and comforting. The four folksongs that appear in the episode—"Camptown Races," "Oh Susanna," "Listen to the Mockingbird," and "Beautiful Dreamer"—function collectively with the Willoughby cues, perpetuating the myth of Gart's dream world.

The non-Willoughby cues are non-diegetic and tend to be dissonant or have many dissonant moments, representing Gart's reality. They tend to be layered melodies with an over-lapping sound, demonstrating both Gart's façade of the successful business executive and suburban socialite that he attempts to be and the man that he actually is.

It's Not a Dream, or Is It?

Both "Twenty-Two" and "Shadow Play" feature a protagonist stuck in a circular dream. Unlike Edward Hall who dreamed in chapters, both Liz Powell and Adam Grant are having—and essentially are trapped in—a recurring nightmare. The results of their nightmares differ, but the music that represents their dream worlds is, in some cases, exactly the same, coming from the episode "Elegy."

In "Twenty-Two," Liz is in hospital for overwork and nervous fatigue. She dreams every evening, in perfect chronology, that she goes to the hospital morgue in the basement, Room 22. The music that plays each time she has this dream is always the same, lending the event a sense of circuitousness. The doctor tells her that next time she falls asleep and the dream begins, which always starts with her hearing the loud ticking of the alarm clock and dropping her water glass before getting out of bed and going to the morgue, she should not pick up the glass. However, as is typical in the series, her fate holds her captive and although she doesn't pick up the glass, she still manages to knock it off the nightstand and the dream continues as usual.

The episode begins in the midst of this dream. Do we see the dream happening or do we see Liz's perspective of the dream? We don't know. We hear a four-note melody, two notes descending a half step followed by two notes ascending a half step to where it began, with another melody attached to it comprised of frequent half-step movements in both directions as we see her leave her room and walk toward the elevator. We also hear trumpet punctuations that descend a wide interval. When we see the nurse emerge from the morgue and say her famous line, "Room for one more, honey," we hear an upper-range piano chord that functions as a stinger, a striking chord that grab's the viewer's attention. Even Rod Serling's opening monologue indicates that it might be difficult for the viewer to determine which aspects of the episode are reality and which are a nightmare, an uncommon problem except in *The Twilight Zone*.

We don't really know what's happening until after the commercial, when we see Liz's agent Barney visiting her in the hospital, and we hear a jaunty euphonium melody, an instrument not typically used on television. The doctor insists that the opening scene was a dream but Liz insists that it was real. As the doctor recounts the dream as she's told it to him, we hear the same music from the opening scene. What confuses the doctor is that although patients are not allowed in the basement where the morgue is, Liz knows that the morgue is Room 22. How could she know that without going there?

The use of the dream scene music allows *us* to question at the end what's a dream and what's reality. When Liz leaves the hospital, we hear the same music as when Barney walks into the hospital to visit her. As she walks through the airport, we hear the dream scene music as she knocks a stranger's vase out of her arms, breaking it. She hears a loud clock ticking and proceeds to her flight to Miami Beach—Flight 22. The gate agent tells her to hurry because they are about to depart. This time, she knows she's awake and that this can't be a dream. As she boards, the stewardess, who is the nurse from her dream, tells her, "Room for one more, honey." She runs down the stairs onto the tarmac and back into the airport where she sees the plane depart and explode in midair. This surely was *not* a dream. So, could the music have represented both dream and reality? Yes. It could have also represented her imagination here. Once she heard that she was on Flight 22, her imagination manufactured the rest to prevent her from taking that doomed flight.

In "Shadow Play," Adam also has the same dream every night. We see this right from the opening courtroom scene where the judge pronounces sentence and Adam mouths the words as the judge says them. His dream always begins at his sentencing and moves through his execution, a little too late for the pardon the governor will give him. When Adam dies, everyone else dies, and the dream restarts. The dream is always the same but each time it's the people who are different. As in "Twenty-Two," much of the music here is recurring. Like Adam, we are trapped amid constantly recurring music with no way out other than the closing credits.

Adam spends the episode trying to convince everyone that, despite being sentenced to death for first-degree murder, he is dreaming and, for this reason, he should be pardoned. Everything always happens not only in the same order but also at the same time in each dream. The music, too, helps to support this. As he recounts to fellow prisoner Jiggs what will happen as he is walked to the execution chamber, we see a split screen, Adam on the right, and on the left, a foggy image of the events with a dreamlike two-note repeated vibraphone accompaniment.

This music recurs through various parts of the dream such as when Adam realizes that he knows each person in his dream from somewhere in his life. We hear the same music here that we hear in "Twenty-Two" during Liz's dream; this is no coincidence. Like Liz, Adam is dreaming, but his dream doesn't foreshadow or save him, he is destined to this fate, forever to be condemned to this event.

Too Darn Hot, or Is It?

"The Midnight Sun" follows two neighbors, Norma and Mrs. Bronson. The first thing we hear is a screeching chord played by the Hammond organ with piano reverberations. At the opening, the piano plays a descending melody revealing that throughout the episode, what the viewer sees directly conflicts with reality; Norma is actually ill and dreaming; in reality, the Earth is moving farther away from the sun (rather than closer) and soon everyone will freeze to death (rather that burn). At several points, such as in the opening cue, the piano plays a descending passage with a flute melody over it, revealing that despite Norma calmly painting, something isn't right. In the majority of the cues, the piano and organ play with liberal reverberation, adding to this effect.

The episode uses a six-note descending minor piano ostinato—or repeated bass pattern—which is sometimes modified depending on its dramatic placement; for example, in one cue the motive is shortened to three notes. It intensifies, often accelerating as the episode continues and bass flute often accompanies it. The flute melody is jagged, not giving us any sense of what key we're in. Like Norma, we're displaced. We can interpret this as Norma's theme musically imitating both the pervasiveness of the heat and the severity of the situation. We hear this theme as Norma tells Mrs. Bronson that she sometimes thinks that she is dreaming and that she'll wake up soon; instead of extreme heat with a midnight sun, it will be dark and cool. As the episode progresses, the melody becomes more desperate, mirroring that of Norma and Mrs. Bronson, with the climax occurring as the ostinato crescendos until Norma screams, jolting us—and her—back into reality. The melody is also associated with Mrs. Bronson as she hallucinates, believing that the waterfall painting is real. Even here, the music accelerates until Mrs. Bronson dies. The music represents imagination in the context of Norma's dream. But we hear the opening music again at the end, showing that not only was this a dream, but reality now is a nightmare.

Where Am I? What Am I? Who Am I?

The music in the episodes discussed here, in some cases, is diegetic and can help the character locate themselves. Most times, the music is non-diegetic, and it helps *us* to understand where the character is and their state of being.

And so we return to Plato's idea that music is both mimetic and yet unreal. How can this music tell us whether the character we're watching is dreaming or awake? Imagining something or experiencing something real? Alive or dead? And how can we use something that Plato believes is unreal to represent and create mental images of something that may itself be unreal? The answer lies in both the instrumentation and the specific musical vocabulary that's used, creating these necessary signs that

Plato discusses and that Aristotle ascribes to mind-altering powers.

Imitations surely can represent by virtue of the signs used; therefore, music can represent through the proper contextual use of these signs. As Aristotle pointed out, their mimesis can be revealing. Like all art, music can only be interpreted correctly if it is done in context. On their own, certain musical techniques and vocabularies might not mean much, but when presented in a specific situation, they contain more meaning than they might have had alone.

9
Machines Who Care

Dennis M. Weiss

Can you find love in a box? Or perhaps in an advertisement in the pages of *Modern Science* magazine? Would you be willing to entrust the care of your children to an electronic grandma? And just what is an electronic grandma anyway?

That's the question Anne raises when confronted with the possibility of an electronic data processing system in the shape of an elderly woman. In "I Sing the Body Electric," Anne and her siblings Karen and Tom have been left bereft after the death of their mother and, while their father George is a loving parent, he's too busy with work to give them the attention they need. Tom shares with his father the latest edition of *Modern Science* and an advertisement from Facsimile Limited.

> **GEORGE:** "I sing the body electric"? Let me see that, Tom . . . "To parents who worry about inadequate nurses and schools, who are concerned with the moral and social development of their children, we have perfected an electronic data processing system."
>
> **ANNE:** An electric? Well, what does that mean, daddy?
>
> **GEORGE:** "An electronic data processing system in the shape of an elderly woman built . . ."
>
> **ANNE:** A woman?
>
> **GEORGE:** Yeah. Sort of a robot. ". . . a woman built with precision. With the incredible ability of giving loving supervision to your family."

ANNE: Can they build a machine like a human?

GEORGE: I don't know.

ANNE: It doesn't . . . it doesn't sound so good.

George, Anne, and her siblings are confronted with a dilemma that has only gotten more pressing since the Ray Bradbury-authored *Twilight Zone* episode aired in 1962. Does leaving your children entrusted to the care of an electronic grandma sound "not so good"?

Today's harried, over-worked parents might be thinking the same thing as Anne, but this doesn't always stop them from handing over their smart phones to their crying children, or maybe even asking Alexa to entertain the rowdy kids. Or perhaps they're contemplating buying a PARO for their elderly and ailing parents. Described as "an advanced interactive robot developed by AIST, a leading Japanese industrial automation pioneer," PARO is a robotic baby seal designed to help soothe and comfort patients with Alzheimer's dementia. As Amy Harmon noted in a *New York Times* article on the use of PARO in nursing homes, these devices are "adding fuel to science-fiction fantasies of machines that people can relate to as well as rely on. And they are adding a personal dimension to a debate over what human responsibilities machines should, and should not, be allowed to undertake."

It Doesn't Sound So Good

Technology theorist Sherry Turkle calls such devices "relational artifacts." They are machines that display behaviors that make people feel as though they are dealing with sentient creatures that care about their presence, relational robots built with psychologies and needs of their own. As Turkle notes, they call forth the human desire for communication, connection, and nurturance. These days, we're surrounded by a virtual flood of such relational artifacts, from Furbies, Aibos, and Tamagotchis, to robotic dogs, humanoid robots such as Cog, Kismet, BINA48, and, yes, even a Japanese therapeutic seal. And then of course there is Alexa, Siri, and "Hey, Google" to attend to us and care for our needs.

Magazines such as *The New Yorker* and *Wired* feature articles about robots that care and embracing intimacy with androids, raising difficult and potentially troubling questions about how we should respond to the growing recognition that our social lives are increasingly mediated by technical artifacts in which the boundary human and thing is disappearing.

Our television shows and movies, too, are populated with story lines in which sociable robots come to care for us and assuage our loneliness, from AMC's *Humans* to Jake Schreier's *Robot & Frank* (2012), and Charlie Brooker's *Black Mirror*, one of whose most entrancing episodes, "Be Right Back," features a bereaved woman using her dead boyfriend's social media feed to order up a replica. Should we be concerned? Do you share Anne's trepidation, "It doesn't . . . doesn't sound so good"?

Robert and Linda Sparrow think we should be concerned. In "In the hands of machines? The future of aged care," they argue that "not only is it misguided to believe that robots could offer care or companionship to older persons but that the desire to place them in these roles may actually be unethical." Alternatively, in "How I Learned to Love the Robot," Dutch philosopher of technology Mark Coeckelbergh spins a fictional scenario straight out of *The Twilight Zone* in which Grandpa's care is administered by a retinue of robotic helpers including CareCap, Robodog, and NanoCare. He concludes that our evolving human-robot relations demand that we change our attitudes and embrace the future of robots that care.

While our love affair with the relational artifacts and sociable robots populating our lives may be relatively new, these themes were regularly explored in *The Twilight Zone* more than fifty years ago. Before the first relational artifact ever showed up on the scene—that would be Eliza, a computerized psychotherapist created in 1964 by Joseph Weizenbaum—Rod Serling and crew were contemplating a future in which we fell in love with robots and electronic grandmas. *The Twilight Zone* was prescient in raising questions that have become more pressing today as our technologies evolve and it offers an instructive take on the complex issues raised by robots that care for us.

Robots in the Land of the Lonely

This debate was central to the very first episode of *The Twilight Zone* to go before the cameras, the 1959 episode "The Lonely," in which James A. Corry is in his fourth year of a fifty-year sentence of solitary confinement on an arid asteroid nine million miles from Earth. And he's profoundly lonely. The captain of a supply ship, Allenby, has tried to alleviate Corry's loneliness by bringing him books, playing cards, the parts to an antique automobile, but these have provided only temporary solace. He's a man dying of loneliness, Serling tell us.

But then on one supply run Allenby secretly brings him something entirely different: Alicia, a robot built in the form of a woman. The manual that accompanies Alicia states that "physiologically and psychologically she is a human being with a set of emotions and a memory track. The ability to reason, to think and to speak." Initially Corry is repulsed by Alicia and feels revulsion at this thing, exclaiming that he doesn't need a machine, comparing her to his antique automobile: "You're just like this heap. A hunk of metal with arms and legs instead of wheels. But this heap doesn't mock me the way you do. It doesn't look at me with make-believe eyes or talk to me with make-believe voice."

Finally, in a heated exchange with Alicia, Corry roughly rejects her, throws her to the ground, and is seemingly intent upon striking her. Whereupon she cries and exclaims that she can feel loneliness too. Alicia at this moment steps out of the category of thing or object and becomes a relational artifact, a more engaging and engaged artifact than Corry's antique automobile has ever been. Overcome, Corry reaches out to Alicia, beginning a strange relationship with her that lasts eleven months. As he notes in his journal,

> It's difficult to write down what has been the sum total of this very strange and bizarre relationship. Is it man and woman, or man and machine? I don't really know myself. . . . I'm not lonely anymore. Each day can now be lived with. I love Alicia. Nothing else matters.

The story takes a dark turn, though, when Allenby returns with news of Corry's pardon. Corry's to be brought home but he can only take fourteen pounds back with him aboard the spaceship. When Corry refuses to abandon Alicia—spoiler alert—Allenby shoots her (it?) in the face and as Alicia crumples to the ground, Corry is shocked to see the wires and vacuum tubes now exposed behind her shot-off face. And thus the debate over relational artifacts, once endearingly broached, is brought to a violent conclusion. As Corry heads to Allenby's rocket ship and back to Earth, Allenby suggests it was all a nightmare.

> **CAPTAIN ALLENBY:** Come on, Corry. Time to go home . . . . It's all behind you. It's like a bad dream, a nightmare. When you wake up you'll be back on Earth. You'll be home.
>
> **JAMES A. CORRY:** Home?
>
> **CAPTAIN ALLENBY:** That's right. All you're leaving behind is loneliness.
>
> **JAMES A. CORRY:** I must remember that. I must remember to keep that in mind.

Finding Solace in the Arms of a Robot?

Already in 1959 *The Twilight Zone* recognizes that in an advanced technological age we human beings, facing the existential crisis of our loneliness and solitude, will turn not to one another but to our technical artifacts for solace. Behind the conflict between Corry, with his love for Alicia and his lack of concern over whether she's a woman or a machine, and Allenby, who is willing to engage in violence to prove his point that Alicia is a mere thing, is a fundamental conflict over how to understand the role of relational artifacts in our lives, a conflict that is even more pointed today.

On the one hand, Alicia may presage a society in which the authentically human has been replaced by simulations, in which our closest ties are to machines rather than other human beings, our loneliness is assuaged not by the company of others but by robot companions, and our sovereignty and autonomy over technology disappear. When Corry is initially confronted with Alicia, he's repulsed and throws her to the ground, comparing her to his antique automobile, arguing that she is a lie, a simulation, not authentically human. Alicia, though, begins to cry and engagingly plays on his human vulnerabilities and his desire for companionship and he is ultimately taken in by this simulation.

On the other hand, Alicia may be the vanguard of a new way of thinking about human-technology relations, in which the boundaries between the two are made more permeable and we recognize that our congress with technology is an inherently human trait to be affirmed rather than denied.

Maybe Corry comes to realize that his life is already inextricably intertwined with technology and that Alicia is simply the most recent and most obvious indication of this? After all, he's imprisoned for causing a death following an automobile accident. His prison is an arid and desiccated asteroid nine million miles from Earth. His imprisonment is enabled by a rocket ship that brings him daily rations and an antique automobile that helps him pass the time. He enjoys neither autonomy nor sovereignty. Perhaps his life is simply a metaphor for the entwinement of humans with their machines. So why not fall in love with a robotic companion and simply complete the circle?

But—on the third hand?—consider Corry's predicament once more. He's been imprisoned in solitary confinement on an asteroid millions of miles from home. He fears becoming an object himself, an inanimate thing sitting in the sand. He's part of a culture that is both willing to objectify him as well as build and box up robotic companions for mass consumption. Why is there a factory building Alicias? What is her purpose? Are there other models of such sociable robots? What consumer need does Alicia fill? There's much we are not told about Alicia, including especially what has led a society to manufacture and sell these sociable robots. And we shouldn't forget the cultural and institutional context in which Corry's loneliness was produced. Alicia is the product of a culture that has chosen to maroon its subjects on a lonely asteroid in a cruel sci-fi vision of solitary confinement and then devise a technical fix for that loneliness by supplying them with robotic companions.

Let's not forget as well that Alicia is female, as are many of our own relational artifacts. Alexa, Siri, Microsoft's Cortana—why is it that our relational artifacts and digital assistants are so often presumed to be female? Alicia arrives in a box, designed to fulfill Corry's needs—her first act is to serve him a glass of water. And when her services are no longer needed, she's (it's?) summarily shot in the head in a particularly violent act and left behind like all of Corry's other things. In the debate over whether Alicia is a mere thing or a human being, we can easily lose sight of the fact that Alicia is also a she, something she shares with Anne's electric grandma.

The Electric Body

Loneliness and the lack of human connection is also a theme explored in "I Sing the Body Electric." Following her mother's death, Anne is, as her Aunt Nedra describes her, "more sickly and hostile every day." The kids are not thriving in the care of baby-sitters and nurses. They are, Nedra says, "like little flotsam and jetsam," having no base or anchor. Fearing that Nedra means to take them away, Tom shares his latest issue of *Modern Science* with his father and they all pay a visit to the showroom of Facsimile Limited. While we learn nothing about Alicia's origins in "The Lonely," in "I Sing the Body Electric" we watch as Tom and Karen pick out the various parts and pieces that are going to make up their electric grandma. As the salesman explains, "These are just the bits and pieces. Just the eyes, the lips, the limbs from which you will choose the elements which will become your, uh . . . grandmother." Tom is drawn to eyes that look like the brown aggies he plays marbles with and Karen wants a grandma with long hair.

Sometime later, a matronly looking woman shows up at the house and begins to entertain Tom and Karen. Grandma delights them by flying a kite and playing marbles. But Anne will have nothing to do with this robotic simulacrum taking the place of her dead mother. Like Corry, she initially rejects and spurns Grandma and calls her old junk. In one outburst, she exclaims,

> I never wanted you here. It was them—father and Tom and Karen. They wanted you, but I didn't. They needed you, but I never needed you. You sit and you talk to her, and you eat the food she makes, and you make believe, father. That's what you do. You make believe as if it were a game. As if she were real. But she's not real. She's a machine. Nothing but an old machine!

Anne is angry that her mother has died and accuses her of having lied to her and left her. In her anger, she runs out into a road and oncoming traffic. Grandma saves her by pushing her out of the way from a van but ends up being struck herself. Just as the kids fear that Grandma has died, she comes back to life and Anne is overcome with emotion, recognizing that Grandma won't die and won't leave her. It's at this moment, as Rod Serling informs us in a rare mid-episode voiceover, that

> the wonderful electric grandmother moved into the lives of children and father. She became integral and important. She became the essence. As of this moment, they would never see lightning, never hear poetry read, never listen to foreign tongues without thinking of her. Everything they would ever see, hear, taste, feel would remind them of her. She was all life, and all life was wondrous, quick, electrical-like grandma.

At the episode's close, the kids are grown and heading off to college and Grandma is returning to Facsimile Limited where she'll talk to all the other mechanical grandmothers and share what she's learned and maybe be sent out to help raise another family or taken apart and redistributed.

Fable? Nightmare?

Where "The Lonely" ended on the note of a nightmare with a violent death, "I Sing the Body Electric" ends on a happier note. As Serling observes in the episode's closing voiceover:

> A fable? Most assuredly. But who's to say at some distant moment, there might be an assembly line producing a gentle product in the form of a grandmother, whose stock in trade is love. Fable? Sure. But who's to say?

Has *The Twilight Zone* had second thoughts about the mistreatment of poor Alicia, shot in the face and abandoned on a dusty asteroid along with the rest of Mr. Corry's things? Grandma gets a happier send off from her charges and looks forward to hanging out with other robotic grandmas, shooting the breeze until she's called back into service. Should we embrace this warmhearted episode about an electric, data-processing care giver? Perhaps not. As in "The Lonely," maybe there are some darker implications to be explored.

While Alicia comes in a box with an owner's manual and Grandma comes strolling down a leafy, suburban street flying a kite and playing marbles, they're both still products, purchased at a factory, designed to fulfill consumer needs. We've seen that there are a lot of unanswered questions about just what consumer need Alicia fills. Grandma, we're told in Facsimile Limited's advertisement, is for parents who worry "about inadequate nurses and schools, who are concerned with the moral and social development of their children." But why are our parents so concerned about the development of their children? And if they are concerned, why are they turning to an assembly-line product in order to address those concerns?

"The Lonely" and "I Sing the Body Electric" clearly tell different tales about our robot companions. Corry is alone and imprisoned on an arid asteroid while Anne and her siblings live in suburbia with a loving dad. But both Corry and Anne are imprisoned in a way in their loneliness and both are bereft of human connection. They're both, as Aunt Nedra notes, like flotsam and jetsam, without an anchor. And it's into this lonely drifting that Alicia and Grandma come, filling a distinctively human need for companionship and care. We can appreciate how, in their loneliness, Corry and Anne welcome the attention of their robotic companions. But we also have to wonder if we want to live in a world where loneliness and companionship are fulfilled by a product you can buy off of an assembly line.

George recognizes that he can provide love for his children. But then he wonders, "But guidance. How do you buy guidance for your children? Someone here all the time. Someone around who cares." But why is George unable to provide guidance and care? He admits he's too busy. Maybe he works too hard and too many hours. But rather than provide guidance and care to his children, he chooses instead to buy them things. A new car. And a new grandma. But what becomes of a society where you can purchase a product designed to love and care? And what are we to make of the fact that Facsimile Limited provides only grandmas? What about grandpa? For all their differences, "The Lonely" and "Electric" are willing to imagine a world in which human companionship and care is hired out as service work to robotic women.

"The Lonely" and "I Sing the Body Electric" leave us with some tough questions about care, loneliness, and learning to love machines that care. As our days and lives are increasingly attended to by our digital assistants and robotic companions, we might wonder, along with Anne, whether this sounds so good.

Fable or nightmare? You be the judge, in the Twilight Zone.

Third Dimension

That Wondrous Land Called Truth

10
Memories Are Made of This

CLARA NISLEY

Once Rod Serling starts his narration, we know we're about to enter the Twilight Zone, where our ideas of reality and existence will be placed in doubt. We call into question our everyday beliefs and entertain beliefs in visions of the past, the future, and alternate realities. Beliefs we might have once dismissed as unintelligible now appeal to us.

We take a journey into the shadows where our ideas in sleep are impossible to tell apart from the ideas when we're awake. As Serling tells us in Season One, there is an experience based in the middle ground between light and shadow; that we've entered, in another dimension beyond that of our everyday beliefs. The fictions that originate in between light and shadow, that begin with scarcely any reason, call us to question our beliefs. The fictions originate from our experiences of the world around us, but beliefs in the Twilight Zone are always formed in a way that gives us a certain peculiar feeling about their nature. Ordinary beliefs that tie together commonplace experiences from the world around us start unraveling once we enter the Twilight Zone.

The Twilight Zone calls us to ask questions about true beliefs when momentary glimpses of light shine through. But, existences that are removed from time and place and lie beyond what we can rationally explain bring us closer to the shadows and take us away from the light. It's impossible to know the difference between our true beliefs and what we imagine is real. The mind once set into motion from some idea in *The Twilight Zone* allows the imagination to rule. So, it's difficult to distinguish our memories from what we imagine.

Not able to distinguish imagination from memory, we have fallen into another dimension. The thin line between ideas and beliefs that our created through our perceptions, memories that explain past existences and those that we do not perceive but imagine acquires such strength that it counterfeits its effect on our beliefs. We find ourselves with beliefs that we cannot justify and go beyond our ordinary experiences.

Although fiction has no force, we find that those fictional ideas in *The Twilight Zone* have the same effect as those presumably true beliefs that we obtain through our senses. People whose existences we have nothing but memories of, now are part of the flight of the imagination. These fictions present us with the same influence on the passions as those true beliefs we perceive as realities. *The Twilight Zone* shows how difficult it is to tell the difference between our true beliefs and our beliefs under the influence of the imagination in the Twilight Zone.

The Belief in Continued Existence

How do we know that things continue to exist when we're not looking at them? One of the greatest of all philosophers, David Hume (1711–1776) took this question seriously, and pointed out how flimsy is our evidence for the supposition that things continue to exist when no one's looking. Our belief in continued existence—even the continued existence of our own selves—depends on memory and imagination.

Belief in continued existence relies on how easy it is for our different perceptions to resemble one another and to be tied together. Some perceptions are of our memories, but as our memories fluctuate and fade, we find that our belief in a continued existence comes from supposed resemblances which may owe more to imagination.

Surprisingly, an episode of *The Twilight Zone* takes up this skeptical concern of David Hume, and makes us doubt that the assumption of continued existence is well founded. Specifically, a long chain of connected perceptions of three spacemen does not prove their continued existence, and as we watch the story unfold, they cease to exist, and finally never did exist.

In "And When the Sky Was Opened," Colonel Clegg Forbes remembers Colonel Harrington, but Major William Gart does not recollect a single event in the past with Colonel Harrington. If we look at this Season One episode, we find that the we have the tendency to imagine that Colonel Harrington, Colonel Forbes, and Major William Gart exist and are independent of our perceptions. But we notice that our belief in their real existences is based on memory and imagination. As we watch, we experience three spacemen disappearing from our sight, as they disappear from our knowledge.

We're bound to question our impressions when we reflect, and find that with each disappearance, the instability of our memory cannot support our beliefs. At the end, the three spacemen have disappeared and what we originally had were the impressions of them. But, now the impressions have diminished and are imperceptible. So, that no one is left, and the events can't truly be said to be remembered.

We find that the three spacemen: Major William Gart, Colonels Ed Harrington and Clegg Forbes have disappeared from the United States Air Force's radar for a day. One of the astronauts, Colonel Forbes, is seen outside a hospital room asking for Major Gart. While in the hospital bed recovering from a broken leg, after the spaceplane X-20 DynaSoar crashed in the Mojave Desert, Colonel Forbes remembers the two astronauts who piloted the experimental spaceship with him. Forbes shows Gart a newspaper headline that reads "Two Spacemen Return from Crash in Desert." Below the headline is a picture of the two spacemen, Colonel Glegg Forbes and Major William Gart before they took off. Gart has no memory of there ever being a third pilot or that there were three men in the spacecraft.

Colonel Forbes remembers Colonel Harrington, his best friend of fifteen years. Forbes must have reasons for believing that Colonel Harrington not only was on the aircraft with him but, as he explains to Gart, that he existed and that all three men had been in the same hospital room the morning before. That's when the screen turns blurry as if in a dream. This kind of effect introduces a skeptical doubt. Was Colonel Harrington really in the aircraft with Forbes and Gart or was it just a dream? Or, is it an effect to show us, the viewers, images from Colonel Forbes's memory or imagination?

We watch as Colonels Forbes and Harrington tease Gart, and just before they leave, Harrington turns to pick up his uniform hat. Underneath the hat is a newspaper, and this time, the newspaper headline reads, "Three Spacemen Return from Crash; All Alive." Then the scene turns to the two men walking into a bar. The bartender recognizes them as Forbes and Harrington who went up in space. While at the bar, Harrington appears sick as he drops the glass of beer from his hand. But Harrington is not sick; he has an unexplained feeling.

He gets up from the bar to call his parents. His parents in Des Moines, Iowa, claim never to have had a son named Ed Harrington. Forbes, worried about his friend, returns to the bar to get Harrington a drink. But, as he heads to the bar, he stops at a table and sees a newspaper with the same picture of himself and Gart that he had originally seen in the hospital room. Harrington is no longer in the phone booth, the broken glass of beer is not on the floor, and the bartender claims that Forbes came into the bar alone.

Here is the difficulty of our story. Why should we say that our knowledge or certainty depends on our perceptions? Well, a belief is justifiable if we have an idea that comes from an original impression. The belief that Colonel Harrington exists is based on Forbes's perceptions and the experiences he remembers. Forbes could not have had a belief of Harrington's past existence without having any memory of Harrington. This means that Forbes's consciousness reveals that he remembers Harrington and believes him to exist. So, Forbes could not have had an idea of Harrington without having some memory of him.

Colonel Forbes cannot have a memory of Colonel Harrington without a definite reference to being in the X-20 Dyna-Soar with Colonel Harrington. Forbes's belief must come from his memory and to have a memory is to have formed some lively ideas of the incidents that he recalls involving Harrington. Forbes's belief is formed by the vivacious ideas with such force and influence that it enforces his belief. But, it must be more than force and vivacity of ideas.

Hume declares beliefs in reality have a character that feel different from fictional ideas. The perceptions that Forbes is having feel real because they're orderly and do not alter from the original impressions he had of Harrington. As we see through Forbes's mind, he recalls images of events and the people he encountered. If these are memories we're watching, then they contain the original impressions of the events and people related to ideas that said to be involved in Forbes's belief.

But beliefs are not only determined by memories of some logical order, force and vivacity; they must also be accounted for by the testimony of others. Forbes's belief is challenged, and this suggests that memory is examined through references to other people and history. We need the testimony of historians or journalists who write about the time and place such as the crash that took place in the Mojave Desert. Journalists wrote the headlines based on those immediately present at the crash or received it through eye-witness testimony.

And here we follow Hume's argument that every link hangs upon another and our senses or memories would not account for a true historical event without the testimony. We find that the newspaper headline, the bartender who doesn't have any recollection of Harrington, and Amy, Forbes's girlfriend who arrives at his apartment wondering where he's been, after receiving a wire to meet him at the bus station at midnight, has no recollection of an Ed Harrington.

The wire he sent to Amy does not read that Ed and I are getting out at 9:00 A.M., but that I'm leaving the hospital at 9:00 A.M. After leaving the bar, we find Colonel Forbes at home making a phone call to his Commanding Officers' Residence. After pleading with Amy about how they had been to dinner, dancing, and doubled dated with Ed Harrington, the Commanding Officer calls. Colonel Forbes asks the General to verify the existence of Ed Harrington who the General was to have known for months. But now the General does not have any knowledge of an Ed Harrington.

The screen turns blurry and we see Colonel Forbes recounting his story to Major William Gart, who concludes that Ed Harrington must have been an illusion in Forbes's mind. Colonel Forbes must call into question the truth of his belief. The lack of testimony undermines the natural function of memory as part of past perceptions. His chain of thought appears to be more the influence of the imagination which seems to easily lead him to believe in the link of his perceptions. But, all of a sudden Forbes has that funny feeling, just like Harrington did, of not belonging, and he doesn't see his reflection in the mirror. Forbes runs out of the hospital room and Major Gart runs after him, but Forbes is not in the hallway.

After the nurse places Major Gart back in bed, he sees the newspaper lying on the tray "Lone Spaceman Completes Journey; Lands in Desert." Was this account all in the mind of Major Gart? On the belief based on testimony, Hume explains that the reason we acquire historical beliefs is from the memories of the characters and communications that we have. But, at the end we watch as the nurse calls for the medical officer. When we see her next, she's talking to him; she tells him that Room 15 is empty. We see that Room 15 is in fact empty of all impressions or memories of the spacemen.

At the end we hear Rod Serling's narration, "Once upon a time, There was a man named Harrington, a man named Forbes, a man named Gart. They used to exist, but don't any longer . . . At least they are no longer a part of the memory of man."

The Matter of a Continued Existence

In "The Trouble with Templeton," we see the problem of continued existence from a different angle. We see a man fondly remember his loving wife who is now, so it would seem, dead. The problem goes something like this: Mr. Templeton believes his wife is dead and upon seeing her, at a speakeasy, he remembers her features, manners, and individual traits. But, these are in the past, and his senses and memory cannot guarantee her present existence. As we've seen from the previous episode, it would be impossible to account for our belief in the continued existence of someone. We now run into the problem of a belief that someone is the same even when that someone is dead.

The episode starts with a man who has been a very successful Broadway actor. He's looking for the memories of yesteryear and a lost first love. Mr. Booth Templeton is an old man reminiscing about his first love, Laura. Mr. Templeton married Laura when she was eighteen, but Laura died at the age of twenty-five. On his first day of rehearsals for the play,

"The Angry Lovers," Mr. Templeton is late. He is berated by the director for walking in late on the first day of rehearsals. Walking out of the theater, he's surrounded by people applauding. He turns and looks at the poster that reads "Now Appearing Mr. Booth Templeton," in the play *The Great Seed*. Underneath the title is a ribbon with the words "1927's Big Hit." Mr. Templeton is recalling memories of his past life. He is told his wife is waiting for him at Freddie's speakeasy.

Mr. Templeton rings the bell and is allowed in by Freddie. When he's admitted into the bar, he searches for Laura who isn't at their usual table. Laura is drinking beer with his best friend Barney and eating a Kansas City steak. She tells her husband to sit and reminds him as she has told him many times before to take off his makeup before he comes into the speakeasy. Booth is confused and reveals that he's not wearing makeup but has grown older.

He tells both Laura and Barney that they've both been memories for years. But, "now, tonight, or today, or whatever it is, and wherever I am in space or time, I have you back again you're alive, you didn't die. Life is going on here. It's as if you never died. Neither of you." But, Laura just wants to have a good time and takes a drink of beer. The first reflection is that he has never experienced that side of Laura. He is bewildered that all this past experience contradicts the Laura he remembers. She's not quite the same person. Her appearance is the same, but her behavior is different from his memories of her. He confronts her and asks why she's so different. He doesn't like "what she's become," but "What did you expect?" she asks. She continues to dance. Booth, disillusioned with her, leaves the speakeasy. As we watch, Laura has stopped dancing, she moves forward and stares, then she slowly fades—apparently, out of existence.

Mr. Templeton is led to regard the world, as something real and stable, and as enduring, even when the speakeasy fades away from his perception. As we recall, Hume says that we have ideas that are copies of our impressions. It turns out, that the ideas of memory maintain the order and arrangement of the original impressions. Mr. Templeton believes that he remembers this order (his beautiful young wife—that lovely girl he was once married to). At the speakeasy, Mr. Templeton verifies his belief by referring to the order of his memory ideas. He remembers the experiences of sitting at their usual table—this was the order and arrangement of his memory ideas.

But, upon testimony from the attendant, he finds that Laura is not sitting at their usual table. So, the original order is not reproduced in the exact way. And so, he remembers Laura at a given time and in some other way. His memory lacks "constancy and uniformity," yet he doesn't think anything of Laura sitting with Barney. After all they're all friends, and seeing Laura sharing a drink with Barney doesn't suggest anything contrary to his recollections of the past. But, he finds a certain amount of consistency in the perceptions, which Hume would describe as a "train" of observations, which continues beyond the perceptions, and creates the belief in continued existence.

Laura looks the same when he perceived her before her death; he ceased to perceive her at one time, but now he's perceiving her once more. Although his perceptions of Laura are different, there is a perfect resemblance that leads him to believe the person he is seeing now is the same person. When he recognizes that his earlier perceptions are different from the perceptions he experiences now, he finds himself in a contradiction. But he glosses over this inconsistency by removing the interruption of his perceptions and supposes that his perceptions of Laura's existence are real. Mr. Templeton hardly notices these interruptions in his perceptions and they're only increased in "vivacity" when he sees Laura. Although it is only an inference he makes, he believes that he sees Laura. The "vivacity" is due to the influence of remembering the "broken impressions" and the tendency to suppose them to be the same.

Booth's beliefs not only require that his memory ideas have a certain order, but also his belief that he has just seen Laura has to have degrees of "force and vivacity." So that when he first sees Laura, his memory ideas "acquire a new degree of liveliness." But, in his encounter with Laura, Booth has a feeling that competes with the feeling he had at the first sight of Laura. Although her features remain the same, her character and actions are different from his memories of them. He has a lively memory of Laura and her personality. Laura's personality currently is quite different. Her disposition, temperament, and distinctive charm has changed. Laura is insensitive to his appeals. He wants to speak to her privately, but she refuses and laughs. She wants to dance. This affects Mr. Templeton's belief. Mr. Templeton's belief is nothing more than the way he viewed Laura. The effect on his belief of Laura could only have approached a memory idea, if the idea approached the impressions of her in "force and vivacity." Laura has been nothing but memories to him for years.

It's Only the Whimsies of Imagination

Mr. Templeton has a present impression and a present memory of Laura. But what Mr. Templeton has are the perceptions of related ideas. The reason is that he would have to place Laura at two different times, or to view the succession of time as unvaried and uninterrupted. His imagination has engaged and his suppose belief in Laura is the "uninterrupted progress" of Mr. Templeton's thoughts. It is nothing more than a succession of what the imagination feigns to be the uninterrupted belief in the same person over time. This is so because the imagination and not memory perceptions in Mr. Templeton's belief is the collection that makes the process of uniting all the perceptions possible.

So, when he sees Laura, he perceives the same person. His willingness to imagine Laura, alive today, would decrease upon serious consideration. Booth Templeton never perceives any real connection in time. His sense of unity and continuity is reportedly felt at each moment. But Mr. Templeton was powerless to maintain a continued focus on any continued existence. The ghosts of his past had put on a performance for him to force him to return to the present. But, for a moment, he had a sense of Laura as an existing, continuous being.

The Causes of Beliefs

We've seen the disappearance of three spacemen. We've also witnessed a woman come into existence after many years of being nothing but part of a man's memory. Both episodes show how we can no longer recall and reproduce in the mind exactly the impressions that we had once remembered. The

three spacemen have been nothing but the temporary impressions that appeared in another's mind. But, the imagination has "feigned" the belief in their external existence.

We should never again suppose that memory alone is responsible for our beliefs in the continued existence of individuals. Memory only supplies us with resemblances
between perceptions that are interrupted. In Booth Templeton's case, the resembling perceptions have been presented
to his senses. He believes the Laura he sees today is identical
to the wife he remembers. His belief arises from the "constancy" of his memory. But, the senses and memories we
count on to explain the world are put to the test in *The Twilight Zone* and are no longer the foundation of rational
beliefs.

11
The Truth about Lying

Don Fallis

Los niños y los locos dicen la verdad, por eso a los primeros los educan y a los segundos los encierran.

—Colombian graffiti

When we journey into the Twilight Zone, we often discover that things are not quite as they seem. An apparently beautiful young woman is actually hideous ("The Eye of the Beholder"). A poor old woman living alone is really a giant alien ("The Invaders"). A seemingly normal swimming pool is a conduit to a secret paradise for lonely children ("The Bewitchin' Pool").

Such surprises can be an enlightening as well as entertaining experience for the viewer. However, *The Twilight Zone* takes us to "another dimension . . . not only of sight and sound, *but of mind.*" It's not just concerned with the things that we perceive, but with how we think about these things and communicate about them. When characters invariably tell other characters about the surprising things that they observe in the Twilight Zone, we enter the domain of the *philosophy of testimony*, which encompasses the ethics and the epistemology of communication.

As the great Scottish philosopher David Hume put it in *An Enquiry Concerning Human Understanding*, "there is no species of reasoning more common, more useful, and even necessary to human life, than that which is derived from the testimony of men, and the reports of eye-witnesses and spectators."

The Twilight Zone takes some interesting positions in this important area of philosophy. We learn something about how to convey—and about how *not* to convey—information to other people. We also learn something about how to evaluate the information the we receive from other people.

The Dangers of Telling the Truth and of Lying

The Twilight Zone frequently makes the case against telling the truth. Characters who try to accurately report the strange things that are going on tend to get themselves into trouble. Jeb and Sport are punished when they tell their parents about visiting Aunt T's gingerbread house by diving into the swimming pool. ("Don't you know what happens to little children who lie? They go to hell and get burned up.") In "Nightmare at 20,000 Feet," Bob Wilson's warning about a gremlin on the airplane's wing simply leads the flight crew to conclude that he's crazy.

Indeed, the protagonists of "A World of Difference," "Mirror Image," "Back There," "Static," "Night of the Meek," "Shadow Play," "Person or Persons Unknown," "Miniature," "No Time Like the Past," and "The Parallel" all tell the truth and are likewise dismissed as being out of their minds. Thus, *The Twilight Zone* definitely seems to endorse the sentiment expressed in the epigraph of this chapter: "Both children and the insane tell the truth. That's why we educate children and lock up the insane."

While the aforementioned characters voluntarily decide to tell the truth, several characters in the Twilight Zone are forced to tell the truth against their will. This never works out well either. In "The Whole Truth," a mysterious little old man unloads on Harvey Hunnicut both a Model A *and* "the absolute necessity to tell the truth," a trait that makes life very difficult for a used car salesman. (The Jim Carrey movie *Liar, Liar* shows that this trait is a curse for lawyers as well.) In "A Piano in the House," Fitzgerald Fortune's new player piano causes people (including Fortune himself) to reveal their true selves.

But even if telling the truth can be dangerous, it's not clear that we should just start lying instead. We all know what happened to "The Boy Who Cried Wolf." And *The Twilight Zone* takes the case against lying even further. Whereas the boy in Aesop's fable only suffers once people stop believing his lies, liars in the Twilight Zone tend to come to a bad end even when their lies *are* believed. In "Hocus-Pocus and Frisby," Somerset Frisby is nearly abducted by aliens who take his self-aggrandizing tales seriously. And in "The Four of Us Are Dying," Arch Hammer is shot to death precisely because his deception is so convincing.

The Twilight Zone seems to be telling us that things will go badly for us if we tell the truth *or* if we lie. If these arguments in the philosophy of testimony are correct, what are we to do? Fortuitously, telling the truth and lying are not the only strategies available to us as testifiers. In a letter to a young fan of his work, the great German philosopher Immanuel Kant wrote that "want of candor . . . is still very different from that lack of sincerity that consists in dishonesty in the actual expression of our thoughts . . . What the honest but reticent man says is true but not the whole truth. What the dishonest man says is, in contrast, something he knows to be false." In other words, instead of telling the truth or lying, we can also just keep our mouths shut.

The contemporary philosopher Ricky Gervais (BA 2:1 Honors in Philosophy, University College London) seems to have missed this possibility in his movie *The Invention of Lying*. Given that no one has yet come up with the idea of saying false things, the characters in this movie seem to be unable to do anything but constantly spout embarrassing truths. Maybe the lesson that we (and Gervais) should take away from *The Twilight Zone* is to be a little more reticent when it comes to what we tell other people.

Deceptive Aliens and Devils

So far, I have focused on the issue of how and when to give information to others. But another important issue in the philosophy of testimony is how to evaluate the information that we *receive* from others. As we've seen, many people tell the truth, whether it be voluntarily or involuntarily. So, we will not be misled if we simply believe what those characters say. (We can also believe anything we read in the *Danzburg Courier* since the linotype machine in "The Printer's Devil" has been modified so that "whatever it writes comes to pass.") But just like in the real world, there are a lot of deceivers in the Twilight Zone who wish us ill.

In the Twilight Zone, the charlatan is often an alien creature. In "Will the Real Martian Please Stand Up" and "Black Leather Jackets," aliens disguise themselves as humans in order to invade Earth. In "To Serve Man," the Kanamits convince everyone that they only have the best interests of humanity at heart when they actually have very different plans for us. (*To Serve Man* is actually a cookbook!) And just by turning the electricity on and off in "The Monsters are Due on Maple Street," aliens fool people into thinking that their neighbors are, or are working with, aliens who are trying to invade Earth. (Of course, in that case, it is at least true that an alien invasion is coming.)

In the tradition of the great French philosopher René Descartes's (1596–1650) "malicious demon of the utmost power and cunning who has employed all his energies in order to deceive me," devils and demons are also regular deceivers in the Twilight Zone. In "The Hunt," the mountain man Hyder Simpson is told by a demon in disguise that he has reached the gate to the Elysian Fields. In "The Howling Man," the Devil convinces David Ellington that he is the innocent prisoner of "raving mad" religious zealots led by Brother Jerome. In "Printer's Devil," the Devil (now in the guise of a gruff old reporter and linotype operator) tricks Douglas Winter into signing away his immortal soul.

But it is not just aliens and devils who pretend to be humans in the Twilight Zone. In "Long Live Walter Jameson" and "Queen of the Nile," beings who can live forever pretend to be mortal. Also, much like the creators of Westworld, scientists in "The Lateness of the Hour" and "In His Image" build robots and fool them into thinking that they are humans.

And when these deceivers are believed, bad consequences typically result. Here are just a few examples: Michael Chambers is on his way to the Kanamit home planet to be eaten. Pete van Horn is shot to death and the rest of Maple Street will never be the same. And when the Devil is released from his confinement by Ellington, it leads to "the Second World War, the Korean war, the hideous new weapons of war."

It should be noted though that not all of the deceivers in the Twilight Zone are malicious. In "Steel," "Steel" Kelly goes into the boxing ring pretending to be a robot so that he can get the money to repair Battling Maxo. In "The Fugitive," Old Ben only pretends to be human in order to avoid being returned to his home planet to resume his role as king.

"The Fugitive" is actually exceptional in another way. Alien deceivers in the Twilight Zone typically try get people to believe false things. But when Old Ben makes himself look exactly like his young friend Jenny, he is just trying to prevent true beliefs. His pursuers know very well that Old Ben is in disguise. But since they can't distinguish the real Jenny from the fake Jenny, they are forced to take both of them back home. In intelligence and counterintelligence terminology, Old Ben is engaging in *dazzling* rather than *mimicking*.

Detecting Deception and Believing Crazy Stuff

Since deception usually has bad consequences for the person who is deceived, we definitely would like to be able to detect it. Unfortunately, humans do not seem to be very good at detecting deception. According to most empirical studies, we only detect lies at slightly better than chance. And we are probably even worse when it comes to more powerful deceivers, such as aliens and demons. As Brother Jerome tells us, "man's weakness and Satan's strength" is that we see him and fail to recognize him.

But there are some things that we can do. For instance, Hume advises that "we entertain a suspicion concerning any matter of fact, when the witnesses contradict each other; when they are but few, or of a doubtful character; when they have an interest in what they affirm; when they deliver their testimony with hesitation, or on the contrary, with too violent asseverations." And sometimes, we can do even better in the Twilight Zone. For instance, the demon tells Simpson that his faithful hound dog Rip cannot come with him through the gate. This is because Rip would have smelled the brimstone and revealed the deceit to his master.

Even in the Twilight Zone, however, there is no foolproof method for detecting deception. Polygraphs clearly don't work very well on Kanamits. And in "A Penny for Your Thoughts," when his quarter miraculously lands on its edge, bank clerk Hector Poole acquires the ability to actually hear other people's thoughts. As a result, Poole is able to detect that Mr. Sykes is lying when he claims that he wants a loan to expand his business. (Sykes is actually planning to use the money to bet on the horses so that he can use his winnings to pay back what he has embezzled.) But it turns out that Mr. Smithers is not really planning to rob the safe and escape to Bermuda. He is just daydreaming about it.

Of course, we can often be fairly confident that someone is saying something false just based on *what* she is saying. For instance, according to Hume, "when any one tells me, that he saw a dead man restored to life, I immediately consider with myself, whether it be more probable, that this person should either deceive or be deceived, or that the fact, which he relates, should really have happened." When it comes to reports of miracles, Hume quite reasonably recommends that we not believe such extremely implausible testimony because deception is much more likely than that the testimony is true. On the same grounds, it seems that we can safely conclude, despite testimony to the contrary, that there is no gremlin on the wing and that our swimming pool is not connected to an alternate reality.

In "Printer's Devil," the Devil convinces Douglas Winter to sign over his soul by arguing almost exactly like Hume: "As a sophisticated, intelligent, twentieth-century man, you *know* that the devil does not exist . . . But you also know that the world is full of eccentric, rich old men, crazy old men doing all kinds of things for crazy reasons . . . Why not humor an old man? It would mean such a lot to me. And if you don't sign it, it would be admitting fear and belief."

But crazy stuff often *is* true in the Twilight Zone. And it can be bad for characters when they fail to believe it. In "Mirror Image," Paul Grinstead doesn't believe that Millicent Barnes is being shadowed by a double until he runs into his own double. In "Shadow Play," district attorney Henry Ritchie does not believe that Adam Grant is trapped in a recurring nightmare. As a result, Ritchie and the rest of his world go out of existence when Grant is electrocuted and wakes up. In "The Big Tall Wish," the aging boxer Bolie Jackson can't believe that he only won his comeback fight because of Henry Temple's wish that the boxers switch places. So, it ends up that he lost the match after all. In "Kick the Can," Ben Conroy does not believe Charles Whitley's claim that playing like a child will make him young. As a result, he is left alone and elderly in the Sunnyvale Rest Home while the rest of its former inhabitants have become children. And although Bob Wilson's flight lands safely, the crew's skepticism nearly leads to a tragedy.

In fact, we should sometimes believe crazy stuff *even if* the person telling it to us is lying. In "Mr. Garrity and the Graves," Garrity is a con artist, but he actually can raise people from the dead. As one of the risen notes, "The man don't do himself justice."

Although David Hume clearly advises skepticism in such cases, a few philosophers claim that, even if certain pieces of testimony are crazy and very unlikely to be true, we should still believe them *just in case* they might be true. In his *Pensées*, the eminent French philosopher Blaise Pascal (1623–1662) proposed what has come to be called *Pascal's Wager*: "God is, or He is not. But to which side shall we incline? Reason can decide nothing here . . . Let us weigh the gain and the loss in wagering that God is . . . If you gain, you gain all; if you lose, you lose nothing. Wager, then, without hesitation that He is."

Basically, if God doesn't exist, it doesn't really matter much whether we believe in Him or not. But if He does exist, there is a huge benefit if we believe in Him, and a huge cost if we don't. So, given the possible consequences, we really should believe that God exists *even if* we think that it is extremely unlikely to be true.

The Twilight Zone may be equivocal on the truth telling versus lying issue. But it definitely endorses Pascal's position on believing crazy testimony. As Bolie tells Henry, "maybe there *is* magic. And maybe there's wishes, too. I guess the trouble is . . . there's not enough people around to believe." In "The Last Rites of Jeff Myrtlebank," when the townsfolk decide that he is a "hant" who has stolen Jeff's body and try to get him to leave town, Jeff (?) argues almost exactly like Pascal:

We're going to stay, and that means just two things: One, if you're wrong about me, then you ain't got nothing to worry about because that means I'm just a poor ol' country boy by the name of Jeff Myrtlebank. But on the other hand, if you're right about me, then you better start treating me pretty nice because you just don't know all the trouble I can cause you. I might wave my right hand and bring a whole grove of locusts down on your crops. Then I might wave my left hand and dry up all your wells. Then I might snap my fingers and burn a barn or two. And then some morning if I get up and I feel exceptionally ornery, I might have the hawks come down and steal your chickens. Yes, sir. You folks better start treating me and mine real nice.[1]

---

[1] I would like to thank Tony Doyle, Alex Hooke, Kay Mathiesen, and Dan Zelinski for helpful suggestions on earlier drafts of this essay.

Fourth Dimension

As Vast as Space and Timeless as Infinity

12
The Twilight Zone on Our Doorstep

TIM JONES

Three questions I'd like to put to you. *What* is the Twilight Zone and *where* exactly can it be found? *How* did it get there?

The answers to these questions are more unnerving than any of the obvious horrors with which Mr. Serling presents us week after week. More unnerving than a talking doll that sets out to kill its owners. More unnerving than a gremlin looking to dismantle your plane when you're 20,000 feet in the sky. More unnerving than meeting the Devil and realizing he's tricked you into setting him free. More unnerving than the thought you might really be a shop mannikin taking a month's vacation; than the thought you're a robot; than the thought you might be dead and just not have caught on yet.

More unnerving, because the answers to these questions point directly back to our own greatest weaknesses and run a great fat highlighter through our own deepest fears. And these aren't fears of anything that comes *from* the Twilight Zone, wherever it is. They're fears of what we put there. Fears of truths we built the Twilight Zone in a desperate effort to get some distance from.

A Stop at the Twilight Zone?

Rod Serling's opening and closing narrations to each episode insist that the Twilight Zone is somewhere *else*. Somewhere usually remote, but which our generally hapless main characters cross into each week in spite of this supposed separation, catalyzing the turning of their worlds upside down.

Often this remoteness is described as though it's between two distinct physical locations. One being where the characters start from and the other being where they end up: the Twilight Zone. We're told about people having moved "into" the Twilight Zone, as though they've crossed a regional or an international border, or that they're positioned on the "outskirts," as if the zone has a range of suburbs that they're moving through on their way to its center. We're told about it having a "threshold," which is a line separating an area from all the places that're not that area. We're told about signposts pointing the way there, just as signs point the way towards your own town or city, or about people taking a "walk around the block" once they've arrived, like they're checking the place out after completing their journey.

This sort of language suggests if you laid out a map on the coffee table, you could point to a region just like you might point to the United States or the United Kingdom and go, "That's the Twilight Zone, right there!" It'd probably have appeared on that map mysteriously overnight and you might even have bought the map from a shady street vendor promising it's what you need, but it'd be there.

These ways of describing the Twilight Zone as though it's a different location, into which—or through which—the show's main characters are newly traveling, rarely match up with what we see on screen. Weird stuff happens to these characters, sure. *Mostly.* Read on to see why I hesitate to say even this. But where, physically, is this weird stuff happening?

We're told that Nan Adams, twenty-seven, took "a detour through the Twilight Zone" on her way towards realizing she died several days before. We never actually see her go anywhere other than US states which we readily recognize as real places. She drives through New York, Pennsylvania, Virginia, New Mexico . . . None of these places occupy a different space that we can identify as the Twilight Zone. You could put this book down and follow her route yourself.

Despite the narrator insisting that Nan has traveled somewhere different, somewhere neither she nor the show's viewers have been before, she hasn't ever left locations that are completely familiar. And this is true for so many of the show's episodes. Count how many times we're told that something has taken place "in the Twilight Zone," when what we've been watching has taken place in a contemporary America that the show's original viewers could see right outside their windows.

Sometimes people go off-world, as with the astronaut in "People Are Alike All Over", who ends up trapped in a zoo on Mars. But this doesn't mean that he's travelled to anywhere called the Twilight Zone. Mars isn't the Twilight Zone. Mars is Mars. It's the same Mars that these viewers could see in the night sky. Even an episode like "The Eye of the Beholder", which doesn't take place in an identifiable part of our world, is still located somewhere that differs only in the ways that work to facilitate that episode's twist and that's otherwise indistinguishable from any other hospital you could visit yourself.

Marking out the Twilight Zone as somewhere completely different in the terms Serling often uses just doesn't hold up. Which makes me wonder why he's so keen to give it a go.

The Monsters Are Due from the Twilight Zone

Whether or not it's right to label the places seen in the show as anywhere other than the real world, stuff is happening in these episodes that doesn't tend to be a part of regular life. Right? Sure. You don't wander up the road while your car's being fixed at the gas station and end up visiting your past. Kids don't fall through the bottom of swimming pools into other realms. William Shakespeare didn't teleport into the room to help me finish this chapter on time. Notice the difference in tense in my last example.

Often this impossible stuff involves literal monsters from out of fantasy, or what're clearly supernatural forces out to get us. The gremlin from "Nightmare at 20,000 Feet"; an evil slot machine; Talky Tina herself. I'm going to stake a claim on these things not existing in the world around us. If the characters in these stories never actually get to the Twilight Zone as an alternative space in the way that the narration often implies, then perhaps the Twilight Zone is where these phenomena come from.

If it's a different place, then it's a different place operating by different rules, where the otherwise impossible events described are entirely possible and where otherwise impossible creatures have a home. And sometimes these different physical laws and these supernatural forces spill out of the Twilight Zone into our own world.

But however easy an answer this would give to at least one of my opening questions, it's not what Serling's opening narration ever describes happening. Or, well, usually—try and find an example that proves me wrong. Whether you can or not, the narration is *much* keener to describe people going *into* the Twilight Zone and to suggest that things have happened to these people once they've slipped inside, rather than stuff coming *out* of it and into a location much like the world we see all around us, in which the clear majority of the episodes more obviously take place.

Why? Because, I reckon, while we can be clear about the unreality of the phenomena themselves, we can't be so sure about the unreality of the lessons that these impossible phenomena reveal to us. We can be entirely sure about these lessons' *reality*, to an extent that might make them unpleasant to hear unless we find a device to keep them safely at arm's length. Unless we position them in a place far away that we can give a weird name like, I don't know, the Twilight Zone.

Let's look at what a few of these lessons tell us. Many of the episodes offer variations on the classic warning to beware of what you wish for. Thanks to the supernatural phenomenon of the episode, characters' wildest dreams often come true, only to take a dark turn leaving the dreamer wishing they hadn't—most literally in "The Man in the Bottle," as the title might suggest, where a guy who wishes to be an all-powerful leader of a modern, European country winds up as Adolf Hitler hours away from his suicide.

Other episodes like "The After Hours," "People Are Alike All Over," and maybe even "The Hitch-Hiker" too warn us that what makes us human—what therefore separates us from what we cast as non-human, or other than human, or less than human—might not be as solid as it seems. Perhaps we're only moments from having anything distinguishingly special in our humanity pulled away from us.

Even the gremlin in "Nightmare . . ." has traveled into our world not primarily to torment Bob Wilson, but to provide a catalyst for the audience to scrutinize its own beliefs. Perhaps those beliefs concern how safe the science fuelling the technology around us might really be and how vulnerable we are when we're dependent on its power. *I* know that gremlins don't exist, any more than the Devil or sentient mannequins. At the same time, I'm a guy who hates flying and looks pretty much as uncomfortable as Bob does as the plane is about to take off.

When I'm flying, my life itself depends on the science carrying this impossibly heavy vehicle through the skies functioning without fault. If it didn't, I'd be dead. But should I really place any more trust in it than I would in the existence of the gremlin when, according to my own ability to explain these phenomena, they might just as well be as fantastical as each other? Do I only deny the gremlin, while accepting the plane's ability to fly, because each of these is the option most conducive to my safety? Might that be the only reason why any of us readily accept anything?

Tell me something makes me safe and I'll believe in it, even when I have no further understanding of what you're telling me. Is Bob then the sane one because he's much readier than I am to accept something that he can see presents a stark threat to his mental and physical well-being? Even if you're not as paranoid about a plane's ability to stay in the air as I am, I hope you can see my point that the gremlin's purpose is not to make us fear gremlins, but to think on lessons that might make us worry about stuff in the world all around us. The lesson might just ask how readily you can trust your own senses.

Lessons applicable to this world, however much they might threaten to dethrone our place as human beings at the center of it, can be accepted, yet lessons that come to us via impossible creatures and phenomena that the natural laws and physics of this world don't accommodate, are more difficult. Not all the show's lessons come from causes whose literal existence can be so readily dismissed, true. A case in point: the readiness of the astronauts in "I Shot an Arrow into the Air" to turn on each other as soon as they believe they're away from human civilization. Or the sheer dependence our sanity has on other people that's revealed by prisoner James Corry running into the arms of an android in "The Lonely." Landing somewhere you imagine to be a distant asteroid will probably be possible at some point in our future and, looking particularly at Japan, lonely people seeking comfort in simulacra is already an actual thing.

The situations that allow for these lessons aren't strictly impossible in the same way as the gremlin or his supernatural friends. Or portals into history. Yet they're not things that could happen at the time of the show's making, so they're technological impossibilities, for the moment, just as many of the other catalyzing forces are supernatural ones. The moral lesson is still being driven by a force that isn't (yet) something that's within the realm of the possible. The unlikelihood of the catalyst being encountered by the viewer still keeps its consequences safely at arm's length.

The Twilight Zone Looks Just Like You

Why is all this so important, given my opening three questions? What is the Twilight Zone; where is it exactly; how did it get there?

It's important because there's a sort of double . . . distancing, we might call it, between the audience at home and what are actually pretty mundane lessons—a distancing I call double because it's created by not one but two fundamental aspects of how these lessons are usually delivered. Two different ways in which these truths are presented to us in a safe way, ripe for us to ignore or deny.

We're selfish. We're easily tricked or manipulated if the right carrot is dangled in front of us. We like to think we're special, when really we're not. We cling to truths that guide our actions but are actually pretty shaky. We don't like to get old. We wish we could return to a past that probably never existed. None of these are that earth-shatteringly surprising, particularly given what's going on in the world right now, at home, or abroad, and across the whole of twentieth- and twenty-first-century history.

These aren't lessons that we need to go into a mysterious, distant realm if we're to discover them. There's evidence of these truths all around us. And yet we're continually shown characters only discovering these truths when they go somewhere that we're *told* is another place (even when it doesn't seem to be), and only usually at the hands of monsters or events that *have* legitimately arrived from a realm operating by different laws from our own. Two attempts to make these lessons strange, when they're not.

It's scary, acknowledging our vulnerability, or the fact that humans aren't as special as we'd like to think. We don't like to be confronted by evidence to the contrary, because it would cause a whole load of existential angst that's tricky to cope with. *The Twilight Zone* allows us to feel that we're dealing with all this, but in a safe way, even when it's presenting itself as something frightening. It accentuates the strangeness of obvious yet disconcerting truths about our humanity. It shelters us from their *mundanity*.

Question the first, for which I'm about to give two answers, submitted for your approval. Two answers that together I hope will answer my second and third questions too. The Twilight Zone is right here. Wherever you're sitting right now, you're in it. It's where this chapter was written. It's where this book was put together, proof-read, printed, sold. Only it's not a mysterious, otherworldly place of shadow or magic. There's nothing strange about it or what we might learn there—not at all.

But this is the Twilight Zone as it really is, that exists in resistance to the Twilight Zone as the narration before each episode attempts to cast it for our comfort. You don't need to worry. The Twilight Zone is somewhere else, impossible, faraway. It might have things to tell us, but these things are so strange, so unlike anything in the real world, that it can only deliver these messages by sending impossible phenomena into our realm. The very majesty of our existence is so solid that it takes events of such an extraordinary nature to upset or uproot it. Everything's cool.

The car dealer from "The Whole Truth" wouldn't physically be able to give you one of these two answers. I'll leave you to work out which.

Taking Shelter in the Twilight Zone

If we buy into what the show's narration tells us, the Twilight Zone is a distant place we're not in any danger of running into.

And we put it there. It was built by *us*, as a repository for truths that threaten our sense of our place in the world. It's a sort of metaphorical shelter at the same time, allowing us to defend ourselves from these truths by highlighting their supposed strangeness. (I realize when looking back over this paragraph that in literal terms a repository can't be a shelter as well, because then all you'd be doing is locking yourself in with what you're trying to protect yourself from . . . But maybe that's the real reason the show can be so unnerving? Watching the show might allow a massive act of distancing, but if you're intent on distancing yourself from something, that very intent becomes what binds you to it. By watching the show, we get locked in with the same fears that we're using it to protect us from.)

Anyway. This brings me to "The Shelter", where the shelter that is the show called *The Twilight Zone* falls apart.

Take Bill Stockton—a man enjoying a birthday party thrown by his family and neighbors. The party is interrupted by a Civil Defense announcement that unidentified objects are hurtling towards American airspace. It's 1961—the height of the Cold War—and so this can only mean an imminent nuclear attack. The Stockton family hurries into its handy garden fallout shelter. There's not enough room for the neighbors, so they're forcibly kept outside. They're not gonna get nuked, because it's a false alarm, but in those moments they've learnt how ready their friendly neighbors are to consign them to their doom.

This episode reminds me of Season One's "The Monsters Are Due on Maple Street", where the titular road collapses into paranoia about the impending arrival of alien invaders. Both episodes show how the civilized values holding our communities together crumble as soon as they're tested and our own selfish drives are brought to the fore. But the ending of "Maple Street" reveals not only that aliens *are* on their way, but that they're using a comic-book device to manipulate the residents' nerves. The craze that rips through the street doesn't come from the people themselves, but from an otherworldly outside influence. This episode seems to draw out a dangerous truth inherent in our character, but then defuses it by showing the cause to be something impossible. "Maple Street" fits the pattern I established earlier.

"The Shelter" does not. There's no otherworldly influence behind the false alarm. No aliens or gremlins. No supernatural force that's taken control of the country's radio waves. What makes the communal links between the Stocktons and their neighbors break down is entirely possible. Correct me if I'm wrong, but I think it's the only single episode of the show where the moral lesson or warning is entirely devoid of any influence either supernatural or driven by technology that didn't exist when the episode aired.

It's not only this lack of supernatural influence that makes "The Shelter" so possible and so unnerving. During the Berlin Crisis of 1961—the same year this episode aired—Soviet Premier Nikolai Khrushchev had overtly threatened the US with nuclear oblivion. This threat was taken seriously enough for President Kennedy to advise American families to ready themselves by building fallout shelters in their backyards. The Stocktons weren't the only family that followed his suggestion. There were door-to-door fallout shelter salesmen too. Toothpaste ads highlighted how the product in question was ideal for use inside one of these things.

The situation here, which reveals the impossibility of people being able to work together in the way necessary for rebuilding society after such an attack, is not just physically possible, but was felt by the show's original viewers to be actively on the horizon. And I'm a pretty optimistic guy myself, but given the tensions building as I write this chapter between the US and Russia, and between the US and North Korea, I'm not sure the threat is entirely one that everyone reading this book would comfortably dismiss as historical . . .

The Twilight Zone Is Walking Distance

"What you are about to watch is a nightmare. It is not meant to be prophetic, it need not happen, it's the fervent and urgent prayer of all men of good will that it never shall happen. But in this place, in this moment, it does happen. This is the Twilight Zone."

What you have just read is Serling's opening narration to "The Shelter." It might not mean to encapsulate much of what I've been arguing here. But it does.

More than the other episodes, this in no way takes place in the Twilight Zone, unless we understand the Twilight Zone to mean the same familiar world of the viewers themselves. There's a tension here, between much of Serling's language presenting the place the audience is about to see as somewhere *else*, and the episode clearly taking place in what could easily be the audience's own home, with the event that disrupts their suburban comfort one frequently discussed in the news and that their own president warned was likely.

I'm wondering now if Serling *is* aware here of how the show usually works to distance us from common yet disruptive fears. Maybe that's why this is, if not the only, then one of the very select few episodes without any technologically or supernaturally impossible catalysts. It's as if he wants his viewers, once this one form of sheltering is removed, to note the disparity between the distancing attempt of his narration and what would've seemed the utter likelihood of the situation that it introduces. Noting in this active way the sheer *possibility* of the feared event unfolding in the same destructive way that it does in "The Shelter" can only help the families watching be less ready to throw away their own human values if (or when) the situation repeats itself off-screen.

The show reveals that the Twilight Zone is not the separate world of mystery or imagination that Serling's narration tells us it is. It's the room you're sitting in right now. The truths it shows its characters could be stumbled upon by you too, the moment you put this book down. Working together, the show and its narration highlight our urge to dump our worst fears and weaknesses into another realm, to cast them as fantastic; the show highlights, too, our urge to believe that only extraordinary events have the power to bring these fears and weaknesses out into the light of day. Because it wants us to be braver than we usually are, it also gives us the opportunity to recognize the failure of these urges, to see the weaknesses we'd love to disown in all their closeness and normality. The show allows its narration to encourage us inside its makeshift shelter, only to shut us in with all the fears and weaknesses we want to shelter from, encouraging us to grow better acquainted.

It's only in the case of a threat that must've felt all too probable that the show *forces* us to see how close the Twilight Zone really is. There's nothing like the threat of nuclear oblivion to make you so impatient about getting your point across. Let's keep an eye on the news over the coming months and hope it doesn't get any closer.

13
No Place Like a Non-Place

FERNANDO GABRIEL PAGNONI BERNS,
JUAN IGNACIO JUVÉ, AND EMILIANO AGUILAR

Empty streets. Empty roads. Empty gas stations. Empty bars. Empty worlds.

The Twilight Zone was many things: science fiction, fantasy, horror, and sometimes, comedy, but it always preferred stories revolving around crisis of identity and paranoia against the backdrop of the American Dream. In this context, the show illustrated the emptiness haunting American citizens in the consumerist 1950s. Even at the time, a host of books and intellectuals criticized the impact of consumerism and conformity in the era. The empty spaces privileged by the narrative were echoes of the emptiness felt by inauthentic, alienated characters.

Rod Serling, creator of the idea and the series, belonged to the school of California horror that included, among others, writers such as Richard Matheson, Charles Beaumont, Harlan Ellison, and George Clayton Johnson. All of them wrote for the show at some point in their careers. These men were, from the early 1950s to the mid-1960s, part of a brotherhood of writers centered in the Los Angeles area. According to Matt Cardin, they "founded their sense of the fantastic in everyday reality and in the experience of characters who might live next door if not in the reader's own house" rather than in foreign monstrosities embodied in figures such as the Count from Transylvania or the exotic walking mummy.

The geographical location is notable: California, and more particularly Hollywood, the place where identities are stripped down and recreated, where people come and go, often unnoticed.

The French philosopher and anthropologist Marc Augé used the term "non-place" to refer to places of transit that do not hold enough significance to be regarded properly as "places." Examples include motorway routes, airports, hotel rooms, and shopping malls. Places where there is no sense of belonging, places that favored lack of connectivity with anything of meaning or with other persons. The contemporary modern world is increasingly characterized by such "non-places." Nineteen-fifties Hollywood might also be classified as a non-place.

Non-places are the best of places to speak about loneliness and alienation. Thus, many of the best episodes of *The Twilight Zone* were constructed around this particular motif: "Will the Real Martian Please Step Up?," "The Four of Us Are Dying," "The Hitch-Hiker," "The After Hours," "The Passersby," "Passage on the Lady Anne," and, of course, the instant classic "Nightmare at 20,000 Feet," among many others.

American Dream or American Nightmare?

Unlike the pulp fiction dominating the markets, the writers of the California school of horror wrote about fantastic adventures taking place in the lives of common people residing in the suburbs. Of course, alien landscapes, rocket ships and amazing planets were part of the stuff of their tales, but all these elements were used to speak about down-to-earth human nature, in a very down-to-earth way.

The Twilight Zone was created in the postwar period, a time when traditional notions of gender were being re-organized. On the one hand, masculinity was framed by fears that arose when women joined the public workplace in record numbers due to the scarcity of men, who were occupied fighting in the battlefield. Many working-class women had always worked outside the home, but the Second World War prompted middle-class and upper-class women to take the jobs that the men of the house (their husbands, sons, brothers, or fathers) left vacant when marching to the front. In a matter of months, many women left the domestic space to fulfill the masculine role of breadwinners.

Further, many men returning from the war were wounded, mutilated, or psychologically damaged with shell shock, thus unable to keep working as they did before 1941. The nation applauded them as heroes, but did not guarantee them jobs. In this scenario, a crisis of identity took place: after many years of working and creating an identity within the public sphere, many women were reluctant to resume their traditional position as the passive domestic partner; men, meanwhile, were jobless heroes. One of the main jobs opening up for middle-class men was that of salesman, a role which competes with that of the perfect husband and father; the salesman earns enough money to support his family but, in doing so, he spends days and weeks away from home.

It was within this situation that the writers of *The Twilight Zone* turned the fantastic from foreign universes to the dark underside of the sunny everyday life of many Americans. The true source of anxieties comes from a potential crisis of identity rather than an alien invasion.

Enter *The Twilight Zone* and the non-places.

The Nearness of You

The privileged site for *The Twilight Zone* to tell stories of identity crisis was the non-place, the space of anonymity. But what exactly is a non-place? The non-place is a term coined by Marc Augé in his book *Non-Places: Introduction to an Anthropology of Supermodernity*. Augé begins with creating an "anthropology of the near," an understanding of "everyday life." As it easy to see, the latter suits perfectly well the philosophy behind *The Twilight Zone*, as the show revolved around what was close to Americans rather than anything exotic or alien.

Augé also coined the term "supermodernity"; the situation created by the changing nature of time, space, and construction of meaning in the historical frame that is our postmodernity. For Augé, the 'non-place' is the new spatial mode born of supermodernity, and it opposed the traditional place, which indicates that a culture is inextricably located within a certain time and place. Non-places, by contrast, are prevalent in the new form of society as spaces created for specific ends, such as transportation. These "supermodern" spaces cannot be defined as concerned in any way with identity. Simply put, the traditional conception of space means that the persons inhabiting it are identified by the shared space. A neighborhood is a good example. Everyone knows you. Even if you're reluctant to get out and meet the neighbors, you'll be recognized as the shy guy or girl living at a particular place. This kind of conception of space presumes a fixed identity and place.

Augé observes how acceleration in transportation and mobility has made an impact on the new globalized culture. This doesn't mean that people didn't travel in previous decades, but the flux of bodily movement has now been ramped up. There are more airports than before, trains take you everywhere, weekends are times for quick escapes, and low-cost air travel has made intercontinental flights more accessible, even to the working class. According to Augé, the non-places are nodes of traffic and movement: pleasure, velocity, and modernity blend together creating "supermodernity."

In "Passage on the Lady Anne" the Ransomes, a married couple facing a crisis, book passage on "The Lady Anne," a very old luxury liner from the past en route to London. Against the wishes of the others, elderly passengers, Eileen and Alan Ransome remain on the ship and, eventually, reconcile their differences. "The Lady Anne," however, is retiring after this final voyage—the boat will be dismantled—so the passengers agree to ditch the young couple. Put in a lifeboat, Eileen and Alan are given a warm goodbye as the old ship and its passengers disappear into the fog without leaving any traces.

The tension between the new (speed) and the old (slowness) frames the story. The first scene establishes the Ransomes as people accustomed to a life full of obligations and urgent demands. He is a businessman who dedicates himself completely to his work to the point that he does not have time to be with Eileen, who in turn works as a stewardess. During six years of marriage, they have shared practically no time together. That's why she insists on traveling by boat, which is much *slower*; she wants to "slow down" time.

The travel agent is surprised at the willingness of the couple to find the slowest means of transportation, in a world of supermodernity where distances become shorter and speed is often the decisive consideration. By contrast with the trend of the times, the "Lady Anne" is the ultimate expression of slowness and an already outdated way of traveling. One of the elderly passengers points out explicitly that the old mode of travel involved a way of life that had more "grace, education, and tradition."

This rejection of speeded up modernity is the lesson that the young couple gets from the "Lady Anne" and it is what motivates them to make this trip. When Alan Ransome gets on the boat he is upset by the loss of time involved in the sea voyage: in one scene he gets confused and asks "When is this going to take off?" His wife quickly corrects him: they are already in motion. After the experience aboard the old ship, they begin to understand the importance of spending time together rather than speeding from one commitment to another.

The episode seems to follows Augé's thinking. Unlike traditional anthropology, concerned with the examination of faraway groups of exotic people, Augé's project dealt with the here and now, ordinary Americans, what's taking place around us, and how supermodernity is affecting us.

One for the Road

We pass more and more time in places of interchangeable anonymity, places such as shopping malls or airports that don't require any sense of community. These spaces made for transit, commerce, and leisure are what Augé calls "non-places," inextricably linked to the relations that individuals have with these spaces: anonymity. Any sense of community has been shattered. In the middle of the road, the husband is turned into an anonymous salesman.

Travel was an important issue in the 1950s. The new consumerist economy promoted traveling as a form of leisure. New cars and faster forms of traveling were available for the postwar generation. *The Twilight Zone* made excellent use of these non-places as geographies of horror and identity crisis.

Shortly after beginning her trip in "The Hitch-Hiker," Nan Adams finds herself being haunted by an omnipresent, disheveled hitch-hiker who keeps appearing along the road. Soon, she accepts the fact that something uncanny is taking place. In fear, she spends days and nights driving non-stop, only finding anonymity wherever she goes. The non-place, in Augé's terms, describes a zone which creates neither singular identity nor relationships. Afraid of the solitary road ahead, Nan invites a young hitch-hiker aboard. He, however, soon abandons her, as he fears her mental stability. It seems impossible to establish durable bonds in the middle of the journey.

Scared to death, she phones her mother, only to discover she is in a hospital after suffering a nervous breakdown following the death of her daughter, Nan. Apparently Nan had died in a road accident, when a tire blew out and the car crashed. After learning the truth, Nan returns to her car and agrees to take the hitch-hiker wherever he wants to go.

"The Passersby" can be read as a companion piece to "The Hitch-Hiker." Lavinia sits on the front porch of her dilapidated house, a casualty of the American Civil War. There, she has been watching a daily march-past, the wounded of a bloodthirsty war. Eventually, she figures out that the wounded are the war's dead. Like Nan Adams, Lavinia refuses to accept the unavoidable fate awaiting her down at the end of the road. Again, the road appears as a non-place; the stripping of identity suggested by Augé is here metaphorized by representing those traveling the road as dead people. The location with real meaning lies ahead: a city in the case of Augé, the afterlife in the world of *The Twilight Zone*.

It can be argued, and rightly so, that both Nan and Lavinia know perfectly well who they are. However, the horror of the tales comes from the lack of knowledge that the women have about their situation: they are dead and refuse to accept that fact. They are alienated from their own selves, unable to grasp the reality of their existence. Their journey to self-discovery is metaphorized through the road, the non-place representing their unconnectedness.

Even taking a respite at the side of the road shapes a non-place. "Will the Real Martian Please Step Up?" revolves around two patrolmen investigating reports of a flying saucer that submerged into a pond. Tracks from the pond lead to a nearby diner, so the patrolmen visit the café to see if they can find the aliens. The people in the diner are all passengers of a bus making a stop while the unstable bridge ahead is checked out. There, and after weird happenings (the lights going on and off, sugar containers exploding), the patrolmen start questioning the passengers who, rather than being six as they were when boarding the bus, are now seven. There is an alien among them. The rapid-fire editing of close shots of everyone's faces increases the sense of suspicion. Any one of them could be the invader.

Augé sees non-places as good marks of the success of the capitalist apparatus of individualization. Finding the alien in "Will the Real Martian Please Step Up?" seems simple: who was not on the bus when the trip began? However, nobody had really paid attention to their fellow passengers, so nobody seems to be sure who was there from the beginning and who was not. All of them are unknown to each other; any sense of community is completely broken. Anonymity has prevailed.

Day Tripper

Airplanes and ships are both specific physical spaces and non-places through which you simply pass without truly belonging there. In an airplane, you're passenger "left window seat, C," not a "real" identity. Only after landing can you recover your proper sense of "I."

If we're thinking of travel as the perfect example of non-place, we naturally think of one of the most famous episodes: the classic "Nightmare at 20,000 Feet" in which Robert Wilson, an airline passenger flying through a storm, catches glimpses of a creature creating havoc on the wing and, even worse, the engine of the aircraft. Regardless of his warnings, neither his wife, nor the stewardess, nor the co-pilot believe him.

Faithfully following Richard Matheson's short story on which the episode is based, the core of the tale is not so much whether the airplane will fall but whether Bob will reaffirm his identity as a sane man. This need for identification with some sense of the normal is what seems to bother Bob most. On the plane, people sleep or do not pay attention to what happens around them, and only the hostesses display a totally fake interest in Bob's claims. What emerges in "Nightmare at 20,000 Feet" is the loneliness of the modern man in an individualistic society that, like "Will the Real Martian

Please Step Up?," favors anonymity. Bob's most crucial struggle is against this lack of interest in himself as a person, not the gremlin tearing apart the engines of the airplane.

"The Parallel" also pursues the theme of identity. Here we're told the story of Major Robert Gaines who makes an orbital trip, spending one week orbiting the planet, having lost communication on radar and radio for a total of six hours. He reappears unconscious and without remembering what happened while he was off planet Earth.

After being questioned by his superiors, Gaines finds that things are not what they used to be at home. His daughter insists that he is not her father. Gaines himself feels different and soon comes to the conclusion that he has fallen into a parallel dimension not too different from our own but with some small differences.

Space travel was a hot topic during the late 1950s and 1960s, the heyday of space competition between the Soviet Union and the United States; but the episode can be analyzed as a critique of supermodernity. Space flight is the most pronounced symbol of non-place, as well of the acceleration of movement noted by Augé.

Rather than roads connecting distant towns, here the non-place is the vast infinity of the universe, a non-place filled with loneliness. Outer space provides a sense of homelessness devoid of meaning; as Siobhan Carroll says, it is a "space antithetical to habitable place." It is, in other words, an extreme example of non-place.

Crisis of Identity, 9th Floor

Since the non-place is a space for anonymity, Augé observes that the relations individuals have with these particular landscapes require certain contractual relations. This heavily contrasts with the anonymity provided by the non-place. When entering and exiting a non-place, such as the border between regions or checking into a hotel, people must affirm their identities. It is the only moment of "identification" in the non-place. Thus, the patrolmen of "Will the Real Martian Please Step Up?" demand identification (name, surname, and ID) from all the passengers as a way to break from the anonymity that comes with traveling.

Only an easily recognizable figure, Abraham Lincoln, can convince Lavinia to accept her state, while Nan learns the truth from her mother, the only point of familiarity within the road. Gaines is identified by his credentials after his return, but he is different nonetheless and cannot pass the check of his own family, which ultimately is the identification that emanates from his real place of belonging.

Identification is needed to downplay, at least to some extent, the overwhelming sense of invisibility, of being, like Nan or Lavinia, undead. When entering a non-place such as an airport or a shopping mall, the individual becomes invisible or, at least, indistinguishable from the masses who pass through it; everyone seemingly goes about their own business with no sense of connectedness or communion with anyone else. They are not there to make friends.

Even if roads and traveling are good examples of non-places, closed spaces, such as hotels or shopping malls are also spaces that produce a non-experience. These sites, rather than providing a stable identity, provide a fleeting one, that of client. In "The After Hours," Marsha White gets into the ninth floor of a shopping mall where she purchases a gold thimble from the only saleswoman working in this desolated area. After a little inquiry, she learns that the building has no ninth floor and later faints when she discovers that the saleslady was, in fact, a mannequin. Marsha wakes later to find herself left behind after store hours. At that time, her ephemeral identity as "client" is of no use any more: the purpose of the space (selling things) is shut down. Then the mannequins come to life and the truth is revealed: Marsha is also a mannequin who has forgotten her true identity as such.

At first, Marsha finds the ninth floor intriguing, as the saleswoman seems to know her name. But what really upsets Marsha is the fact that the saleslady asks her if she is happy. This little intrusion of intimacy in a place dedicated to anonymity is the bell that rings alarms in Marsha's head. Nobody expects intimacy and care in a non-place.

The need for identification brings some sense of relief amidst a sea of anonymity. But *The Twilight Zone* being the show it is, identification can be fatal. In "The Four of Us Are Dying," Archie Hammer uses his talent for replicating the face of any man he sees to profit from the dead. All his plans go well. As Johnny Foster, a deceased trumpet player, Archie seduces Johnny's fiancé and makes plans with her to run away. Knowing that he needs money to finance his love affair, he imitates Virgil Sterig, a local ruffian and steals the money Virgil was killed for.

The episode takes place in various places, but two are recurrent; the streets and the hotel where Archie goes to plan ahead and changes his face. The hotel room then is turned into the perfect example of a non-place, a location where identities are interchangeable. The way in which the streets are filmed is especially striking. Neon advertising and lights are displayed in awkward positions, almost falling into Archie. Rather than being a safe place, the streets of the episode offer an expressionist aesthetic pointing to something going awry.

In the streets, with gunmen giving him chase, Archie imitates Andy Marshak, a local boxer. He succeeds and fools the gunmen. However, amidst all this anonymity that is Archie's main weapon, somebody recognizes him: Andy's father thinks that Archie is his son, and wanting to exact vengeance on him, shoots and kills Archie. Ironically, Archie's doom was recognition. To both Archie and Marsha, the blow comes from issues of intimacy taking place in non-places.

Unknown to the many writers for *The Twilight Zone*, writing forty years before Augé, many episodes followed Marc Augé's logic of the non-place, the site for anonymity typical of the modern age. Shopping malls, hotels, ships, all of them are reconfigured as scenes of a crisis of identity that follows the shifting of traditional roles and identities taking place in the 1950s.

The long, winding road with no clear light at the end is the ultimate example of going nowhere, a shattered identity in the bag, while Beverly Garland singing "One for My Baby (and One More for the Road)" resonates heavily, as it does in "The Four of Us Are Dying."

14
The Science of Alternate Realities

DAVID MORGAN

The Twilight Zone's own opening narration describes itself as another dimension—both a "fifth dimension" and a "dimension of mind." But what does that really mean?

There are a number of ways that the idea of alternate or "higher" dimensions arises in mathematics and science, from the mundane structures of Euclidean geometry, to the speculative spacetimes of string theory. Each of these notions of a "dimension" carries its own unique philosophical questions and conundrums. And in many cases, thinking about higher dimensions also invites us to imagine "parallel universes" of the sort that played a major role in the *Twilight Zone* series.

What is a "dimension" anyway? Mathematically speaking, it's simply the number of co-ordinates needed to specify a location in some space. A piece of graph paper represents a two-dimensional Euclidean plane. You need two numbers to locate a point on the graph. These are the familiar x and y Cartesian co-ordinates you may remember from algebra or geometry class.

To specify the location of a point in the room you are sitting in would require not two but three numbers—the distances from two perpendicular walls, plus the distance up from the floor. The universe of our experience is a three dimensional one, and as far as we can tell from our senses, the universe we inhabit has only three spatial dimensions.

This doesn't stop us from thinking about spaces with four or more dimensions. We can't picture them, draw them, or even satisfactorily imagine them, but if we think about them mathematically, we can draw conclusions about them. For example, consider a one-dimensional line that has length "L." Slide this line perpendicular to itself a distance L and you have a 2D square with size L^2. (We call this 2D size "area.") Move this square perpendicular to itself a distance L into the third dimension and you make a cube with a size of L^3. (We call this 3D size "volume.")

Suppose we moved this whole cube a distance L into the fourth dimension, perpendicular to itself. What would that make? Whatever that object is, we can't draw it, or sculpt it, or even close our eyes and imagine it, since we are limited by our three-dimensional bodies and our experience of three-dimensional space. But nevertheless, we can give this new object a name—a "hypercube"—and use the rules of mathematics to deduce that its size in four dimensions is L^4.

We can use mathematics to extend this pattern into as many dimensions as we want. And when we imagine spatial dimensions that are greater than the three-dimensional space we live in, it's not long before we ask ourselves whether or not these higher dimensions actually exist outside of our ordinary three. This gives rise to the notion of a "parallel universe." In this context, we can imagine a parallel universe as another universe with the same number of dimensions as ours, but which is "offset" by some amount in the invisible fourth dimension.

Again, this is hard to picture, so we can take the analogy down a dimension. Imagine a universe that is strictly two-dimensional, like a plane from Euclidean geometry with length and width, but absolutely no thickness. Now imagine another universe stacked on top of that one, "above" it, in the third dimension. And another, and another, like a stack of paper. The residents of each 2D universe would be two-dimensional themselves. They would not be able to look "up" or "down" or likely have any way of knowing that another universe existed right next door to their own. Unless of course, there was some way to cross through the higher dimension.

In one of the most memorable *Twilight Zone* episodes, "Little Girl Lost," six-year-old Tina disappears from her bedroom. Her parents can still hear her voice, but she's nowhere to be found. Eventually her dog disappears as well. As luck would have it, the family has a friend, Bill, who is a physicist, and physicists know all about such things. Bill correctly identifies the issue—behind Tina's bed is a portal into "another dimension." (I can't help but see the parallel dimension of "Little Girl Lost" as a clear precursor to "The Upside-Down" of the contemporary Netflix hit series *Stranger Things*.) They manage to rescue Tina from the other side of this interdimensional portal just before it closes. The closing narration by Rod Serling confirms physicist Bill's interpretation of a parallel universe situated in a higher dimension, but reveals that physicists were never again able to open the portal.

Time as a Dimension

A fourth spatial dimension is one place to situate a parallel universe, but you may have also heard people say that "the fourth dimension is time." But how can time be a dimension when time is so different from space?

The nature of time has been a topic of interest to ancient philosophers (Plato and Parmenides) and modern physicists (Einstein and Hawking) alike. For philosophers, questions about time include such conundrums as: "Are the past, present, and future equally real?," "Can statements about the future be true or false in the present?" and "Why does time seem to have a 'flow' and a 'direction' when space does not?"

One important twentieth-century contribution to our understanding of the relationship between time and space is Einstein's view that time can be thought of as a "fourth dimension," placing it on an equal footing with the ordinary three dimensions of space. As we often do when discussing higher dimensions, we can visualize this idea by considering a situation with one fewer dimensions than our ordinary 3D world.

Many readers have probably made a simple "flip book" animation, where you draw a picture on each page of a small notepad, and then change that picture slightly on each page so that when you riffle quickly through the pages with your thumb, the picture appears to move. This rudimentary animation can be thought of as a 2-dimensional space—each page of the flip-book is a 2-dimensional drawing. The vertical dimension, the thickness of the notepad, represents time. As you flip through the thickness dimension of the notepad, time progresses, and the objects in the 2D "universe" move and change. By analogy, our own changing universe can be thought of as a series of static three-dimensional instants that "stacked" in the fourth dimension of time.

This geometrical interpretation of time wasn't unique to Einstein, and others before him had visualized time this way. But the approach of putting time and space on equal mathematical and geometrical footing was an important aspect of the theory of relativity. Since, according to Einstein's theory of relativity, moving through space changes your measurements of time, it's important to stop considering time as something entirely separate from space as Isaac Newton did. The two are connected, and the unification of space and time into a four-dimensionsal "space-time" made this connection explicit.

Einstein's special theory of relativity permits a limited sort of "time travel" in that it allows for different observers who are moving through space at different speeds to experience different amounts of time between events. This is the idea of "time dilation"—that time flows more slowly for an observer aboard a rocket moving close to the speed of light than it does for another observer who considers themselves "at rest" relative to the rocket. (Of course, the very question of who is moving and who is "at rest" is a relative one. Hence, "relativity.")

The existence of the phenomenon of time dilation means that we aren't all necessarily moving into the future at the same rate. This means that an explorer in a very fast-moving rocket could depart from Earth and zip around the galaxy at close to the speed of light, then return to Earth to find that more time had elapsed for the Earthlings than aboard their spaceship. This means that, in some sense, they have "time-traveled" into the future.

The "fast-forwarding" through time permitted by the theory of relativity is certainly interesting, and it is a staple of some science-fiction stories about time travel into the future. For example, it's essentially the mechanism that transported astronaut George Taylor into Earth's post-apocalyptic simian future in *Planet of the Apes*.

The first draft of that classic movie's screenplay was written by none other than Rod Serling. Serling also penned the story for the *Twilight Zone* episode "A Kind of a Stopwatch." In this episode, the boorish Patrick McNulty gets his hands on a stopwatch that somehow has the ability to stop time for everyone but him. When he breaks the stopwatch during an attempted bank heist, he suddenly finds himself effectively alone in a time of his own. While the complete cessation of the flow of time isn't permitted by the theory of relativity, this episode plays with the idea that time is malleable and need not flow the same for everyone.

Time and Time Travel

The idea that time is not absolute and may be more connected to space that we had thought leads to an obvious question. If time is just a "dimension" like space, why is it that we can travel in any direction in space, but only one direction in time? One question of interest to both philosophers and physicists is whether or not time travel is possible—either physically possible, logically possible, or both.

The Twilight Zone explores notions of time travel in several episodes. In "Walking Distance," ad executive Martin Sloan finds himself suddenly in his childhood hometown, where he encounters both his younger parents and himself as a young boy. In "The Odyssey of Flight 33," a planeload of passengers finds themselves transported back to the age of dinosaurs, and struggles to return to 1961. But for all its frequent forays into the topic of time travel, *The Twilight Zone* did not often wrestle with the philosophical problems and paradoxes that time travel stories so often create.

The most-discussed philosophical issue raised by the possibility of time travel is the so-called "Grandfather Paradox." This paradox can be phrased as a simple question. If a time machine existed, could you travel back to a time before you were born and kill your own grandfather? The paradox created by the scenario is that if you kill your grandfather, you can never be born, so how do you exist? Some philosophers insist that these sorts of paradoxes alone are enough to establish that time travel is impossible. It's not just a physical impossibility, but a logical impossibility. Others see it merely as proof that whatever a time traveler does during his or her foray into the past must be those things that already happened in the past, so that actions of the time traveler were and always have been eternally true events.

For example, if you ask, "Could I go back in time to 1930 and assassinate Adolf Hitler before he rose to power?," the answer would be "No" because we know that Hitler was not killed in 1930. For this to happen would logically contradict a known true fact about the past and cause it to be false. But if you ask, "Could I go back in time to 1963 and assassinate President John F. Kennedy?," the answer might be "Yes." But only if the JFK assassination conspiracy theorists had been right all along, and there was a "second gunman" on the grassy knoll—you, a time traveler from the future. In other words, you can kill JFK in the past, but only if you did kill JFK in the past. Such a scenario is strange, but it involves no paradox.

The Grandfather Paradox was dealt with in the *Twilight Zone* on a couple of occasions. In the episode "Back There," Professor Peter Corrigan (played by Russell Johnson, who would later play a much more famous professor on television) has a discussion with his colleagues about whether a time traveler could alter past events. For example, could you travel back to before the stock market crash of 1929 and cash out before the stock market began to tumble? Professor Corrigan argues that his actions could potentially alter the circumstances of the crash—an impossibility, as the crash is a fixed moment in history that can't be changed. When Corrigan does find himself inexplicably transported into the past, he also finds himself faced with the opportunity to stop the assassination of Abraham Lincoln. He fails, but finds that some historical events wound up changed in other, smaller ways. This leads to the philosophically unsatisfying implication that some events in the past can be altered, but others cannot.

By contrast, the *Twilight Zone* episode "No Time Like the Past" presents a more philosophically consistent picture of time travel and its associated paradoxical nature. In this episode, Paul Driscoll travels back in time with the express goal of altering history. But at every turn he is thwarted. He's ignored when he tries to warn residents of Hiroshima, found out by a hotel maid when he tries to assassinate Hitler, and even winds up causing a fire he wanted to prevent. The message of the episode is clear—past events are eternally true. Driscoll couldn't kill Hitler in the past because it's a fact that he didn't kill Hitler in the past. And the schoolhouse burned down because Driscoll had always been the one who burned it down.

Infinite Universes and Infinite Possibilities

There's another way to escape the Grandfather Paradox, which is to say that when a time traveler arrives in the past and makes a change, they bring a new universe into being, creating a new history from that point forward. This new universe exists alongside the old one—parallel to it, if you will—as a new timeline with new facts. This is another sense of the idea of a "parallel" universe. But there are many other notions of parallel realities that arise in physics and philosophy. And we don't need to invoke time travel to encounter them.

One scientific concept that forces us to confront the possibility of multiple parallel worlds is the notion that, if the universe is infinite in both space and time, then everything that could possibly happen must actually happen at some point in space and time. (This is a consequence of something called the "ergotic hypothesis" in physics, which basically says that every microscopic arrangement of matter and energy in a physical system is equally probable when taken over some appropriately long time.) Even if the probability of some event is very, very small—any very small probability times "infinity" gives a finite likelihood. With an infinite amount of time and space for things to happen in, everything possible becomes certain. This means that there is some other version of Earth somewhere where you aren't reading this book, as well as some version where you wrote this book. There is even some version where you look like one of the monstrous, vaguely-pig-nosed denizens of the world where Janet Tyler awakes in "The Eye of the Beholder."

This philosophical thought experiment is nothing more than that, and we need not concern ourselves with the reality of such arguments, since modern cosmology reveals that our universe is neither spatially nor temporally infinite. There

have been thirteen billion years or so of cosmic history since
the Big Bang, and our universe contains a few hundred
billion galaxies with a few hundred billion stars each. These
are large numbers to be sure, but still infinitely far from
infinity. So while there may be Earth-like planets elsewhere
in the physical universe, we would never expect to encounter
any exact copies or almost-exact copies of ourselves in the
cosmos. But there are other avenues of thought that lead us
from established scientific ideas into speculation about not
just parallel worlds within our own universe, but entire
universes that could exist parallel to our own.

Quantum Mechanics and Parallel Realities

One of the most puzzling theories to emerge during the early
part of the twentieth century is the theory of quantum mechanics. There's nothing particularly difficult about the formal physics of quantum mechanics—it's a part of every
sophomore physics major's coursework, and the calculations
made possible by quantum field theory and modern particle
physics have given us some of the most precise mathematical
predictions ever confirmed by experiment. But at the same
time, one of the lasting philosophical issues facing physics is
the question of how to interpret the probabilistic nature of
quantum theory.

In classical Newtonian mechanics, the laws of physics
allow us to calculate a precise trajectory for an object
through space and time. Newton's Laws allow us to calculate
the orbit of the Earth around the Sun as precisely as we
wish. But in quantum mechanics, the behavior of subatomic
particles is not described by a single definite path through
space. Instead, the behavior of a subatomic particle is described by a quantum mechanical wavefunction that only
gives the probability of various outcomes. The question of
what actually happens when a quantum-mechanical probability becomes an observed result is still the source of much
debate among physicists and the source of considerable confusion within popular treatments of quantum mechanics.

The most common way to deal with this transition from
probability to actuality is to simply acknowledge that when
we observe a quantum system, we have to interact with it,

and when we do so, we introduce a change into our description of the situation. Before we make our observation, the theory demands that we describe a system using a wavefunction which handles all of the potential outcomes probabilistically. But after we've made an observation, only one of the potential outcomes is actualized as "real." So the old wavefunction is no longer a useful description of the situation. This transition is sometimes referred to as the "collapse" of the wavefunction.

What does this all have to do with parallel universes? It turns out that some physicists have side-stepped the question of what happens when one possible outcome becomes the "real" one by postulating that *all* of the possible states of a quantum mechanical system are actually realized in multiple parallel versions of our universe. Every event and interaction at the quantum level gives rise to multiple copies of the universe in which each possible outcome of the interaction occurs. These multiple copies of the universe split from one another, but exist side-by-side, a staggering number of parallel realities superimposed upon one another at every instant. This is the "Many Worlds Interpretation" of quantum mechanics.

Notice that the proper terminology is "Many Worlds Interpretation" and not "Many Worlds Theory." That's because the Many Worlds idea adds nothing new to the equations of the theory of quantum mechanics, or to the predictions of the theory itself. It is merely a way to interpret the meaning of the act of observation within the context of the theory. There is no way to experimentally determine whether or not the Many Worlds idea is true, because we only have access to whatever version of the universe we find ourselves in at this instant. Whatever parallel realities may exist are not our reality, so we have no access to them. In fact, many philosophers would argue that to claim these other universes are "real" when there is no way to confirm or deny their existence is not only unscientific, but ontologically suspect as well.

Parallel universes that exhibit only very slight differences from our own—the result, perhaps, of quantum mechanical roads not taken—can also be found among the episodes of *The Twilight Zone.* One of them is "The Parallel." In this episode, Major Robert Gaines, an astronaut, experiences an incident while in orbit that causes him to lose consciousness. Upon returning to Earth he begins to notice small differences from the reality he knows. The discrepancies start out small. People call him "Colonel" instead of "Major." His house has a white picket fence he doesn't remember. But the differences gradually become more pronounced. When the people around him claim to have never heard the name "John F. Kennedy" before, Gaines realizes that he has slipped into some sort of alternate reality—a universe that looks the same in most respects, but where some things have, for whatever reason, turned out differently. Perhaps Gaines, or his consciousness, has strayed from his original reality into one of the many alternative quantum realities that exist side-by-side with our own.

Cosmology and the Multiverse

While quantum mechanics requires us to think about the meaning of observing the smallest things in the universe, modern cosmology forces us to wrestle with the structure of the cosmos as a whole.

The fact that the Big Bang theory tells us that our Universe is "expanding" tempts us to visualize the universe as expanding "into" something, like a balloon expanding into the space of the room that contains it. It is not necessary to imagine some region outside the universe (and many cosmologists would caution against doing so) but it's almost unavoidable, and in some cases, imagining this higher-dimensional space outside of our three-plus-one-dimensional spacetime has some attractive advantages. And once we imagine a higher-dimensional space outside of our universe, it becomes possible to imagine other universes existing within this space as well. Modern physicists and cosmologists sometimes speak of the "multiverse," a higher-dimensional construct in which perhaps an infinite number of alternate universes are embedded. The idea of a multiverse emerges naturally when we're confronted with the task of picturing the structure of the cosmos as a whole. The other universes could have different numbers of dimensions than ours, and even entirely different laws of physics from our own. Our own universe could even have come into existence when two of these higher dimensional universes interacted or collided.

If the multiverse is real, and also infinite, then we return to the possibility of there being an infinite number of copies of not just our Solar System and Earth, but our entire universe. These parallel universes would exist separate from us in a higher-dimensional space, not superimposed on our own like the quantum copies of Many Worlds.

Serious physicists and cosmologists discuss the idea of the multiverse and other universes as a real possibility and as an answer to some nagging questions that plague our fundamental theories of physics. For example, why does the universe have the particular laws, particles, physical forces, and physical constants it does and not some other ones? Why isn't the charge of an electron twice what it is? Why is gravity trillions of trillions of times weaker than electromagnetism instead of billions of times stronger? For decades, our attempts at a unified theory of nature have tried to provide a convincing answer to this question, and all such attempts have failed. But the idea of the multiverse sweeps that question away with a wave of its multidimensional hand. The laws of nature are essentially random, and somewhere in the multiverse there exists some universe, possibly infinitely many universes, with any permissible set of natural laws, physical constants, and spatial dimensions you could imagine. We just happen to live in *this* one.

Whatever cosmological issues the idea of a higher-dimensional multiverse pretends to solve, it's hard not to feel like it's a bit of a cop out, and somewhat lacking in scientific seriousness. After all, can we even speak scientifically about a universe outside of our own?

One of the most widely-accepted notions among scientists is philosopher of science Karl Popper's claim that what demarcates scientific ideas from non-scientific ones is that scientific theories can be falsified by experimental evidence. In other words, a scientific theory is not actually scientific if you can't imagine an experiment that could be done to prove it wrong. It's almost impossible to imagine an experiment whose results would probe the existence (or lack thereof) of universes outside of our own, since the universe is, essentially by definition, everything we can possibly observe and measure.

If it's impossible to know that the multiverse is out there, then is it really a scientific idea at all? With no ability to travel into it or even experimentally confirm its reality, the multiverse and its many parallel realities will likely forever remain a dimension of mind, and a land of imagination.

Fifth Dimension

Our Twisted Imaginings

15
The Twists and Turns of Second Chances

JOHN V. KARAVITIS

The twist ending. Say whatever you'd like about *The Twilight Zone*, but talk about any episode will focus on its twist ending. It's the unexpected turn of events at the end of every episode that defines this television series.

Are twist endings special? They may simply be a clever way to leverage irony in telling a story. You expect one ending, and you're surprised to see another, contradictory, even shocking ending conclude the story. Or perhaps twist endings may suggest that there could have been a better way that events could have turned out. In some episodes, the main character does get a chance at a do-over—a second chance at Life. A chance to appreciate the path traveled, and to learn from their past mistakes. A chance to go back and choose the other fork in the road.

But really, aren't thoughts about second chances just wishful thinking? Or do *The Twilight Zone*'s twist endings reveal a specific philosophical idea about Life? If the purpose of twist endings is to suggest the possibility of second chances, then would it be wrong to ask for a second chance, if you could? Or to reject one, if it were thrust upon you?

The Twilight Zone can be more than just entertainment. It can be a guide on how to live your life. To see this more clearly, we'll look at three different types of episodes. And as *The Twilight Zone* is a television series from my youth (and many of yours), we'll start from that perspective. Let's look at episodes that are all about *nostalgia*.

Things—We—Were Better Back Then!

Nostalgia is a sentimental longing or desire to go back to what we believe were happier, simpler times. Such feelings can arise when you're reminiscing about past accomplishments, or, more likely, present failures. Nostalgia can also arise when you're feeling frustrated or overwhelmed by your daily routine. But the important thing about nostalgia is how we respond to it.

Feelings of nostalgia can be so overwhelming that they can lead to obsession with the past. In "The Sixteen-Millimeter Shrine," Barbara Jean Trenton, an aging actress, relives her past glory by obsessively viewing the movies that she starred in. Her agent tries to get her out of her house, for her to live a little. "It's nostalgia, it's nice, but it's not true. It's phony." She refuses to accept her agent's counsel. "If I wish hard enough, it doesn't have to be phony." In "A Stop at Willoughby," Gart Williams, an ad agency executive, is overwhelmed by the pressures of his work and the high expectations of his wife. During a train ride home, he falls asleep and dreams that he's on a different train that has stopped at a small town called Willoughby. It's also not November 1960, but July 1888!

During an argument with his wife, he tells her how he feels. "I would prefer . . . a job . . . where I could be myself . . . where I wouldn't have to climb on a stage and go through a masquerade every morning at nine o'clock!" In "Kick the Can," Charles Whitley, a resident of Sunnyvale Rest, a home for the aged, wants to leave, but can't. One day, he sees a group of kids playing "kick the can." "It's almost as though playing 'kick the can' keeps them young," he muses. Later, chatting with Ben, a fellow resident, he asks "What happened, Ben?" Ben's reply is straightforward. "We grew up, that's all." Charles rebels against this. "You decided that you were an old man, and that has made you old."

In "Of Late I Think of Cliffordville," Bill Feathersmith, a rich tycoon, bemoans the lack of real challenges in his life. "I wish I could go back to Cliffordville and begin again . . . That was the kick. Getting it, not having it." The Devil—in the form of a beautiful young woman, Miss Devlin—offers to send him back. He accepts, and finds himself back in Cliffordville, 1910. Unfortunately, nothing is as he remembered.

The technological advances that he had depended on to make his fortune won't be available for decades. And although he looks young on the outside, he's still seventy-five years old on the inside!

Main characters who turn to nostalgia and become obsessed with the past in a sense all die. Barbara Jean Trenton ends up "living" in the celluloid world of one of her past movies. Gart Williams jumps off of his commuter train while it's moving. In "Static," an elderly man retreats into a delusion of years gone by. The elderly residents of Sunnyvale Rest who decide to play "kick the can" vanish in the middle of the night. In "Young Man's Fancy," a newlywed groom abandons his bride and returns to his life as his mother's boy. Bill Feathersmith fails at reliving and re-conquering his past, and is returned to the present as a janitor, with no memory of what he had once been.

But this doesn't mean that nostalgia is always futile. There are episodes where the main character experiences nostalgia, but eventually comes to see the folly of his wishful thinking. In "Walking Distance," Martin Sloan, V.P. in charge of Media at an advertising agency, is out for a Sunday drive in the country. Stopping at a gas station a mile and a half from the town where he grew up, he decides to walk there and visit. Incredibly, Martin finds himself back in the time of his youth! At first, his parents refuse to believe him; but his father comes to believe that he is his son. Martin explains, "I had to come back, Pop . . . I just want to rest, I never stopped running." But his father knows that he can't stay. "You have to leave here," he tells Martin. "Maybe there's only one summer to every customer."

In "The Trouble with Templeton," Booth Templeton, an aging actor, confides to a close friend, "I hadn't had many contented moments in my life." Later, after a difficult meeting regarding a new theatrical production, he finds himself back in 1927. He sees his first wife in a nearby speakeasy, and tries to talk to her. But she just wants to drink and dance and enjoy herself. "Why don't you go back where you came from? We don't want you here," she tells him.

In "The Incredible World of Horace Ford," Horace Maxwell Ford is a toy designer who behaves like a little kid, right down to his childish temper tantrums. He's always reminiscing about his childhood. "I was ten. Boy, what great, great times!" One day he goes for a walk in his old neighborhood. He sees the same kids that he knew when he was a child, and gets beaten up by them. Clearly, Horace's childhood was not as happy as he remembers it.

In nostalgia episodes where the main character acknowledges the futility of fleeing to the past, he has a chance to move forward with his life. Martin Sloan drives back to the city, knowing that he has to live his life in his own time. Booth Templeton finds renewed vigor to bring to his latest theatrical acting role. Horace Ford acknowledges that his memories of the past were sugar-coated. "We remember what was good, and we black out what was bad."

In each of these episodes, the main character saw the past as being a better time than the present. But this shouldn't surprise us. As psychologists know, memories can be selective. (Apparently, the Devil knows this, too. "It's not my fault that your memory is imperfect," Miss Devlin chides Bill Feathersmith.) We tend to focus on the good times in our past, and downplay—or even forget— the bad. That's just the way we are. But if the main character is able to learn from his nostalgia, then he's able to acknowledge his situation and the feelings it engenders. He can put the past and the present into perspective, and move on.

Nostalgia does not provide a second chance at Life. Running back to the past is not the answer. The past is unalterable. The past is dead. At best, we can use it to put things in perspective and move on. You can only succeed by going forward. Given this, is there another category of episodes that can teach us something about second chances? Of course there is.

If Only We *Could* Go Back, Things Would be Better!

Episodes that use time travel as a device to explore the possibility of second chances are a step up from episodes that focus on nostalgia. With nostalgia, we dream about going back and re-living our lives. With time travel, we're invited to think about actually being able to do it.

Many people seem to believe that, if you could somehow go back to the past, you could change the future; or, if not, then the past would be a better place to live in. But that's not what we see in *The Twilight Zone*. In "Back There," five gentlemen relaxing in a men's club are discussing time travel and whether past events can be altered. One of them, Peter Corrigan, soon finds himself back on the evening of the assassination of President Lincoln. He tries to warn the police; but, thinking he is either drunk or crazy, they arrest him! John Wilkes Booth succeeds in killing Lincoln.

In "No Time Like the Past," Paul Driscoll is tired of the constant threat of nuclear annihilation. He wants to use a time machine to go back and alter the present by changing the past. All of his attempts fail. Convinced that the past cannot be changed, he decides instead to flee to the past, to Homeville, Indiana. There, he inadvertently causes the fire which burns down a schoolhouse and seriously injures twelve children. Driscoll realizes his folly. "The past is inviolate. The past is sacred. It belongs to those who live in it."

In "Once Upon a Time," Woodrow Mulligan is a janitor in 1890 who works for a scientist. The scientist has created a "time helmet," which accidentally brings Mulligan forward to 1962. There, Mulligan meets Rollo, an electronics scientist. Unhappy with the present, Rollo has the time helmet repaired so that *he* can go back to the past. Mulligan grabs onto Rollo just in time, and both men are sent back to 1890. Unfortunately, Rollo is still unhappy, because there are no modern conveniences in 1890. Mulligan puts the time helmet on Rollo and sends him back to 1962.

Attempts to use time travel to go back to the past and "fix" things always fail. It's only in two time-travel episodes that the main character is successful; and in both, the time travel is directed *forward*, into the future. In "The Last Flight," a cowardly World War I fighter pilot discovers that he has to return to the past to save his wingman, who will one day become a hero in World War II, and later an American Air Force general. "Time was giving me a second chance." He succeeds. In "100 Yards Over the Rim," a settler heading west in 1847 winds up in 1960, and discovers that his son, who's very ill, is destined to become a famous pediatrician. He must return to the past with penicillin in order for his son to survive. He too succeeds.

Overall, we see the same pattern with time travel that we saw with nostalgia. The past is unalterable. The past is dead. You can't go back. Even if you could go back, you could not change the future. You can only succeed by going forward.

A Third Look at Second Chances

The third type of episode deals directly with second chances. Sometimes second chances are not what they seem. Sometimes, you get a second chance because *someone else* thinks you need one. In "Mr. Bevis," James W.B. Bevis, an eccentric young man, is fired from work ("Sixth job I've lost this year"); his antique car is totaled; and he's evicted from his apartment. While consoling himself in a bar, he meets his family's guardian angel. The angel gives Bevis the chance to relive the day, but with changes: new clothes, rent paid in advance, a new car, and a clean desk at his job. "If you want the day to end differently, you're going to have to be just a little bit different, Mr. Bevis." Bevis, however, has no use for all these changes, and asks to have his old life back.

In "Cavender Is Coming," apprentice angel Cavender is given one more chance to win his wings. He's assigned to Agnes Grep, a clumsy young woman; and he's given twenty-four hours to make her happy. Cavender makes Agnes wealthy and gives her access to high society. But she loses her apartment and none of her old friends recognize her. Cavender asks, "Don't you want to be happy?" Agnes tells him "I *was* happy." Cavender tells her "You are the richest woman I know." Cavender then returns to Heaven, where he finds that he has indeed earned his wings. Agnes is happy, and *Cavender* has earned *his* second chance!

At other times, you might find yourself getting what appears to be a second chance, but it does you no good. In "A Nice Place to Visit," Henry Francis "Rocky" Valentine is a small-time hood who's shot dead. His guardian angel, Pip, has been instructed to supply him with everything he wants. Rocky gets everything he asks for: beautiful women, the best clothes and food; and he wins at every game of chance he tries. After a while, this becomes tedious; and Rocky can stand no more of this boring paradise. Thinking he must surely be in Heaven, he asks to go to "the other place." Pip laughs and replies "This *is* the Other Place!"

In "A Game of Pool," Jesse Cardiff is a pool shark who dreams of being the best. He wishes he had had a chance to play Fats Brown, the greatest pool player of all time. "I'd give anything to play him one game . . . anything." Jesse gets his wish, and Fats appears. The stakes are "life or death," and Jesse accepts. While they're playing, Fats tells Jesse "There's more to Life than this pool hall." Jesse retorts, "You didn't get to be the best by sitting on a park bench." Fats acknowledges this, but explains that he still found time to *live*. "But I've made love . . . swam in the ocean . . ." Fats tries to warn him. "You may win more than you bargained for." Jesse wins, and takes Fats's place, but not as he imagined. Now in Limbo, *he* is the one whom future pool players will want to challenge.

In "The Man in the Bottle," Edna and Arthur Castle, owners of a curio shop, acquire a bottle which holds a genie. The genie grants them four wishes. "But be careful what you wish for," he admonishes them. The first wish is trivial, and the next two are disasters. Arthur's last wish is to have everything return back to normal.

Sometimes second chances come out of nowhere, but they can be lifesavers if they arrive at the right moment. In "A Passage for Trumpet," Joey Crown, a trumpet player and alcoholic, throws himself in front of a truck. He finds that he's now in Limbo. There he meets the angel Gabriel, who tells him that he has a choice between Life and Death. "You've got a choice . . . There's still time." Joey decides to go back to Life and take advantage of his second chance.

In "Dust," Sykes, a traveling salesman, enters a squalid little town and sells five-strand hemp rope to a hangman, just in time for a hanging set for that day. He also sells "magic dust" to the father of the man about to be hanged. The man is hanged, but the rope breaks. The parents of the victim are asked whether they want the condemned man to be re-hanged, and they refuse. "One victim is enough."

In "Night of the Meek," Henry Corwin is playing Santa Claus at a department store. He gets into an argument with the store manager, and is fired. Wandering the streets, he comes across a large duffel bag full of presents. He distributes these presents to the poor and the neighborhood children. "I guess what I've really wanted is to be the biggest gift giver of all times." Henry then stumbles across an elf, and a reindeer-driven sleigh. He gets his wish—a second chance at living the life he always wanted.

In "I Dream of Genie," George P. Hanley buys an Arabian lamp as a birthday present for Ann, a secretary with whom he is infatuated. Too embarrassed to give it to her, he takes it home. The lamp contains a genie, which allows Hanley *one* wish. After thinking over various scenarios, none of which help him win Ann's love, he decides to become a genie and help other people!

But sometimes you may find yourself having to make your own second chance. In "Printer's Devil," Editor Douglas Winter is despondent at the failure of the *Danzburg Courier*, a newspaper that he has run for years. As he is contemplating suicide, Mr. Smith arrives and makes him an offer. Smith will give Winter the money he needs to be current with his bills, as long as he can be the linotype operator and a reporter, too. Winter agrees, and headlines and stories are printed right before they happen! Winter eventually sells his soul to Smith/the Devil, but only regrets this when he discovers that his fiancée, who has spurned Smith's advances, is to be killed in a car accident that evening. Douglas uses the linotype machine to write a new headline, one where his fiancée is saved, and his contract with the Devil made null and void!

Moving Forward

We've seen that nostalgia isn't the answer to living a better life. Even if we could somehow travel back in time, still, the past can never be changed. Lastly, we see that just being given a second chance is not enough. You have to know yourself well enough to properly take advantage of that second chance and move on, to live a better life. But all of this seems more like common sense than anything else, doesn't it? Where's the philosophy in second chances?

When you have regrets and find yourself being nostalgic, or wishing for a second chance, you're living in the past. It's only when you stop to consider why you're wishing for a second chance, and then take steps to address the problems in your life, that you're going to be able to move forward. A model of living that acknowledges these two perspectives was proposed by Danish philosopher Søren Kierkegaard in his work *Either/Or* (1843).

Either/Or proposes that a person can live either in the *aesthetic* world, or in the *ethical* world. If you live in the aesthetic world, you're enjoying life in the moment. It's always about what you want *now*. So you're always living the same story. You never move on. You fail to experience more of the possibilities that Life has to offer. You never commit to building a real history that you can look back on in your later years and appreciate. In the aesthetic world, your life begins to sound like a broken record; and you will eventually find yourself in despair.

"A Nice Place to Visit" and "A Game of Pool" both perfectly depict the despair that awaits the person who lives in the aesthetic world. "Rocky" Valentine thinks he's got it made. *Getting everything he could possibly want out of life*—beautiful women, the best clothes and food, winning at every game of chance—*turns out to be a mind-numbing, soul-crushing experience.* Sure, he's got what he's always wanted. But in the end, all that it's gotten him is an eternity of despair. He decides he'd rather be in Hell than experience all of this; yet that's exactly where he's been all this time!

Jesse Cardiff has done nothing with his life except practice pool every moment that he could. His monomaniacal drive led him to a point in his life where he had never given himself a chance to experience all the good things that Life has to offer: travel, friendships, and love. Fats Brown knows what's in store for Jesse, and tries to warn him, albeit somewhat obliquely. But Jesse is trapped in a prison of his own creation. Jesse has wagered and won an aesthetic life—in Limbo—which he realizes only too late will be full of despair.

To live in the *ethical* world, you have to take active and conscious responsibility for your actions and your life. You'll think through the possible consequences of your actions, and you won't let what's happened to you in the past dictate how your future will unwind. Your life isn't a broken record of the same experiences over and over again, regardless of how good they might seem to be at first. And you'll more than likely find yourself one day looking back at your life with no small amount of satisfaction, no matter how difficult the road you traveled was.

Episodes that we've reviewed where the main character learns from his experiences and decides to live in the ethical world—to be more responsible for his choices, and to think about the consequences of his future actions—are the episodes where the main character earns a second chance. "Printer's Devil" perfectly depicts the transition from the aesthetic world to the ethical world. Editor Winter has had only one thing on his mind for years: the *Danzburg Courier*. Unable to accept its failure, and in despair, he's ready to throw his life away. After he accepts the Devil's offer, he remains focused on the newspaper above everything else. But when he tries to break free of the contract, the Devil tells him the kind of world he's really been living in. "You thought you'd get everything for nothing. That's not how Life works!" Only after Winter decides to take responsibility for his past actions is he able to break the contract with the Devil and reclaim his life and his soul. By taking responsibility for his actions, and by doing what's right for its own sake, he finds real meaning in his life. As Kierkegaard said, "Life must be understood backwards, but . . . it must be lived forwards." Winter can now move forward.

This chapter may have been a long road for you to travel to discover that even something as mundane as a second chance could have a deep philosophical meaning. It's only natural to ask yourself "What if" in times of crisis or regret. It's "What could have been" that really makes us human, don't you think? I mean, we don't just react to our environment based on instinct. We plan and we hope. We laugh and we cry. We live and we learn. But, if we can muster a little bit of courage and perspective, we can do what many of us find difficult to do at times: move on. And we should, because moving on makes more sense than standing still, or dying in the past.

At the beginning of this chapter, I asked if it were wrong to ask for a second chance, or to reject one. I believe that Kierkegaard gave us the answer when he said, "Life is not a problem to be solved, but a reality to be experienced." Remember that the next time you find yourself wishing you could go back and do things differently. If only you could somehow erase your past mistakes and make things "right." Everyone makes mistakes. Not everyone learns from them.

Keep moving forward.

16
The Pleasure of the Twist

Stephen Scales

In the final moments of a classic episode of *The Twilight Zone*, Pat shouts to Chambers "It's a cook book!" Suddenly our impression of the benevolent and gracious Kanamits is flipped on its head; what we had seen as wonderful developments in a lesson about the possible benefits of encountering a more advanced alien race turn into sheer horror . . . and we love it!

In several episodes of *The Twilight Zone*, the storytellers take us on a ride through anomaly and confusion which is resolved in the acceptance of a new way to see the world. Our view of what is in front of us is shattered and rebuilt, and we enjoy it immensely. Since so many episodes of *The Twilight Zone* employ what we call a "twist," the series should lead us to take a philosophical look at the phenomenon and ask why it is so pleasurable for us.

A twist ending really begins long before the ending. It starts when the storyteller plants seeds of cognitive or emotional dissonance in the minds of the viewers. We're given subtle clues that there's something wrong with our ordinary understanding of the events unfolding in front of our eyes. A buildup of signals tells us that things are not as they seem, that a new and more penetrating understanding is required in order to grasp the truth of the constructed world in which we're standing.

Finally, when we grasp the twist ending, light dawns over the whole of the story; what we grasp is not a singular proposition, but a new way to interpret all of the information we have been given. Everything that was anomalous suddenly fits together in a new light; we see the world, or at least the fictional world of the story, anew.

These developments are analogous to the process of scientific revolutions as they are described in Thomas Kuhn's great work in the philosophy of science, *The Structure of Scientific Revolutions*. Looking at the actual history of scientific developments leads Kuhn to attack two of the central tenets of the traditional view of how science works: the idea that science is a cumulative enterprise, and the idea that there can be any scientific observations which do not already presuppose a theory.

The Traditional Image of Science

In the first section of *The Structure of Scientific Revolutions*, Kuhn describes the history and philosophy of science which preceded him. The traditional image of science presents scientific development as a process of the accumulation of the facts, theories, and methods which are then affirmed in scientific textbooks. Science is pictured as a search for the truth about nature which is inexorably driven by reason toward the acceptance of more and more items in a cumulative catalogue of truths.

The acceptance of scientific theories is based on a rational comparison between the theory and the hard empirical data, and this comparison is straightforward because there is a clear distinction between observational and theoretical statements. Although theories are speculative attempts to explain the observed phenomena, observations are unquestionable; they are simply given.

The Myth of Cumulative Growth

But when Kuhn looks at the actual history of science (as opposed to the idealized version given in textbooks) he's forced to reject this view in favor of a model that acknowledges that there are two types of activity in the history of science: normal science, and scientific revolutions.

Normal Science proceeds from an educational initiation into a science that provides fixed answers to the most basic questions in the field. These answers are simply taken for granted, not questioned, in the ordinary course of normal science. Kuhn connects the concept of normal science to what he calls a "paradigm," a taken-for-granted way of looking at the world. Each paradigm is built around an example of successful scientific practice and provides its followers with a shared coherent view of the world and a pattern for conducting scientific activity.

Kuhn describes normal science as a sort of puzzle-solving activity based on downplaying the importance of anomalies or problems which crop up. The normal scientist sees failures of fit between the theoretical framework and the world not as a reason to reject or even question the theoretical framework, but rather as a puzzle to be worked out. Normal science plows ahead, firm in the conviction that any apparent anomaly will be resolved. Although the scientists working within a shared paradigm may be blinded to the possibility of the falsity of some of their most fundamental assumptions, if it were not for the restriction of vision which their confidence in the paradigm allows them, they would never be able to focus their attention so narrowly upon a small range of particular problems, so that they can investigate nature in depth.

Every theory has its strengths and weaknesses, but normal science is confident that the weaknesses of the accepted view can be worked out, that the world can be made to fit into the conceptual boxes the dominant theory supplies. But this is not always the case. Sometimes the anomalies just seem to get more and more intractable. New problems come up and the dominant theoretical framework may be altered in some ad hoc way in order to accommodate new findings.

Anomalies begin to multiply and become more troubling. The hold which the dominant theoretical framework exerts over the minds of scientists raised under it begins to loosen. Suddenly, alternative answers to some basic questions in the field are no longer just for "fringe elements." Kuhn explains that when normal science can no longer handle or ignore anomalies which bring the basic commitments of the science into question, then alternative views begin to proliferate until at last a *paradigm shift* occurs. What were the basic truths provided by the old paradigm are displaced by the basic truths of a new and more successful paradigm. Kuhn refers to these events as scientific revolutions. He says they are "the tradition-shattering complements to the tradition-bound activity of normal science."

Thus, Kuhn's new image of science is, in the first place, contrasted with the traditional image in that the history of science is not seen as a cumulative growth towards truth, but rather as a series of periods of normal science centered on accepted paradigms, punctuated by the scientific revolutions which create and destroy those paradigms.

When scientists cannot force nature into the conceptual boxes provided by the existing paradigm under which they work, they are sometimes forced to see the world anew. As Kuhn says, these events involve "coming to live in a different world" in which all of my previous observational experience may have to be reinterpreted. Just like the twist endings in *The Twilight Zone*, the paradigm shifts that Kuhn describes involve "the previous awareness of anomaly, the gradual and simultaneous emergence of both observational and conceptual recognition, and the consequent change of paradigm categories and procedures often accompanied by resistance" (*The Structure of Scientific Revolutions*, p. 110).

So many episodes of *The Twilight Zone* give us hints that something is anomalous or "off." After her car accident, Nan Adams (in "The Hitch-Hiker") is told that "by rights, you shouldn't have called for a mechanic. Somebody should have called for a hearse." She says that she has a feeling that "things are a little wrong." We, and she, later learn that she has been dead all along.

The distraught Jana (in "The Lateness of the Hour"), says that "something's not right", and searches for pictures of herself as a girl. We (and she) later learn that she is an android with programmed memories. The codebreaker, Chambers (in "To Serve Man") tells us that, when we should have been preparing to defend ourselves, "We milled around like frightened farm animals", and we get the Kanamits' ominous command to "simply trust us;" All of these foreshadowing clues (not to mention the often ominous and eerie music that is so characteristic of *The Twilight Zone*) tell us that there is a failure of fit between our ordinary understanding of what we are seeing, and a darker reality behind it. And when we finally do reach the twist endings, of these tales, we "come to live in a different world."

The Myth of the Given Observation

According to the traditional image of science, observations are simply given as theory-neutral arbiters of which theory we should adopt. The facts are the same facts for whichever theory wants to explain them. Kuhn explains that in actual scientific practice, theory and observation are not so easily separated. What counts as an observed fact for the Ptolemaic astronomer, who assumes that the Earth doesn't move ("I can see the Sun moving around us!") is not a fact at all for the Copernican who believes that the Earth orbits the Sun. This is what is meant by saying that the facts, or the observations, are "theory-laden." Facts can only be observed from within a theoretical framework; we cannot make theory-neutral observations. What counts as a fact for us is, at least in part, determined by which theoretical framework we are committed to.

But Kuhn's claims about theory-ladenness are not confined only to scientific observation statements. Kuhn outlines several psychological experiments which bear on the extension of the theory-ladenness of observations to the human perceptual process itself. It's not just what we *say* about the world that is colored by the theoretical lenses we bring to the task of observation; it's what we *see* (or hear, taste, smell, or feel). Kuhn lays out strong empirical evidence that these characteristics are built into the nature of perception.

One psychological experiment he describes involves briefly displaying anomalous playing cards (for example, a red four of spades or a black six of hearts mixed into a regular deck) to subjects. At first, the subjects identified the cards as normal. They would call the black six of hearts a six of either spades or hearts, assimilating their visual experiences to categories they already had prepared (their theory of playing cards, we might say). But as the exposure time increased, they would hesitate and be unsure. Then quite suddenly, the majority of subjects would finally come to recognize the anomalous cards for what they were. Kuhn says:

Until taught by prolonged exposure that the universe contained anomalous cards, they saw only the types of cards for which previous experience had equipped them. Yet once experience had provided the requisite additional categories, they were able to see all anomalous cards on the first inspection long enough to permit any identification at all. Still other experiments demonstrate that the perceived size, color, and so on, of experimentally displayed objects also varies with the subject's previous training and experience. Surveying the rich experimental literature from which these examples are drawn makes one suspect that something like a paradigm is prerequisite to perception itself. What a man sees depends both upon what he looks at and also upon what his previous visual-conceptual experience has taught him to see. (*The Structure of Scientific Revolutions*, pp. 112–13)

So, even at the most basic level—the level of what we see right in front of us—our observations are actually influenced by our prior theories. What we see is influenced by what we expect to see. And this is not really very difficult to understand if we consider that perceiving things involves several layers of brain functioning. It should come as no surprise that the judgements we make about what we see are, at least in part, determined by the theories embedded in our brains. And speaking of brains . . .

Reasoning from the Bottom Up

In the field of artificial intelligence, theorists began by trying to copy what humans do when they think in sentences. We can call this the "top-down" approach, because it starts from quite advanced human skills in using language.

According to the top-down approach, rationality is viewed as the transformation of sets of sentences (representing beliefs) into other sets of sentences according to certain rules, such as consistency and coherence. But does the fundamental character of rational thought really consist in the correct manipulation of sentences?

Nonhuman animals and human infants are not linguistic creatures. They don't manipulate sentences at all. And yet, we don't want to say that they're utterly lacking in intelligence or unable to learn. Just like us, they can use incoming information in order to restructure themselves internally, to make better use of future incoming information so as to achieve their aims.

Very often, people who can perform certain tasks very competently would be unable to explain in sentences just what they are doing. If they tried to do this, we might recognize some similarity between the sentences and what they were doing, but we would feel that something had been left out. Think of tying shoelaces, recognizing faces, catching a ball, or even more general areas like "behaving morally." I know how to tie my shoes, recognize my mother's face, drive a car, and tell right from wrong, but if you ask me for a list of sentences which really capture these practices, I would be unable to provide one.

Since the early 1980s, Paul Churchland has been pursuing a different approach. Whereas early attempts to think about artificial intelligence began with the most sophisticated processes in which linguistic intelligent creatures engage (sentence manipulation) and asked what sort of underlying operations could possibly produce or account for such cognitive activities, Churchland went for a bottom-up approach.

Churchland's bottom-up approach, also called "connectionism," begins with the fact that cognitive activities are activities of the nervous systems of real animals in the world and focuses on the study of the nervous systems of those real animals.

The first thing we notice about these systems is that, unlike the very fast serial computers on our desks at home, they do not process information serially at all. They work by processing information in a massively parallel way. The hundred billion neurons inside my skull are interconnected by about one hundred trillion connections. There is no CPU in my brain, no bottleneck through which all of the information the brain processes must pass. There are only interconnected neurons. They are very simple cells, but so massively interconnected as to border on the infinite.

In contrast to the top-down approach, connectionists like Paul Churchland have used the actual structure of the human brain to build systems that can learn new concepts based on input from the world around them. These "artificial neural networks" are able to recognize faces, translate written texts into spoken language, and solve a host of other cognitive problems that serial computers can't solve.

Rather than being primarily sentence-crunching devices, it appears that human brains primarily work with "prototypes." The prototypes we use to understand the world are not sentences. They can include property-cluster prototypes (cat, chair, briefcase), causal sequence prototypes (cooking food with heat, pouring liquid from a tilted container), social interaction protoypes (you shouldn't disclose things you've been told in confidence, you should respect other persons), superordinate prototypes (why planets move on elipses, why heated metals expand). None of us can explain these things in a list of sentences culminating in a logical proof, but we can all recognize and understand them because these prototypes have become embedded in our brains as we have grown up and learned how to operate in the world.

The Pleasure of the Twist

The connectionist program in neurophilosophy has made great progress in providing us with new understandings of such basic concepts as learning, recognition, theoretical understanding and even large-scale conceptual changes like the ones that Kuhn describes in the sciences. But conceptual shifts do not happen only within scientific communities; they happen to each of us in our daily lives.

Long before language even existed, the ancestors of humans evolved so that they got pleasure from learning in this way. We receive "error messages" which reshape the pathways in our brains, in order to allow for this new learning. And we enjoy the sudden burst of insight when we come to understand that what we had grasped under one prototype is better (more simply, more powerfully, more accurately) grasped under another one. Our world turns upside down for a moment and then settles into a clearer picture which allows us greater control of the world around us.

When we suddenly come to learn something new, our brains get a jolt of pleasurable chemicals (primarily dopamine, serotonin, and endorphins: the same chemicals released when we "get" the punchline of a joke). In our evolutionary prehistory, this fact certainly supported our species' movement to global dominance. Creatures who get pleasure from figuring things out, or learning to see things in a new and more penetrating way, will have greater survival success. Not only will they get pleasure from learning from their elders, but also from coming up with innovative improvements to the lessons passed down to them ("Hey, we can get even more marrow out of these bones if we split them with a sharp flaked-rock rather than just crushing them with a blunt rock."). These jolts of pleasurable neurotransmitters were the reward that helped to lead us from mere biological evolution into cultural evolution and so to the top of the animal kingdom. We also feel this pleasure when we watch some of our favorite episodes of *The Twilight Zone* (especially, in my case at least, the ones with terrific twist endings).

A twist ending triggers the deployment of a prototype that had not been engaged in our understanding of the story up to the end. In "To Serve Man" we're suddenly forced to reinterpret what we had understood as benevolent actions as evil. In place of our conception of the Kanamits' actions under the prototype of "helping behavior," our prototype of "livestock" is sickeningly engaged in connection with humans.

The twist activates our prototypes for cannibalism, and of our use of nonhuman animals as food. We immediately look backwards across the story and struggle to reorient ourselves. We had understood the bringing of world-peace and unlimited energy supplies as compassionate and friendly actions; now they appear as a horrible step in the process of efficiently domesticating, fattening, and slaughtering humanity so as to harvest our flesh for food. It is this re-examination of all that has come before under a new prototype (or paradigm) that makes twist endings so much fun.

The twist endings that appear in all five seasons of *The Twilight Zone* often prefigure twist endings of more popular movies that appeared later. The realization that a space-traveler is actually home on Earth ("I Shot an Arrow into the Air," 1960, "Probe 7—Over and Out," 1963) was used to stunning effect in the original *Planet of the Apes* movie in 1968. The recognition that an important character in the story is really a nonhuman android (in "The Lateness of the Hour," 1960) gave *Blade Runner* its cult classic status in 1982. And the shocking revelation that a lead character is already dead (in "Judgment Night," 1959, and "The Hitch-Hiker," 1960) made *The Sixth Sense* movie into a smash hit in 1999. But the themes that made *The Twilight Zone* unique in its time have also given a twist to all of our cultural expectations since the series first aired.

The thin line between reality, dreaming, and madness, aliens among us, paranormal events, time-travel, and inanimate objects coming to life are now part of our shared library of story-prototypes. Seeing *The Twilight Zone* has changed our outlook not only on other TV and movie experiences, but on our social existence and the world around us. It has turned many of our understandings and expectations on their heads.

And that's just a small part of what we love about *The Twilight Zone*.

The Dimension that Can't Be Named or Numbered

17
A Shadowland Called the Twilight Zone

TRIP MCCROSSIN

"I can give you a lovely front room overlooking the square," the innkeeper says to the dapper gentleman who's just come seeking "accommodations," in "Deaths-Head Revisited," episode nine of Season Three of Rod Serling's *The Twilight Zone*, which aired on November 10th 1961.

"Would you care to see it?," she continues, with palpable hospitality, until he turns to say, curtly, that he's "sure it will be satisfactory," and her face betrays equally palpable disquiet. "Yes," he asks, staring at her menacingly, "anything wrong?" Might it be, she asks in turn, that she recognizes him as among the Nazi SS officers who, stationed nearby, frequented the inn during the war? "I spent the war years on the Russian front," he deflects, untruthfully we soon learn, and begins to taunt her to divulge, reluctantly and painfully, what he seems clearly already to know, which is that the "prison or something you had here" was a concentration camp, that the "here" is Dachau, and that the "camp, it's that group of buildings up on the hill."

"But most of us would like it burned to the ground," she adds, unbidden, now palpably defiant. It's a sentiment he rejects, storming out in anger. And it's one that Serling means for us to reject as well, though on very different grounds than the "nostalgia" that animates Mr. Schmidt, formerly Captain Gunther Lutze, cruelly overseeing the camp until the end of the war. He was "a black-uniformed strutting animal whose function in life was to give pain," Serling offers in his opening monologue, who "shared the one affliction most common amongst that breed known as Nazis: he walked the Earth without a heart." Unfortunately for Lutze, having returned now to the scene of his heatless atrocities, "a place like Dachau cannot exist only in Bavaria," Serling concludes, as "by its very nature, it must be one of the populated areas of the Twilight Zone."

Nor, it seems, can a place like Dachau exist in only one episode. It comes into play again, a little over fourteen months later, in "He's Alive," episode four of Season Four, airing on January 24th 1963. Ernst Ganz, reluctant father figure to budding neo-Nazi Peter Vollmer, having survived heroically for nine years in Dachau, is killed ignominiously by Peter, at the behest of a "phantom from another time," a "resurrected ghost of a previous nightmare," residing now in "a shadowland called the Twilight Zone"—the governing architect of Dachau himself, Adolf Hitler.

Given that there are other camps that Ganz could have survived, needless to say, this connecting thread is surely emblematic of a broad thematic connection between the two episodes. The earlier one is "Serling's statement on the Holocaust," we learn from Gordon Sander, in particular "in reaction to the then-ongoing Eichmann trial," airing seven months after it began, three months after it ended, and only a month before its verdict and sentence were handed down. The later episode is his statement on the trial's aftermath, then, what it may or may not have accomplished. All the more interesting, Serling's perspective appears to have matured in the interim. More interesting still, the perspective he appears to come to in the later episode appears to be closer than the earlier episode's to a perspective that began to emerge a little over three weeks later, on February 24th 1963, with the first of five installments in *The New Yorker*, in February and March, of Hannah Arendt's *Eichmann in Jerusalem*.

We'd already been put on notice by the Holocaust being the general setting of the two episodes. And "He's Alive" is a conspicuous allusion to the famous "It's alive!" proclamation by Victor Frankenstein in James Whale's 1931 movie adaptation of Mary Shelley's *Frankenstein*. And now we've the idea that the thematic move from the first episode to the second is toward Arendt's perspective, which according to Susan

Neiman, is "the twentieth century's most important philosophical contribution to the problem of evil." Serling's concern here, in other words, is with this very problem, the problem of evil analyzed by Susan Neiman—the perniciously difficult-to-satisfy "need to find order within those appearances so unbearable that they threaten reason's ability to go on," as when (at times seemingly incomprehensibly) bad things happen to (at least relatively) good people, and (at least relatively) good things to (at times seemingly incomprehensibly) bad people.

The Original "Black-uniformed Strutting Animal"

Fans of *The Twilight Zone*, tuning in to "Deaths-Head Revisited" on that Thursday, November 10th 1961, would likely have felt their ears prick up even before Serling's opening monologue, listening to Lutze's exchange with the inn keeper, and then, a few minutes after the monologue, seeing Lutze mysteriously imprisoned in Dachau, and listening then to his exchange with the ghost of his former prisoner, Alfred Becker. "I functioned as I was told," he offers in response to Becker's accusations.

"Why have you come back," Becker muses, "changed your name," given that you were "quite safe down there in South America?" The deal is sealed when, midway through the episode, Lutze's on trial before Becker and those who, like him, suffered and died at Lutze's hand. Without being named, one such as Lutze, who'd been in the news of late, surely had to have come to mind—one Adolf Eichmann.

He'd escaped an Allied detention camp in January of 1946, the news would have been, and fled to Argentina in 1950, as Ricardo Klement, but had finally been captured relatively recently, on May 11th 1960, by agents of the Israel Security Agency, Shin Bet, and removed to Israel nine days later to stand trial. Controversy over these actions grew in subsequent months, so much so that in August, it reached the United Nations Security Council, which resolved in the end that Argentina's sovereignty had been violated and that it was owed reparations. And they remained sufficiently controversial throughout the following Autumn and Winter to justify a feature film, *Operation Eichmann*, chronicling Eichmann's crimes, flight, and capture, which appeared on March 15, 1961, just shy of a month before Eichmann's trial began.

Operation Eichmann

The movie, a "docufiction" in the current vernacular, produced in black-and-white to give it the unmistakably feel of a documentary, has many of the hallmarks of being rushed into production, presumably in order to capitalize on (though hopefully also to reflect sincerely the importance of paying attention to) history as it's unfolding. It's nonetheless a remarkable document, most notably for its conspicuously fictional first minute or so. The only bit of genuine artistry in the movie, this is a telling snapshot of the public's perception of Eichmann, or so its writer and director, Lester Cole and R.G. Springsteen, must have imagined.

The screen is shrouded in darkness, but for a light shining down from the top left portion of the screen, on Eichmann standing in the dock. A beat of a bass drum and a brief drum roll and he begins chillingly to dress down those who have tried and sentenced him.

> Justice. Justice! Who are you to speak of justice? All of you out there, staring at me, as if I were an inhuman monster, a grotesque beast. You there, smug and self-satisfied, now that I have been captured. You will learn of true justice. And you will get it. *From us!*

As the camera begins slowly to move in on him, and a drum roll builds to a crescendo, he continues.

> Even now, at this moment, while I stand here, forced to perform in your circus, your travesty of a trial, we are rising again, once more growing in strength, in Germany, in Argentina, in America. You will put me to death, but you will stop nothing. Hang me, but watch. As you spring the trap on the gallows, look at my dangling feet, and you will see them dancing above the millions I have sent to their graves. *Heil Hitler!*

The drum roll reaches its crescendo, ominous music follows, the title and credits roll, and a narrator, David, whom we meet again halfway through the movie as the leader and moral compass of Operation Eichmann, introduces himself.

"I am one of the survivors of the hell and holocaust that was Nazism," we learn. "Even now," he goes on, "so many years later, I still must remind myself that Adolf Eichmann was not only a beast and grotesque monster, but the final end product of a political process. Adolf Eichmann was a Nazi."

Queue the chronicle of Eichmann's crimes and capture, allowing David to confront his tormenter finally in the film's concluding scene. "I regret nothing," Eichmann boasts, "I do not repent. *Kill me!*" But David, who has steadfastly resisted such expediency and satisfaction, has other plans.

"That's too easy, too quick. You're going to stand trial, Eichmann. People are going to see you. They're going to study you. They're going to learn how one man can become responsible for the torture and murder of six million human beings—*six million!* The world will learn, and they'll *remember!*"

Against the backdrop of David's stirring lead-in, Eichmann's trial begins just shy of a month later, on April 11th 1961, lasting a little over four well-publicized months, ending on August 14th. When "Deaths-Head Revisited" aired three months later, on November 10th, roughly a quarter of the way through Season Three of *The Twilight Zone*'s five seasons, the anticipated verdict was only a little over a month away, on December 12th, his death sentence pronounced only a few days later, on December 15th. Less than a day before the season's finale, provocatively entitled "The Changing of the Guard," after a roughly six-month appeal process in the wake of sentencing, and a little over a year after his capture, Eichmann was hanged shortly after midnight on June 1st.

As David had hoped, as a result of evidence presented at trial from nearly eight months of taped police interrogation, from May 29th 1960, to January 17th 1961, and from Eichmann's own statements and demeanor there, and upon his execution, people did see and study him. And from their seeing and studying—some of it more symbolic, as from Serling, some of it more factual, as from Arendt—we've struggled in different ways to understand.

Operation *Lutze*

Even with the benefit of the ongoing trial, though without the directness of Arendt's experience, nor her eventual perspective, Lutze appears to be akin to the Eichmann of *Op-*

eration Eichmann. Serling's introductory monologue reflects this, as does the rest of Becker and Lutze's initial exchange, punctuated by intermittent wailing in the background, the former calling the latter to account for the "ten million human beings who were tortured to death in camps like this."

"You were never a soldier," Becker insists, in response to Lutze's futile attempt to take refuge in no longer being one. "The uniform you wore cannot be stripped off," he continues, being "part of you, part of your flesh, part of your body," a "piece of your mind, a tattoo," holding up his arm to reveal his own, "a skull and crossbones burned into your soul." "I was a *soldier*," Lutze again insists. "No, Captain, you were a sadist," Becker responds, "a monster who derived pleasure from giving pain," which elicits Lutze's "I functioned as I was told" variation on the earlier soldiering defense, and again the wailing, louder now, and again Lutze, "What *is* this *noise?*" It ought to be obvious, Becker muses.

> Strange that it should disturb you so. It never used to, Captain. When your victims screamed you weren't so sensitive. But now, they are not screaming. No, they are reacting. They just heard you offer the apology for all the monsters of our times. "We did as we were told." "We functioned as ordered." "We merely carried out directives from our superiors." Familiar, is it, Captain? It was the Nazi theme music at Nuremberg, the new lyrics to the *Götterdämmerung*, the plaintive litany of the master race as it lay dying. "We did not do, others did." Or, "Someone else did it. We never even knew that it was being done." Or, "We did it, but others told us to."

The litany falls under the rubric of the so-called "superior orders" plea, more typically dubbed the "Nuremburg defense," for its prevalence during the post-World War II Nuremberg Trials, in 1945 and 1946, as later in Eichmann's. By whatever name, the defense fares no better for Lutze, in the trial that ensues shortly after the above exchange, than it did for Eichmann, as the reading of his guilty verdict a month later made clear.

More telling here than Lutze's trial and verdict, however, which are clearly foregone conclusions, is his sentence. "Your final judgment will come from God," Becker pronounces, but in the interim, it's "the unanimous judgment of this court that from this day on, you shall be rendered insane." It's "not hatred, but retribution," Becker insists, "not revenge, but justice," which in the Twilight Zone means proportional punishment. "You shot down hundreds of people with machine guns," Becker pronounces, "hung others up to die a slow death," and performed "unmentionable" experiments on still others, "do you feel their torture now?" Indeed, he does.

"He is screaming through pain," the doctor tending to Lutze reports, or worse, "agony," and yet "there isn't a mark on him." But then "what could happen in two hours to turn a man into a raving maniac?" In a word, he concludes, "*Dachau.*" "Why does it still stand?," he pleads, "why do we keep it standing?" It ought to be obvious, Serling concludes.

> All the Dachaus must remain standing—the Dachaus, the Belsens, the Buchenwalds, the Auschwitzes, all of them. They must remain standing because they are a monument to a moment in time when some men decided to turn the Earth into a graveyard. Into it, they shoveled all of their reason, their logic, their knowledge, but worst of all, their conscience. And the moment we forget this, the moment we cease to be haunted by its remembrance, then we become the gravediggers. Something to dwell on and to remember, not only in the Twilight Zone, but wherever men walk God's earth.

As David in *Operation Eichmann* thought it "too easy, too quick" to kill Eichmann, without an intervening trial at least, Becker and his ghostly cohort must be thinking similarly about Lutze. Whereas Cole and Springsteen conceived of David in this way *before* Eichmann's trial begins, in early April of 1961, Serling is conceiving of Becker and company *after*, its beginning or perhaps even its conclusion, in mid-August, but still before its verdict and sentence, in mid-December. In David's language, then, Serling would have to reckon that the "people of the world" *had* learned from the trial, and so *would* presumably remember, to at least a degree.

What if Cole and Springsteen had been writing from *Serling*'s vantage, though, might they have chosen to have David think that killing Eichmann even *after* the trial, executing him that is, would *still* be "too easy, too quick," and *worse*, would deprive us of an additional opportunity to remember, by continuing to share the world with him, albeit imprisoned for the remainder of his shameful life? Indeed, this seems clearly to be at least part of what Serling is imagining in having Lutze *not* perish as a result of what he's imagining, as Edward Hall had perished in "Perchance to Dream," for example, episode nine of season one. Surely it's worse to be driven to live agonizingly insane by what one's imagining, that is, and so just as surely this would be a more fitting punishment for the likes of Lutze, and by extension Eichmann.

And this also nicely leaves open the possibility of avoiding the "and worse" concern. "He's so full of sedatives he doesn't even know he's on Earth," the doctor says, just before his apparent wish to see Dachau demolished, "but I want him in the hospital, and I want him strapped to a bed." He's agonizingly insane *and* imprisoned, then, in a manner of speaking, and one imagines as well, appropriately at risk of being revealed as Lutze. It's not such a stretch, after all, that Bavarian hospital and related authorities would likely be curious about the identity of someone with a relatively generic name, discernibly Germanic accent, recently returned from *South America*, who goes insane, within the span of two hours, while visiting *Dachau*. And of course word might get around, perhaps the doctor visits the inn, chats with the innkeeper, two and two come together to make what they make, and so on and so forth.

Contemporaneous television programming nicely acknowledges, just shy of a month after "Deaths-Head Revisited" aired, a way that the storyline could have remained mostly intact, while nevertheless ending with Schmidt written to be more explicitly revealed as Lutze. Serling could have explored this, but, interestingly, chose otherwise.

Operation *Kleinerman*

The programming in question is the thirteenth episode of Season Five of *Perry Mason,* Samuel Newman and Bernard Kowalski's "The Case of the Renegade Refugee," which aired on December 9th 1961, and which also reasonably reflects the Eichmann trial.

"One of the top Nazis in Hitler's Germany," Lawrence Vander, a reporter posing as an executive of Space Associates Limited, confides to Cliff Barlow, the company's Director, in the episode's introductory scene, "is in the United States, in Los Angeles, an executive working in your company" under a false identity. We're led to suspect that this "renegade refugee," one Max Kleinerman, is posing as Harlan Merrill, the company's Assistant to the Comptroller, who's soon accused of murdering Vander in order to maintain his cover. Convinced of Merrill's innocence, however, and with the assistance of Father Paul, the Superior of the St. Francis Retreat, where the company's executives are spending the weekend when the murder occurs, Mason is able ultimately to flush out the real culprit, of course.

In the episode's penultimate scene, Mason asks fellow executive Arthur Hennings, who's taken the stand to testify against Merrill, "Could there have been certain circumstances, which made it necessary for you to claim that you saw the defendant on the path th[e] night [of the murder]," such that "if Merrill were guilty, it would have solved a problem for you?" When he resists, Mason appeals to the "religious peace" he'd learned earlier that Father Paul had helped him to find. "I'm sure you know this portion of St. Francis' Prayer," Mason offers: "Grant that I may not so much seek to be loved as to love; for it is in giving that we receive; it is in pardoning that we are pardoned; and it is in dying that we are born to eternal life."

"You have the life of Harlan Merrill in your hands," Mason continues, and, having earlier recorded the pained look on Henning's face upon hearing St. Francis's Prayer, the camera pans down to show him clutching a Rosary and Crucifix, and he recants. Insists that he didn't kill him, Vander was nevertheless after *him*. He lied about Merrill to conceal his identity, that is, because he "was afraid to face the truth." "I'm not afraid anymore," he confesses, visibly relieved, "I'll take what comes. My real name is Max Kleinerman."

The analogous move on Serling's part would have been, that is, to have Becker and company condemn Lutze to be driven *temporarily* insane by experiencing himself what he'd done to them, reconnecting him eventually, Kleinerman-style, with a moral compass that would have him reveal himself as Lutze, ready now to "take what comes." Clearly, though, while Newman and Kowalski add to the range of interpretations of the likes of Eichmann, at the time at least, it wasn't Serling's. He wanted us to learn and remember, but to learn and remember simply that there are monsters among us, by their very natures irredeemable. He wrote Lutze to be one, and to lead us to think of Eichmann similarly.

Operation *Vollmer*

At the time of "Deaths-Head Revisited," Serling was unwilling to contemplate a Nazi war criminal with a retrievable moral compass, as Newman and Kowalskee had managed to do. Granted, writing in the wake of the trial, he was able to offer a slightly more nuanced view of the likes of Eichmann. Nonetheless, if the introductory scene of *Operation Eichmann* was meant to reflect the culture's general sense of what the likes of Eichmann look and sound like, Lutze reflects, generally speaking, this same sense. Much can happen, however, in fourteen months.

Serling's introductory monologue in "He's Alive" is, as always, chilling. The following first portion it, however, is also amenable to being fleshed out in a way that better reflects movement away from "Deaths-Head Revisited."

> Portrait of a bush-league Führer *named Peter Vollmer. A sparse little man who feeds off his self-delusions and finds himself perpetually hungry for want of greatness in his diet. And like some goose-stepping predecessors, he searches for something to explain his hunger and rationalize why a world passes him by without saluting.*

What's in play is not only Vollmer and his relation to his predecessors, but the sad *inspirations* of this *aspiring* neo-Nazi, and *their* relation to *those* of his *then-aspiring* predecessors. Serling could have written of Vollmer instead, that is, though considerably less elegantly, that "like some goose-stepping predecessors, he searches as they searched for something to explain that hunger, that want of greatness, and rationalize, as they rationalized why a world passes him by without saluting, as at a similar point in their lives it was passing them by." The implication, in other words, is that Vollmer's goose-stepping predecessors, including presumably a certain "black-uniformed *strutting* animal" named Lutze, were once also merely *aspiring* Nazis, for reasons similar to those that now inspire Vollmer.

"When you were a little kid," Ganz reminds Vollmer, "I used to find you crying at my door late at night," a "little boy with so much fear in him," a "quaking, whimpering boy who cried on my couch; who still cries on my couch." The cure for this, Vollmer comes to believe, all too familiarly, is to find fault not in oneself, but in others, at first this or that individual in particular, but soon enough in their ways of being more generally, as this or that *type* of person, giving way eventually to xenophobia and the various hatefully destructive responses all too prevalent in Serling's era, as in ours. "It's not hate," Vollmer insists, haltingly, "it's a, a point of view, it's a *philosophy*," which yields Ganz's chilling observation.

> Ah, I know the philosophy. I know it quite well. Nine years in a place called Dachau. You know who put me there? Peter Vollmer. A lot of Peter Vollmers. Frustrated men, sick men, angry men.

Vollmer struggles, but ultimately fails to reconcile Ganz's self-professed "sentimentality, softness, the 'weakness' that makes a man his brother's keeper," being the very reason he's the beloved father figure, with his also being among those he "scream[s] about on street corners." And so he falls deeper into "the sewer," as Serling writes, beckoned from the shelter that Ganz has once again offered him, even while knowing that he should instead simply "close the door," to the beginnings of Hitler's ghostly seduction. "Your success," he tells Vollmer, "will be my success."

Vollmer ultimately fails, however, and so the ghost fails as well, *in this instance*. It's playing the long game, that is, the point Serling brings us around to in his concluding monologue. "Where will he go next, this phantom from another time, this resurrected ghost of a previous nightmare?," Serling asks, as the audience tracks a shadow proceeding along a wall, leaving the scene of Vollmer's mortal attempt at escape from police custody.

Anyplace, everyplace, where there's hate, where there's prejudice, where there's bigotry. He's alive. He's alive so long as these evils exist. Remember that when he comes to your town. Remember it when you hear his voice speaking out through others. Remember it when you hear a name called, a minority attacked, any blind, unreasoning assault on a people or any human being. He's alive because through these things we keep him alive.

We can't help but realize, in other words, that Serling would have us, in thinking about the two episodes together, equate Lutze not with Hitler, but with *Vollmer*, or more precisely Lutze's *origins* with Vollmer's.

Operation *Real-time Eichmann*

There are certain similarities, some of them eerily prescient, between the artfully frightening first minute of *Operation Eichmann* and Arendt's *Eichmann in Jerusalem*. "Bragging was the vice that was Eichmann's undoing," she reports early on, and in particular there's the example she gives. "I will jump into my grave laughing," he boasted, "because the fact that I have the death of five million Jews on my conscience gives me extraordinary satisfaction." This can't help but recall the movie's introductory invective, but the recollection is nonetheless tempered by her earlier description of Eichmann. He was "the man in the glass booth built for his protection," after all, "medium-sized, slender, middle-aged, with receding hair, ill-fitting teeth, and nearsighted eyes, who throughout the trial keeps craning his scraggy neck toward the bench."

The perspective on Eichmann that Arendt presents is nonetheless distinct from the Eichmann of *Operation Eichmann*, and so from Lutze in "Deaths-Head Revisited," in ways that make Vollmer in "He's Alive" feel at least somewhat of a foreshadowing. Which is to make no particular claim about what popular culture Arendt may or may not have consumed. Rather, it's to claim only the possibility, nicely often in play in the history of ideas, that even a perspective as novel as hers comes to us with momentum not easily acknowledged.

This is no more evident than in the idea, ever controversial, with which she closes the principal text of *Eichmann in Jerusalem*. The "lesson that this long course in human wickedness ha[s] taught us," she concludes, speaking of Eichmann's trial and execution, is "the lesson of the fearsome, word-and-thought-defying banality of evil," the turn of phrase becoming the book's provocative subtitle, in its post-periodical form: *A Report on the Banality of Evil*.

What's lost in the subtitle, however eye-catching, is a subtlety found in the text. It's not so much that the personification of evil may be surprisingly banal, which is hard to deny in comparing Eichmann at trial with the "beast and grotesque monster" of *Operation Eichmann*. It's also, and more importantly, that its development in the world is the "end product of a political process" of a broader sort: the fearsome, and all too common, defiance of language and thought—fearsome because it surely leads to a defiance of others, a denial of their natures, of their existence even, that's equally so.

"The longer one listened to him," Arendt tells us, in a manner eerily evocative of Ganz's exchanges with Vollmer, "the more obvious it became that his inability to speak was closely connected with an inability to think, namely, to think from the standpoint of somebody else." It was impossible to communicate with him "not because he lied, but because he was surrounded by the most reliable of all safeguards against the words and the presence of others, and hence against reality as such." Reflecting back some years later, in 1972, on the controversy that developed immediately in response *Eichmann in Jerusalem*, Arendt stood by its central contention.

> Some years ago, reporting the trial of Eichmann in Jerusalem, I spoke of "the banality of evil" and meant with this no theory or doctrine but something quite factual, the phenomenon of evil deeds, committed on a gigantic scale, which could not be traced to any particularity of wickedness, pathology, or ideological conviction in the doer, whose only personal distinction was a perhaps extraordinary shallowness. However monstrous the deeds were, the doer was neither monstrous nor demonic, and the only specific characteristic one could detect in his past as well as in his behavior during the trial and the preceding police examination was something entirely negative: it was not stupidity but a curious, quite authentic inability to think.

Still, the controversy persists to this day, both in academic circles and in more popular media, though perhaps without quite the ferocity of its first few years. As Mary McCarthy wrote in a letter to Arendt four months later, in September of 1963, the fierce nature of the backlash was, she thought, "assuming the proportions of a pogrom." It would have been very difficult indeed, then, if possible at all, to neglect it in thinking about World War II in the months leading up to September 17th 1965.

Operation *Klink*

That evening, the pilot episode aired of a new television series, by Bernard Fein and Albert Ruddy, with the provocative tag line, "If you liked World War II, you'll love *Hogan's Heroes!*" This was far from their only provocation.

The pilot's introduction, prior to credits rolling and the episode proceeding, suggested serious business. "If you liked" experiencing the drama, heroism, etc., of "World War II, etc.," it seemed the tag line must be saying. Produced in black and white, it opens with the view from above, as a military-style drum beat pulses, of what appears to be a POW camp, with "Germany 1942," in large Gothic script, center screen. Cut then to searchlights in guard towers panning back and forth, a boot kicking open a door, and prisoners filing hurriedly out onto snow-covered ground. Cut again, to one barracks in particular, a German officer more lazily urging its prisoners to exit, who do so less hurriedly. And cut yet again, to a building labeled "Kommandantur," another German officer emerging, clearly the other's superior.

To have seen *Operation Eichmann* is naturally to imagine that the latter's Eichmann, the former his subordinate, Lieutenant Colonel Rudolf Höss, the actors in question being Werner Klemperer and John Banner, in the film and again here. We are just as naturally shocked, however, to learn that they are instead Colonel Klink and Sergeant Schulz, and that *Hogan's Heroes* is a *situation comedy*, set in a German Prisoner of War camp, Stalag 13, run so incompetently that it's been infiltrated by a band of faux-POWs, led by Colonel Hogan, working over a laugh track for the Allies.

It would be uncharitable to think that Fein and Ruddy were unaware of their provocation. It would be unreasonable to think that they could have anticipated whom precisely they'd provoke. Well before the series was designated the fifth worst in *TV Guide's 50 Worst TV Shows Ever*, that is, in 2002, at least in part for the slight it reflected to the veterans and victims of World War II, it earned the scorn of one Rod Serling.

His daughter Anne recalls that in the Sterling household, watching *Hogan's Heroes* was "never allowed," her dad having "a particular abhorrence of this show and no tolerance for how it perversely twists what happened in Nazi prison camps into something remotely comical." Which abhorrence would later figure prominently in his January 15th 1968, address to the Library of Congress, as a "weekly mirth-filled half hour that shows us what kind of a swinging ball could have been had in a Nazi POW camp" was "a good working example of th[e] phenomenon of national hedonism as it is mirrored in our mass media." "We used to recognize our enemies," he mused.

Through the good offices of *Hogan's Heroes*, however, we meet the new postwar version of the wartime Nazi. He's a big, bumbling fat-head whose crime is stupidity, but nothing more. He's kind of a lovable, affable, benign Hermann Goering. Now this may appeal to some students of laughter who refuse to allow history to get in the way of their laughter. But what it does to history is to distort; what it does to a recollection of horror that is an ugly matter of record is a distortion that is inexcusable. Satire is one thing. It bleeds while it evokes laughter. But a rank diminishment of what was once an era of appalling human suffering is in no way proper material for comedy.

The outrage is palpable, and understandable. It's all the more so against the background of Serling's earlier and withering portraits of Lutze and Vollmer, as struggles with the legacy of Eichmann, and so with the problem of evil, more so still in light of the demonstrable maturation of his response to it, as the earlier portrait yields to the later one.

He returned yet again to the perspective a few years later, in his Commencement address at Ithaca College, on May 13th 1972, a little over a year after *Hogan's Heroes* came to close, a little over two years before his untimely death, on June 28th 1975. "There is in this country unhappily and currently a strange, convoluted sense of morality," he warned, "and a selective moral outrage that goes with it." By way of example, he contrasts two cases prominent at the time, which together can't help but recall the problem of evil. "We can jail a Father Berrigan for the destruction of draft records, and pursue his punishment with a single-minded ferocity," he bemoaned, but "a young infantry lieutenant named Calley, found guilty of complicity in the deaths of over a hundred innocents, women and children included, is moved to more comfortable quarters by presidential edict, and permitted daily visitation by his girl friend."

On the road to the address, film, television, and philosophy had conspired to offer an array of competing perspectives on the likes of Eichmann—the grotesquely monstrous Eichmann of *Operation Eichmann* and Lutze of "Deaths-Head Revisited," the confessional and repentant Kleinerman of "The Case of the Renegade Refugee," the unrepentant, but banal Vollmer of "He's Alive" and Eichmann of *Eichmann in Jerusalem*, and finally, sadly, the "inexcusably distorting" caricature that is Klink. Serling's untimely death, already tragic, of course, is all the more so given the tenor of the address, and the knowledge that, so pleased he was with the way "He's Alive" turned out, he'd contemplated a feature-film version, which would surely have added usefully, provocatively, to the above array.

History repeats itself, someone very clever once said, first as tragedy and then as farce. But what if it does so, in some instances at least, in order to force us to look again at what lies in between? In this case, what's traditionally thought to lie there is Arendt's rightly famous account of how fearsomely, all the more so for how banally, we allow ourselves to let go of thinking and empathy as our most effective tonics against not only suffering the likes of Eichmann, but *becoming* his like. What lies there as well are Serling's portraits of Lutze and Vollmer, and what the latter teaches us about the former, and the hope that if they can help us to think more carefully still, might we someday rid the world of their kind.[1]

---

[1] I'm grateful, first and foremost, to Susan Neiman, for my interest in, comprehension of, and attachment to the problem of evil. I'm also grateful to Sue Zemka and her trusted companion, Fergus, for giving me the space and encouragement to work through the early stages of this. I'm grateful to Sue in particular for her happy observation that I'm channeling here Marx's enduringly clever view of history. I'd also like to thank the folks in

my "Problem of Evil in Philosophy and Popular Culture" seminars, during the spring semester of 2018, in the Honors Program and Byrne Family First-year Seminar Program at Rutgers University, for their helpful ideas, and those who make these programs possible, then and now, including Vanessa Coleman, Paul Gilmore, Jennifer Jones, Muffin Lord, Matt Matsuda, Angela Mullis, Julio Nazario, James Register, and Mary Jo Zachary. Needless to say, none of them are responsible for what I've managed, for better or for worse, to do with their insight and assistance. Finally, I'd like to thank the volume's editors, for patience and understanding far and away beyond the call.

18
War Means Fighting and Fighting Includes Philosophizing

ROBERT S. VUCKOVICH

Often a lull in fighting means something is brewing. When it comes to what's presented in *The Twilight Zone*, that something has a sinister dimension. One side in the American Civil War not only becomes capable of fighting its enemy without resistance, it has the opportunity to easily turn the tide of war in its favor. Bringing an end to war, though, is not entirely peaceful. How victory is achieved will not sit well with those who have lost and, surprisingly, with some of those who would win.

This sinister element makes it possible for the Confederacy to gain the upper hand against Union soldiers amassing near Gettysburg. Upon reconnoitering a town in a secluded valley, Sergeant Joseph Paradine discovers that a manual on witchcraft is responsible for rendering a Union patrol motionless and thus defenseless against any attack; an extraordinary version of shooting fish in a barrel. Given this opportunity to take possession of this magical aid, the stunned scout then realizes that the Confederacy can easily win the war. Enabling one soldier to determine such a favorable outcome seemingly undermines all the hard-fought efforts, including all of the bloodshed both sides have endured so far. Some fighting—not the blazing guns sort—would still persist should Sgt. Paradine rely on the Devil's handbook. Here's where the philosophical dimension opens up in the episode "Still Valley."

Questioning the use of a demonic device has a lot to do with how the intended user rationalizes a very tempting

195

predicament, rather than thinking how evil it is for wanting the Confederacy to win. It seems decisively easy to take the easiest path to victory, but Sgt. Paradine's conscience views this situation as more perplexing. His whole being becomes a moral battlefield.

Instead of regarding Sgt. Paradine's taking the handbook in the same manner as his trading his soul to the Devil, consider that some underlying principle in this soldier has created a conflict between his desire to win and his approach to winning. Even before encountering Teague, the witchman who imparts the handbook to Sgt. Paradine, this scout is hell-bent on discovering what his brothers-in-arms need to know to continue their fight. He has no second thoughts about risking his life for the Confederacy. Yet his acquiring the handbook is not without a snag.

As Rod Serling narrates in a fragmented opening, perhaps that "outpost not found on any military map" depicts Sgt. Paradine's deeply rooted value network.

How Low Will You Go?

What stands out as Sgt. Paradine ventures alone into the valley is his commitment. He is impervious to the "yellow" that would eat at his insides, unlike Dauger, his young scouting companion who first refuses to investigate the town for fear of being killed and, moments later, suggests they surrender. Whatever happens, Sgt. Paradine is prepared to accept his fate. It seems unfitting to call him desperate.

The first sign of weakness emerges when Sgt. Paradine, after finding Union troops in a bizarre state of suspended of animation, deems it safe to pilfer their supplies for himself. One cannot reprimand a hungry man who has pledged "nothing to the Confederacy expect a lack of sleep" for acting this way. Besides, since the enemy can't do anything, the enemy doesn't. Strategically, Sgt. Paradine takes advantage of this situation.

Important to what then develops is that his willingness to immediately sate his hunger temporarily suspends his prime directive to survey the enemy. Shirking his duty as such not only makes Sgt. Paradine vulnerable to an attack, it exposes an apparent oversight to his making rational sense of what befell the enemy. Could all this be a trap? This lapse in his mental focus does not go unnoticed, for unseen eyes have been scouting the scout.

Before examining Sgt. Paradine's encounter with the witchman, let's rethink the scout's activities. As trite as feeding a hungry body seems, it also signifies his immediate recognition of a situation and the grasping of a golden opportunity. This soldier gives in to an intense personal need because defeating that need now becomes possible.

An individual's opportunistic reaping of benefits at the expense of another featured in Plato's *Republic*. In Plato's rendition of the myth of Gyges, Glaucon, Plato's older brother, tells of a lone individual discovering a magical device to go undetected when taking possessions not his own. What further develops is not an admonishment for stealing items; it has a lot to do with the moral strife associated when a person attempts to gain the upper hand without appearing unfavourable. As Glaucon explains,

> a really unjust person . . . doesn't want simply to be unjust but actually to be so . . . he has contracts and partnerships with anyone he wants; and besides benefiting himself in . . . these ways, he profits because he has no scruples about doing injustice. In any contest, public or private, he's the winner and outdoes his enemies . . . benefiting friends and harming enemies. (*Republic*, pp. 37–38)

This account of how a crafty yet very committed person operates applies to Sgt. Paradine, for this soldier in the context of war intends to outdo his enemies. He later admits to his own and the Confederacy's desperation when he eventually returns to camp with the handbook. Yet what moral strife troubles Sgt. Paradine so much that would demonstrate that "he has no scruples about doing injustice"?

As a fighter, Sgt. Paradine confronts a Union patrol head on. Due to their suspended state, a perplexed Sgt. Paradine does not fire on the enemy in cold blood. We may see that action as a sign of fairness with how this Confederate handles this unbelievably odd situation. Then again, Sgt. Paradine has limited ammunition to fight. He would fail in his mission to report the Union's position and strength should they instantly come alive and fire at him. Though no one ever fires a shot, this soldier remains committed to the war, for he's nervously prepared to take prisoners. Never does he abandon this will to win.

Winning under those conditions comes across as too easy, which inadvertently is difficult to pass up. It is a favorable time for a lone soldier to make such a difference in the war. From a pacifist's viewpoint, nothing could be more tempting than ending the war. Winning the war, however, is really what counts for this Confederate. So if ending it is no different than winning it, what does Sgt. Paradine really have to lose?

Colluding with the Devil

Teague's introduction to the story adds to the quandary Sgt. Paradine finds himself in. Their brief encounter provides the soldier with a supernatural account of why the enemy troops are incapable of fighting. Skeptical of this magical influence, Sgt. Paradine is then frozen still for not believing Teague. Holding Sgt. Paradine captive enables Teague to convince the Confederate that the handbook renders the user unstoppable. Even prior to casting a spell on Sgt. Paradine, Teague drops a bombshell by saying that he could have killed him using the handbook. Most stupefying about that claim is that a fragile, seemingly harmless, old man posesses such a devastating weapon.

Sparing Sgt. Paradine reveals that the witchman has something in store for the soldier. Freezing both the Union soldiers and Sgt. Paradine is a persuasive sample of what a handbook on witchcraft can do. Yet the handbook itself is not sinister. Although it supplies the user with many menacing functions against anyone who poses a threat, it, by itself, remains idle. Associating with this witchman, however, is cause for concern.

Aristotle (384–322 B.C.E.) is one philosopher who spent time discussing the quality of human relations. The relationship between two individuals varies in accordance to how each one values the other and what the other might have to offer. In Aristotle's assessment of those friendships based on shared pleasures, a common interest is what unites two individuals.

The common bond between the witchman and Sgt. Paradine relates to their hatred for Union soldiers. The sole inhabitant of the valley announces his disdain after freezing Sgt. Paradine, so as to narrow the soldier's focus and demonstrate that they're fighting a common foe.

Although Aristotle does not specify what shared pleasures can consist of, there are occasions when questionable characters form bonds because of what they deem pleasurable. "Bad men," he writes, "can be friends for a short time, while they take pleasure in each other's wickedness" (*Nicomachean Ethics*, p. 483). Having convinced Sgt. Paradine that they are on the same side, the witchman offers his comrade the handbook.

One person's relinquishing the handbook places the burden on the recipient to follow the same path as his predecessor. For getting Sgt. Paradine to assume the role of the witchman, Teague has committed one final accursed act without the use of witchcraft. In fact, he informs Sgt. Paradine that he is "in league with the Devil" for possessing the handbook. Even though it is Sgt. Paradine who accepts the witchman's offer to use the handbook, it's Teague who uses the soldier to do the dirty work. "The base," in Aristotle's negative characterization of using others, "try to get more than their share of advantages, and take less than their share of labors and public burdens" (p. 543). Recruiting Sgt. Paradine to fulfill the witchman's own suggestion to freeze the whole Union army seems more in line with corrupting the soldier as opposed to assisting him. This arrangement makes us wonder whether Teague was the Devil.

Instead of viewing this scenario in Faustian terms where an individual deeds his soul to the Devil in exchange for some benefit, we see that one agent exploits another who is quite desperate to accomplish something and incapable of doing so on his own. Sometimes in the midst of war, an alliance may be formed between two parties because they share a similar objective. Yet there may be a shift in one party's values that weakens his evaluation of reaching that objective. In Sgt. Paradine's case, he discovers that he alone is fighting a different kind of battle, which is more private than civil.

Into the Depths of the Valley of Darkness

As Glaucon suggests, a person aims to outdo his enemies without reservation. For Sgt. Paradine, he is leery of possessing the handbook, even when he takes it. Still, he conjures up a spell to immobilize a large company of Union troops just outside the valley. This willingness to use the handbook trumps his initial reluctance.

Testing the handbook not only serves to convince Sgt. Paradine that he can change the outcome of the war, it serves to augment his commitment to fighting it. No longer does desperation fuel this soldier's drive, for once he relies on the handbook, the fighting will cease and winning the war is most assured. Sparing his Confederate brothers-in-arms from becoming casualties in the looming battle at Gettysburg would present itself as a splendid bonus. The prospect of losing seems quite absent from Sgt. Paradine's mind.

Without the possibility of being defeated, it's difficult for Sgt. Paradine to appreciate this Confederacy victory. No credit or praise can be attributed to the Confederacy for valiantly marching into Washington uncontested. Plus, Sgt. Paradine must give the Devil his due. He urges a superior officer to call "muster on the Devil." Promoting the Devil in this manner indicates that some within the Confederacy are willing to embrace such an alliance for the sake of victory, one lacking a whole-hearted effort.

Note how desperation once again grips Sgt. Paradine. Though Dauger and the Lieutenant become more than eager to have Sgt. Paradine use witchcraft to defeat the enemy, it is this new witchman who impresses on the others that they are in the same league as the Devil. There's no need for Sgt. Paradine to demonstrate the handbook's effectiveness on his comrades, as Teague did to him, for a fellow Confederate scout, Mallory, substantiates that many Union soldiers have inexplicably been rendered inactive outside the town. Receiving this confirmation is the proof that Sgt. Paradine needs to go on using this devilish approach to win.

Don't Wanna Do Your Dirty Work No More

With the Confederacy's triumph resting on Sgt. Paradine, the lone soldier soon realizes that the sole condition for ending a war involves renouncing God. Religious devotion is not specifically examined in this episode, so as not to make the Civil War a holy crusade. Though the religious conflict between good and evil is apparent, it is the dissociation from what is deemed just that now troubles the soldier. Since it is one soldier doing the Devil's bidding, the moral dilemma is whether he will go through with it.

It seems puzzling at first that the prospect of an easy victory can generate such personal anguish. In spite of Sgt. Paradine's simplistic view that God is good and the Devil is bad, this soldier must determine whether he sides with either good or evil. Such determination gets problematic when factoring in his having to disappoint his brothers-in-arms should he not renounce what is typically deemed good. It's a troubling decision either way.

This extraordinary dilemma comes to an end when Sgt. Paradine tosses the handbook into a campfire. Pledging an allegiance to the Devil has lost its appeal. For one soldier, this particular path to victory has become an exercise, one of militaristic proportions, in succumbing to temptation. Taking the handbook can primarily be viewed as Sgt. Paradine's failing to comprehend the scope of this one act. Clearly he misjudged what he was going to do and, most importantly, who he was dealing with.

Damned Legacy

One thing that lingers is a sense of shame which Sgt. Paradine has to carry with him regardless of the eventual outcome of the Civil War. Don't forget that Sgt. Paradine was apprehensive even before he conjured his first spell. Prior to destroying the handbook, he emphatically points out that if he resorts to using the handbook against the enemy, "it'll be the Confederacy that's damned." This admission has far reaching implications, in that such an act, if followed through, taints an individual's standing as well as those closely associated with him. So, Sgt. Paradine is essentially damned if he does, but how does he fare if he doesn't?

The sad reality, even in the Twilight Zone, is that although Sgt. Paradine may have avoided public opprobrium for relying on the devil's handiwork to thwart an enemy, he has not spared his brothers-in-arms from the ravages of war. It is absurd that the sole hope to end the fighting and the possibility of not getting his comrades killed comes from an alliance with the Devil.

Not giving peace a chance in this fashion boils down to a strategic blunder on Sgt. Paradine's part. It also places him is an awkward relation to those with whom he fights alongside. Should he take comfort for possibly saving the souls of those fighting for the Confederacy despite putting them back into dire straits? As easy as casting the handbook to flames is, Sgt. Paradine may still have a tougher fight with a personal demon.

Post-Demonic Stress Disorder (PDSD)

Sgt. Paradine's final words about needing to bury this demonic conflict unearth something distressing. Brushing this episode aside has sinister overtones just like colluding with the Devil does. Part of Glaucon's account of and praise for an unjust individual consists of his never letting others know about his wrongdoing. Being successful in such a secret undertaking is to be "to be believed to be just without being just" (*Republic*, p. 36). In Sgt. Paradine's case, burying all associations to the handbook and its architect is deemed a fitting way to eliminate them as though they had never existed and no wrongdoing had happened, yet alone been considered.

Can an individual still have a shameful, or to a lesser extent a questionable, standing if no one ever finds out?

If Sgt. Paradine wants to believe that a dark episode of his life has been entirely annihilated, then he must, to paraphrase Glaucon, continue on through life fooling himself. Maybe when Sgt. Paradine dies, it is then he has successfully accomplished that personal mission of burying his shame for good.

Winning Isn't Everything

For a drama on war, it sure ends on a grave point. That's rather bizarre, because nobody is killed, unless one counts the killing of some Confederate soldiers' hopes.

Still, there's fighting. This fighting has more to do with bruising the human spirit than damaging bodies. Without seeing any visible harm, a person not associated with the conflict might question how it's even possible for anyone to have lost anything. Then again, consider that one side's failure to capitalize on an easy victory that would end the war is really devastating to that side. What plays out for Sgt. Paradine becomes the most fantastic element to this drama as opposed to the Devil's attempt at influencing the outcome of war.

Missing out on that kind of victory is a victory of a different sort and not a complete loss. Sgt. Paradine does not surrender the principle that values fairness above all else, even in times of conflict, yet he comes awfully close to giving it up. His uttering a single word could have done it. Perhaps Sgt. Paradine has something eating at his insides. It might even be something "yellow," a different sort of yellow, a core principle which is afraid of surrendering what matters most.

Anyone notice the back and forth struggle going on here—a veritable tug of war?

We could argue that Sgt. Paradine and his weary troops are in no different a situation than before the scout ventured the valley. Still, their will to fight has gained new ground.

A moral lesson about whether to associate with seemingly like-minded characters during a war stands out. It is a challenge for those involved to accept the assistance of an overly accommodating ally, especially one who brandishes a so-called weapon that will make a difference in how the war is fought. For desperate men, it is worth a shot.

It's also worthwhile for a Devil or a rogue to prey on such desperate individuals, especially one soldier who is committed to winning for his side. Blinded by an offer to be victorious on a grand scale shows how Sgt. Paradine is easily used by someone who despises the same enemy. The hope of such gain minimizes the fear of any loss. So, if the Devil delights in someone accomplishing a complete victory and ignoring the prospect of losing, then some good must come from losing.

A Pyrrhic Loss

This episode with the Devil threatens to get hardened soldiers to lose sight of losing. Being overly optimistic leads them to temporarily ignore a reality grounded in conflict. No important victory should be without some conflict. Sgt. Paradine eventually grasps this notion once the Confederacy has been given an opportunity to seize the upper hand by magical means.

Such a realization illustrates two types of losing: on one side, winning a war with a little help from a friendly Devil signifies a loss of the personal toil associated with fighting in the war. On the flipside, an individual's not giving in to taking an easy and seemingly underhanded victory represents loss of a rare opportunity. Taking advantage of that opportunity would have involved a conditional surrender, a surrender of what a desperate fighting man holds sacred.

Although Sgt. Paradine does not lose what he values, there remains some lingering regret for almost claiming such a tempting victory. Perhaps there is in a fighting man's conscience a barrier to winning at absolutely *any* cost. Fighting to protect that barrier may hold greater importance than victory.

Preserving the will to fight serves as a slight victory to those accustomed to losses, great, small, or absurd, for there are victories worth fighting for, but victory should never be simply handed to the victor.[1]

---

[1] The title of this chapter is an adaptation of the famous remark attributed to Confederate General Nathan Bedford Forrest, "War means fighting and fighting means killing."

19
Looking Like Number 12

LARRY ALAN BUSK

At the age of nineteen, everyone in Marilyn's world undergoes "the Transformation," a complete cosmetic makeover that replaces all physical features according to one of a set of predesigned models. A choice of new bodies is provided by "the Bureau." It's about time for Marilyn herself to transform, and her mother thinks that Number 12 suits her perfectly. Both Marilyn's mother and their housekeeper have changed into model Number 12 and so look identical, distinguishable only by nametags.

But Marilyn doesn't want to have the Transformation. She harbors deep worries about losing her sense of identity and grave doubts about the stifling uniformity of her culture. She tries without success to confide in her friend Valerie (Number 8) and her uncle Rick (Number 17); she consults the family doctor (Number 17 again), and eventually confronts one of the chief engineers of the Transformation process (Number 17 yet again). They see Marilyn's reluctance at first as immaturity and then as a kind of pathological illness. With decaying patience, they try to convince her that Transformation is an important part of growing up, that being beautiful and perfect is preferable to being mediocre and different, and that she will learn to appreciate this in time. They suggest she take a glass of "Instant Smile" to feel better. Marilyn resists and tries to escape. Eventually, however, she gives up and is transformed into Number 8, the same model as Valerie. She emerges from the operating room, exuberant and bubbly, to find her now identical friend waiting for her. "And the nicest part of all, Val," she exclaims, "I look just like you!

A Disturbing Episode

"Number 12 Looks Just Like You" has been called one of the most chilling entries in the *Twilight Zone* catalog. But what's so disturbing about this particular episode? There are no monsters, aliens, or magic powers. We might call it "social commentary." But what exactly is being commented on? What is it about this episode that we find so unsettling, so uncomfortable, so creepy?

This might seem an odd question for a philosopher to ask— perhaps it's better left to a psychologist or a television critic. But philosophy can do more than just puzzle over logical paradoxes and ethical conundrums. Philosophers have also inquired into the nature of *subjectivity*. In common parlance, to call something "subjective" typically means that it is partial, limited, or biased. "Subjectivity" is also sometimes conflated with "personality," the particular qualities of a given individual.

Philosophers have used the word in a somewhat different way. For our purposes, think of it like this: a way of relating to the surrounding world as a world of objects distinct from one-self. In simpler terms, subjectivity is the capacity at work when you say the word "*I*"—the positing of a being, your *self*, who is the "subject" of thoughts, feelings, desires, actions. This is not your "self" in terms of your hobbies, your personal biography, or your hair color, but your quality of agency, or individual identity. Subjectivity refers to more than just the ability to perceive your immediate environment or to recognize objects ("that's a dog, that's a cat"); it involves an active and analytical disposition toward the world. Things are not just passing by in a stream of raw data; subjectivity allows us to react to the world, interpret it, question it, and to inquire into what is concealed beneath what is immediately present.

Some philosophers have argued that the *form* of subjectivity is not something eternal and unchanging. They think that the very structure of the relationship between the "I" and the world of objects, rather than a permanent fixture of the human mind as such, is shaped by the forces of history, culture, economics, and politics. As the world changes, the nature of subjectivity changes with it. This might mean that subjectivity grows more discerning, more refined, more robust. There might also be historical conditions, however, in which subjectivity is diminished in some of its capacities, particularly its active and critical function; social-political-economic reality might develop in such a way that the self becomes less of a self. It is the dramatic representation of *this* possibility that is so profoundly disturbing in "Number 12 Looks Just Like You."

What exactly is the relationship between the unsettling world depicted in this episode and a philosophical account of subjectivity? What is it about Marilyn's story that is not only horrifying but also eerily familiar? We can get a better handle on this by examining a classic theory of the changing nature of "the subject" under modern conditions: the concept of "the culture industry" made famous by two German philosophers of the mid-twentieth century, Max Horkheimer and Theodor W. Adorno.

Trouble in Paradise

In the early 1930s, Horkheimer and Adorno were forced to flee the Nazis and came to the United States. The two émigrés traveled to California by car in 1941, and it was on this trip that the idea of the culture industry crystallized. Under totalitarian regimes, the cliché image suggests, everyone is made to be the same; things are uniform, administered, and drab. In free societies, by contrast, the individual is autonomous, and the free reign of self-expression is paramount.

But as Horkheimer and Adorno drove across the United States of the 1940s, they noticed something unsettling: in spite of obvious superficial differences, the character of American life bore a striking resemblance to the nightmarish authoritarian world they had escaped. There was no mandatory Hitler Youth, of course, and they did not fear for their lives as Jews. What they observed, rather, was that the same *form of subjectivity* that helps produce (and is in turn produced by) totalitarian regimes was present in a profound and frightening way in mainstream American society.

To understand this distressing form of subjectivity, we first need to explore Horkheimer and Adorno's concerns about the increasing monotony and homogeneity of mass consumer culture. The word "culture" is related to the word "cultivate." In its original sense, culture referred to that which *cultivates* human beings—enriching them, improving them, developing their best qualities and allowing them to flourish. Art, education, and tradition are so many ways of nurturing our capacity for growth, self-direction, and the creation of a good life. But to Horkheimer and Adorno, the American consumer society does not seem to have this kind of 'cultivation' as its goal. On the contrary, cultural creations are churned out according to predictable formulas and standardized models, intended for passive enjoyment rather than active engagement. Movies and music are 'products,' made like any other product by adhering to strict rules and leaving little room for spontaneity, creativity, or variation. This gives cultural production the quality of an assembly line in a factory, and so Horkheimer and Adorno give this tendency the oxymoronic name "culture industry."

In the dystopian world of "Number 12," people can attend "culture class"—but books, including literature like Dostoyevsky and philosophy like Plato, are banned. Culture is dolled out like food rations, but anything with too much complexity or too much depth is not allowed. Nothing politically subversive is allowed either. This is the logical result of the culture industry as Horkheimer and Adorno understand it. While it may not be necessary to literally ban books, culture becomes increasingly administered and one-dimensional. This happens to such an extent that artistic integrity and political dissent are phased out without any formal legal decree. Indeed, we get the sense that most of the characters in this episode wouldn't think of reading even if it were legal. Marilyn complains that all anyone ever talks about is "electronic baseball" or "super soccer." "There's got to be more to life than that," she says.

Subjects or Subjects?

At this point we might reasonably ask: what does the culture industry have to do with subjectivity? Most movies and music (and now, TV) might be formulaic, flat, and uninspired, but that has no bearing on the development of the self. This is where Horkheimer and Adorno see things differently. They argue that as cultural objects are integrated into the system of industrial production, so too they become integral to the *production of subjects*. Culture, as the result of our creative, intellectual, and moral life as a society, also shapes our subjectivity. What happens when the self becomes a part of the industrial production line, when a mechanized and standardized system goes beyond making chairs or refrigerators and starts making *people*? Social critics sometimes use the word "commodification" to refer to the process by which aspects of life that were previously outside of the production process are assimilated into it. If culture itself is *commodified*, what happens to subjectivity?

Horkheimer and Adorno argue that the subjects produced by the culture industry have an overwhelming tendency toward conformism, the dissolution of those qualities that make a subject a subject. As we said earlier, subjectivity requires an active, critical, and reflective engagement with the world in a way that goes beyond its immediate appearance. This capacity is systematically diminished in the subjects tutored by the culture industry. Rather than cultivating us, this kind of culture does exactly the opposite.

Think about the term "mindless entertainment." For Horkheimer and Adorno, the point is not that the people who consume these mass cultural objects are mindless, or even that the products themselves are mindless, but that they *produce mindlessness* in the consumers. They do this not through any overt, explicit propagandistic "message" (although this is still an important aspect), but in subtler ways. Stereotypical characters suggest that people really are simple and easily categorized. Happy endings tell us that all's well in the world. Formulaic plots and bland uniformity get us used to the idea that there are no surprises, that everything is neatly intelligible without too much work on the part of the audience, and that difference from the norm is quaint at best and pathological at worst.

The most disturbing aspect of this diminishing subjectivity, however, is the dwindling capacity for critical *resistance*. Horkheimer and Adorno see contemporary capitalist societies as oppressive and self-destructive: class and other hierarchies keep most of the population in a subordinate and powerless position, and a system based on the profit motive requires a constant turnover of production and consumption, creating enormous amounts of waste and fueling environmental degradation. Because of these ugly aspects of modern life, it's necessary to weaken the capacity for resistance in order to maintain the status quo. The culture industry fulfills this role by deadening the qualities of subjectivity that might lead anyone to resist: imagination, spontaneity, and critical insight. The culture industry encourages conformity to the given state of affairs not because this state of affairs is good, but simply because it is given. This kind of conformism is one of the key factors in the development of fascism and totalitarianism.

Horkheimer and Adorno are *not* claiming that ten evil men are sitting around a table on the top floor of a skyscraper somewhere plotting to ensnare the masses with their sinister designs. Rather, they think that the necessities of the system—the all-powerful profit motive—lead to the ever-increasing integration of all aspects of life under its sway. All of the requirements of the labor process—deference, consistency, passivity—are transferred to the cultural world. Free time is now an extension of work. If we cease to be subjects in the proper way, we become 'subjects' in a different sense— subjects *to* the prevailing socioeconomic reality, in the same way that a king has subjects.

The subjects (in both senses) of this society are therefore not the free, autonomous beings they regard themselves as being, and the distinction between the lush consumerist paradise and the grim totalitarian hellscape is not as strong as it seems. Rather than real choice, difference, or freedom, what the culture industry provides is the *illusion* of choice (all "brands" are ultimately identical), the perpetual recurrence of the same way of life, and the "freedom" to adapt to the needs of the system whether you like it or not. The "individuality" or "self-expression" offered by this industry is also a ruse: you express your self and your individuality only through the products you buy—products which, by definition, are available to anyone with the same discretionary income. The subject becomes just another commodity. But above all, for Horkheimer and Adorno, the culture industry fosters a form of subjectivity that is appropriately conformist: the ideal worker-consumer, with little desire and no ability to resist, content to remain a cog in a machine they can neither understand nor control, and pacified by the delusion that they are autonomous, self-expressive, and free.

Model Numbers and Mannequins

In "Number 12 Looks Just Like You," the self is a product mandated by the powers-that-be and marketed in home catalogs. Individuality is expressed through one of a set of sanctioned, predetermined models. The people in this society are under the impression that their choice of number represents their true nature, their inner being, when actually it represents their complete integration into the system as mindless and passive components with no discernible inner life. "Don't you have any feelings, Val?" asks a desperate Marilyn. "Of course I do, silly," her friend replies, "I feel . . . good!" Valerie feels good—aided by a glass of Instant Smile—because she is incapable of feeling anything else.

For the subjects so desensitized, the value of the transformation is self-evident, and no one close to Marilyn can comprehend her resistance—difference from the norm simply isn't intelligible. "No one's ever been forced to take the Transformation if he didn't want it," her doctor explains. "The problem is to figure out *why* you don't want it—and to make the necessary correction." He can't help but see her lingering sense of critical subjectivity as a problem to be solved. Only in the end does Marilyn appreciate the full gravity of this diminished faculty of resistance—"They can't understand! They can't understand!" Eventually, even Marilyn herself can't resist.

Perhaps "Number 12" is so disturbing because it embodies our anxieties about the declining qualities of subjectivity under the weight of the culture industry. The tendencies described by Horkheimer and Adorno and brought to terrifying life in this episode have only intensified in the subsequent decades. It would be too easy to regard the story as representing the fear of communism; rather, it represents our fears about our own society, about what it means to be a subject in the era of mega malls, targeted advertising, credit card debt, Prozac, and the latest superhero film reboot.

The Twilight Zone has a penchant for exploring this kind of anxiety. This is not the only episode built around elements of the culture industry and the diminished subjectivity that goes with it. In "The After Hours," a young woman named Marsha discovers to her shock that she is actually a department store mannequin. The mannequins are allowed a two-week furlough to explore the outside world once a year, and Marsha overstayed hers, becoming so enamored with life outside the store that she forgot what she is.

Think about what it means to *be* a mannequin: something lifeless, inert, plastic, a pre-molded model used for whatever the sales effort requires, a dummy, a cog in the machine. Horkheimer and Adorno's point is that the culture industry produces subjects that are like mannequins, props used by the system for its own ends, without any capacity or desire for a critical engagement with the world. It also produces subjects that know their place and will not try to alter their circumstances—in exchange for some modicum of permitted "fun." Just as there's no escaping the process of repetitive labor and facile consumption, Marsha's employer cannot permit her to leave except for a brief, prearranged vacation. Two weeks of "free time" and then it's back to work for Marsha. Yet, like Marilyn, she yearns for something more, to live "as if we were like the others, the outsiders, the real people." She yearns to be a subject. But instead she's a plastic doll.

Hope for the Hopeless?

This perspective on the culture industry and its effects on subjectivity might seem bleak and hopeless, especially the emphasis on our diminishing capacity for resistance. Conditions may have deteriorated to such an extent that fighting against the dismal tide is no longer possible. Horkheimer and Adorno are often called overly pessimistic for entertaining this view. Indeed, both "Number 12 Looks Just Like You" and "The After Hours" would be candidates for the distinction of bleakest *Twilight Zone* ending. Marilyn's protests go unheard, and in the end she's happily assimilated into the system; after some wistful hesitation, Marsha resigns herself to her post in the women's wear section.

In spite of all this, Horkheimer and Adorno's position is ultimately a hopeful one. These episodes of *The Twilight Zone* are hopeful too, dreary as their endings might seem. The sheer existence of Marilyn and Marsha—and likewise the sheer existence of Horkheimer and Adorno's theory—shows that there is still some subjectivity left, that the culture industry hasn't been *entirely* successful in undermining our capacity for critical resistance. However faint, these dissident characters represent a glimmer of hope in an otherwise hopeless world.

But don't get me wrong here: a single individual can't do much to change things on her own, and philosophical theory can probably do even less. If a better future is possible, it depends on our collective struggle and not on some inevitable historical trajectory or an unshakable faith in the purity of the subject. Overzealous optimism can be just as dangerous as overzealous pessimism. There is a warning against both in Serling's closing narration to "Number 12":

> *Improbable? Perhaps. But in an age of plastic surgery, body building, and an infinity of cosmetics, let us hesitate to say impossible. These and other strange blessings may be waiting in the future—which, after all, is the Twilight Zone.*

20
The Totalitarian Zone

JOHN ALTMANN

You are about to read a chapter dedicated to showing you one of the most horrific ideas ever realized within the human mind through the lens of another time. The idea, you ask? One simply called *totalitarianism.*

This political system has a government wielding absolute power over its citizens, who no longer have any personal beliefs, dreams, or tastes, but instead live their lives in the service of another entity simply known as the State. If the State is strong then you are strong and if the State is weak, then you are weak and you may even be viewed as the cancer the State needs to cut out of its own body to restore its strength. Because in the world of totalitarianism, strength is everything and no matter the cost even if that cost is human life, the State will become strong.

The lens through which we will be looking at totalitarianism was crafted at a time when the United States was finding its moral bearings after the atrocities of World War II and the Holocaust. The fantastical roamed the Earth in the form of *The Twilight Zone*, one of the most critical shows as it relates to Nazi Germany and totalitarian regimes. Consider the chapter you are holding as a time capsule and within it, *The Twilight Zone's* best episodes that expose the nature of totalitarianism.

But a word of caution as we embark on this journey. The nature of totalitarianism is not a fixed and unchanging thing. It transforms with the ages and while this chapter is indeed a time capsule, it is also a time machine, traveling to the futures depicted by *The Twilight Zone*'s spiritual successor *Black Mirror* and shows how totalitarianism has transformed and evolved to the point of being quite distinct from its twentieth-century incarnation. With this word to the wise given, welcome to *The Totalitarian Zone*.

He's Alive and Quite a Speaker Too!

The first item that we have dusted off from our time capsule comes from the time of the Cold War. During that time we see an insignificant Neo-Nazi movement being led by a man named Peter Vollmer, a man who can manage to draw only the smallest of crowds—and those who do attend usually end up beating up Vollmer and his friends. Frustrated with his situation, Peter wonders what it will take to get his movement off the ground.

One night he is visited by a shadowy man who gives Peter advice on how to grow his movement. The biggest piece of advice that Peter's adviser from the shadows gives is how to speak to energize and excite his crowds. The man from the shadows teaches him how to speak with fire and conviction, which in time will make his crowds grow larger in number. What Peter's shadowy benefactor taught him could be described as the art of rhetoric.

The purpose of the art of rhetoric is persuasion, at least that was the conclusion drawn by the ancient Greek philosopher Aristotle (384–322 B.C.E.). For Aristotle and for Peter's ally from the shadows, the main key to speaking persuasively as it relates to growing his Neo-Nazi movement, is understanding his audience on an emotional level and speaking to their frustrations. The emotions of Peter's audience are anger towards minorities, fear of nuclear war with the Soviet Union, and weariness at the current state of the economy. Peter begins to appeal with greater and greater mastery to these emotions and soon, his crowds grow quite large. As the size of his crowds increases, so too does the threat that is carried within his message. Peter's success with rhetoric is similar to that of all the great totalitarian dictators in history, whether they be Benito Mussolini, Francisco Franco, or Peter Vollmer's mentor who dwells in the darkness, Adolf Hitler himself.

Unfortunately for Peter Vollmer, his powers of persuasion were not enough to save his life. In the end, Peter was gunned down and left to die in the gutters as Hitler resumed his roaming of the Earth, looking for the next sad and angry individual to groom as his successor. But let's remember before we put the life of Peter Vollmer back in our capsule, that the power of rhetoric is timeless, and so long as speakers choose to wield it to target others that do not look as they do, or to breed hatred and violence under the guise of championing a worthy cause, the threats of rhetoric are also timeless. Such is the case of Peter Vollmer, an insignificant and insecure man who became a Nazi to feel like a somebody, and whose life saw its end before his choices extinguished the lives of others.

Difference Is to Be Despised

The next stop on our journey of understanding totalitarianism and the horrors that humankind are capable of is the year 2000 (as 2000 was foreseen in 1960), a time that for many was hailed as Armageddon by way of machines but in reality, came in the form of the beautiful. Because in the year 2000 ugliness no longer exists, and men and women when they reach a certain age, undergo an operation that transforms them into people who are free of imperfection in every way.

Our tour guide as we travel along this world of the stunning and handsome? A young woman named Marilyn, a woman who thinks with her own mind and uses her own voice and in light of this very fact, has opted not to be transformed. Marilyn appreciates who she is and does not wish to look like everyone else, for it is as her father taught her after he was transformed: "If everyone is beautiful then no one is." Marilyn's mother and her friend Valerie, both of whom were transformed, cannot understand why Marilyn is so resistant to the idea of the transformation even as she tries explaining to both of them the conversations she had with her father.

Marilyn is soon forcibly taken to a doctor to determine the cause and nature of her behavior, and the doctor becomes concerned when Marilyn asks him if he's ever read Socrates, Aristotle, or Dostoevsky. The doctor is alarmed by Marilyn's questions, as he reminds her that those books were banned years ago. The doctor sends Marilyn to a room to keep her under the thumb of the system, and while there she is visited by her mother and Val. When Val tries speaking to Marilyn alone, Marilyn informs her that her father killed himself because he couldn't stand what the world had become and who he had become upon being transformed. Later that night, Marilyn tries to escape but is ultimately unsuccessful, and is transformed into model number eight in accordance with the system. Upon completion of the treatment, Marilyn excitedly declared to Val that "The best part of all Val, is I look just like you!"

This society of the stunning, this control of bodily appearance and intelligence in the name of sameness, is a hallmark of any totalitarian regime. The Italian philosopher Umberto Eco (1932–2016) noted in one of his most famous essays, "Ur-Fascism," that one of the defining characteristics of regimes like Hitler or Mussolini, where Eco grew up, is a fear of difference. In the world Marilyn inhabited and the world her father struggled against, they were considered a danger precisely because of their difference whether it was in how they looked, how they thought, or both. So as we remember the life of Marilyn before she became like everyone else, remember that freedom of expression means so much more than eye-popping clothes, how you style your hair, or the language you use. Freedom of expression means being able to truly be who you want to be, without fear that doing so could cost you your life.

Following Orders and the Banality of Brutality

Our final journey into the past comes in the form of the life of SS Captain Gunther Lutze, who one day decided to visit the Dachau concentration camp and relish the memories of his days as captain and the lives he tormented. What Captain Lutze did not prepare for however, was for his trip down memory lane to turn into a nightmare.

During Captain Lutze's visit to Dachau, he comes across a man named Alfred Becker, who was a former inmate at the concentration camp and whom Lutze believes to be in charge of maintaining the camp. While touring the grounds of Dachau, Becker reminds Lutze of all the cruel and inhumane things he did while serving as an SS Captain during the war. Lutze's defense against the charges of his malice was that he was just following orders, that he was functioning as he was told, and that he had no choice. Unfortunately for Captain Lutze, these excuses ring hollow to the ghosts of his past who would put him on trial and ultimately, find him guilty.

Captain Lutze's reasoning about only following orders, was a common line of argument employed by many Nazis who were tried for war crimes in the aftermath of the Holocaust. One trial that was particularly notable, was that of Adolf Eichmann, who was convicted of his crimes and hanged for them. Like Captain Lutze, Eichmann denied any sense of personal responsibility and claimed that he was just following orders. One person present at Eichmann's trial, was the writer and political theorist Hannah Arendt (1906–1975), who concluded that Eichmann had been a product of what she called the banality of evil. In Arendt's mind, Eichmann did not necessarily possess hatred in his heart for Jews or any of the other victims of the Holocaust, the moral failure of Eichmann's actions was that he never *thought* about them at all.

This lack of self-reflection, of internal dialogue in the midst of his actions, is what permitted the evil of Nazism to become as widespread and powerful as it was. For Eichmann, according to Arendt, sending Jews to gas chambers was as routine and mechanical a process as a secretary filing paperwork. Eichmann, and those like him, carrying out orders like machines just like Captain Lutze, they are the real face of Nazi Germany. It is a face that while its vitality is connected to the past, the memory of it must be carried by all of us as we march towards the future both as a species, and you, dear reader, on this journey through the evils of man.

Blue Bear Spectacle

We have stepped into a world that, though it is called future, many people would frighteningly declare is our present. We're gazing into this world through the eyes of a struggling comedian named Jamie, whose claim to fame is being the voice actor of a blue cartoon bear named Waldo. Waldo is quite popular with the British public, so much so that Waldo is preparing for his own television pilot. The producer of the television series, Jack Napier, suggests that Waldo run for Parliament to build publicity for the show. Jamie does agree, though with considerable reservation about mixing Waldo with the world of politics. Jamie's concern would prove to be well founded, as the injection of Waldo into the election would turn everything upside down.

When Waldo enters the political arena, he does so on a platform of crass humor and of insulting his competition. Waldo is a candidate who lacks substance, he's nothing more than an empty vessel and an image with which any political vision could come to life. Jamie knows this, but much to his horror the general public doesn't care, as they love the idea that Waldo is so critical of the status quo and to them represents a genuine alternative. This alternative soon becomes a living Hell for Jamie, who begins to grow fearful that Waldo might win. Jamie feels responsible for this possibility, for he had agreed to impersonate Waldo on national television and he performs scathing critiques of all the other candidates with that airtime.

Jamie has tapped into the general public's anger, and because Waldo is nothing more than an image, when Jamie no longer wants any part in the parliamentary race or Waldo as a character, Jack takes the controls and with them, Waldo becomes a figure of violence that will sic mobs on both Jamie and the candidates he lost the election to. In the end despite losing that election, Waldo goes on to become a symbol of global authority, a totalitarian Hell served to you courtesy of a cartoon bear, and a public all too eager to embrace him.

What does this eagerness say about what humanity has become? Whether we're discussing a blue bear or an orange-haired real estate mogul turned President, our affinity for the new and exciting, the symbols that buck against the status quo, must be grounded in some kind of reasoning. Philosopher and cultural critic Guy Debord (1931–1964) had arrived at the conclusion that we're living in "the society of the spectacle." What this means is there's no authenticity anymore, or genuine human interaction. All there is, is the image which acts through the will of the people and their relationships to each other and their society.

In the case of Waldo, the people's anger, distrust, and hunger for change from their current political climate, is realized through this crass, empty, blue cartoon bear rather than any kind of meaningful human activism. Because of the people's apathy and willingness to consume the image of Waldo and to embrace him, they had willingly signed on to realize an authoritarian nightmare. When we think about what we have permitted ourselves to embrace and to consume, a President who became a reality television star and who rode a wave of criticizing and mocking the world around him and those who share it with him, I ask you, as we depart from this world whether we are not living in our own Waldo moment.

Resistance as Just Another Product

In our final journey together, you are now witnessing a world where Debord's idea of the image and the spectacle is taken to the limit. A world that is powered by low-class citizens on exercise bikes who work to earn virtual currency, that is used in their day-to-day lives or to customize their personal avatars. One citizen who lives in this digital dystopia is a man named Bing, who is living comfortably in this world because he has fifteen million credits he has inherited from his deceased brother. Bing is not just content with being comfortable however, he wants more and what he wants is something real. He gets something real when he overhears a woman named Abi singing in the bathroom. While in any other world this encounter would be beautiful, for both Bing and Abi it is an encounter that signals the beginning of immense suffering.

Bing convinces Abi to audition as a singer on the reality show *Hot Shots*, and even goes as far as to use all of his credits to purchase her ticket for her. When she gets to the show and sings for the judges, they cut her off mid-performance and suggest that rather than singing, that she should consider doing porn instead. Abi, having just taken a cup of compliance at the urging of a producer before her audition, agrees, much to Bing's horror. Bing is so distraught about putting Abi in the position to be taken advantage of and when he sees her in a porn commercial, he shatters the screen and is about to kill himself with a shard of glass. But what starts as a suicide attempt soon becomes a plan for Bing, as he decides to earn back fifteen million credits and go on to *Hot Shots*. When he gets there, he fakes a dance routine but soon shocks the judges and the audience by pulling a shard of glass out and holding it to his throat. What proceeds from this act of defiance is a speech from Bing about how everything around him is not real and that anything genuine and authentic cannot be handled by this world.

It is a passionate speech by Bing, but one that is turned around on him by the judges treating it as just another act. Despite Bing's protests that he's serious, the judges call his speech "stuff" and offer him his own show to speak with the same fire he always does. In the end Bing accepts the offer and the shard of glass that was once a revolutionary symbol, has become nothing more than another product to give to your avatar. It is Debord's understanding of the image taken to the extreme, where revolution has a price tag. In this era that Marxist theorists call hyper-capitalism, turning resistance into a commodity or a trend is no longer the stuff of bleak science fiction, but our very reality. Such was the case of Bing and his glass shard, born from anguish and fury towards the system, it becomes complicit in its very functioning. Perhaps this is the greatest fear of a totalitarianism that need not call upon bombs and tanks—that there is no way and no hope to resist it.

Can Totalitarianism Be Turned Back?

In the world of *The Twilight Zone* which brilliantly captured the world of its time through the fantastical, totalitarianism had very clear signs. Charismatic speakers, conformity to the will of the State, and soldiers who follow orders and don't think for themselves. But we have ventured far beyond the dreams and nightmares that dwell in *The Twilight Zone*, and instead have found ourselves in a world where we are left staring into a *Black Mirror* that reflects back the very worst we are capable of.

The totalitarianism of our world is one where politics have become another medium of entertainment, where any and all human interaction is mediated through screens, and any pushback against this world becomes profit in the same breath. Revolutions reduced to hashtags, martyrs for noble causes reduced to a social media trend. Is there any way to break the cycle? Any way for human beings to free themselves?

The correct answer to this question will not be found in these pages, dear reader. Because the truth is a matter of such complexity and importance that it can't be boiled down to a single chapter. The truth is found by engaging the very world that finds itself in turmoil.

By connecting with your fellow man, by educating yourself on the nature of your government and its values, and discovering the values that you uphold and whether they are more just than the values of your government, you resist it, however you can, whenever you can. Because no matter how massive the totalitarian regime, they all crumble under the power of the human conscience in action.

This is a truth that is not unique to *The Twilight Zone*, and it is one that shines through even the blackest of mirrors. That is because it is a truth whose power endures across ages and dimensions, and dwells instead in the hearts and minds of every human being on Earth.

So long as that truth continues to persist in these same spaces, there will always be a chance to free yourself from *The Totalitarian Zone*.

21
That Unnamed Zone
We Call Freedom

ALEXANDER E. HOOKE

> JUSTICE, n., A commodity which in a more or less adulterated condition the State sells to the citizen as a reward for his allegiance, taxes, and personal service.
>
> —AMBROSE BIERCE, *The Devil's Dictionary*

If we follow current political disputes, it seems that "libertarian" and "liberal" are assumed to be inherent opposites—though libertarianism is practically the same as what we now call "classical liberalism," liberalism as the word was understood 150 years ago.

Which political perspective encourages compassionate immigration policies, respects the right to abortion, welcomes gays and lesbians as valuable citizens, and supports the legalization of marijuana as well as assisted suicide? Faced with this question, my guess is that most people would answer "liberalism." It turns out the correct answer is both—libertarian and liberalism.

Despite their considerable overlap, though, they do have serious disagreements about the meaning of freedom, its moral and political significance, its place in civil society, and the relationship between the quest for and experience of human freedom with respect to the powers and authority of the State.

It's a tenuous and sometimes testy relationship. Liberals tend to encourage more active roles for government to advance various options for citizens. Libertarians are suspicious of relying on a central authority that has the option of dictating to competent adults what they should or should not be doing in their personal lives.

This is more than an academic issue. The tension between a liberal and libertarian endures because its adherents have different takes on how freedom is related to justice and whether humans can be trusted with too many individual freedoms.

This ongoing tension is central to *The Twilight Zone*. Rod Serling does not directly talk about liberals and libertarians, but his narrations and plots often illuminate an ambivalent attitude towards the State and institutions that distrust or attempt to define the limits to individual freedom.

Underscoring this ambivalence is Serling's uneven perspective on human nature. On the one hand, he depicts numerous human endeavors that embrace happiness, beauty, justice and truth. On the other hand, he often acknowledges what a miserable lot humanity can be.

Consider his introduction to the episode "People Are Alike All Over." "You're looking at a species of flimsy little two-legged animal with extremely small heads whose name is Man." In this episode an earthling arrives on Mars and discovers that its inhabitants look just like him. At first he feels relieved by this discovery. Indeed, they look more peaceful and harmonious than his fellow citizens back on Earth. But soon he finds himself locked in a large cage—it resembles a house found in the suburbs—as if he were a rare species to be stared at and pitied by the cautious Martians.

"The Monsters Are Due on Maple Street" offers a more cynical variation. Afraid of an alien invasion, long-time neighbors become suspicious of who among them might be the real alien and thus a traitor. Soon they are accusing one another and ganging up on who they believe is the culprit. Serling sardonically notes, "There are weapons that are simply thoughts, attitudes, prejudices—to be found only in the minds of men."

In "Eye of the Beholder" a young woman undergoes her final cosmetic surgery that might correct her natural ugliness. She is understandably scared and desperate. If the operation again fails, she will be exiled to an area where the other misfits dwell. No, she cries, how can anyone decide and forcibly remove those who do not fit the norm? No, she sadly mutters, "The State is not God."

This cursed woman is not making a plea for theocracy. Rather, she expresses a damning indictment against any group of people who, through coercive laws and oppressive enforcement, seek the powers of a god that can undermine or destroy human freedom. Such groups evoke Ambrose Bierce's insight that, for many, justice is a fancy word to disguise an antipathy towards freedom rather than one of the seven cardinal virtues designed to defend human freedom.

The State Is Not a Shepherd

One of the most compelling depictions of the state appears in "The Obsolete Man." While Marc Scott Zicree rightly notes that this episode is a bit overhanded in portraying the antagonist, his claim that the theme foreshadows a neo-Nazi world is misleading. There are no caricatures of Hitler and goose-stepping soldiers. The enemy is not some distorted and contrived image of a Jew, homosexual, or Communist. Here the enemy is a simple librarian.

His name is Romney Wordsworth. As portrayed by Burgess Meredith, perhaps the most endearing *Twilight Zone* actor, the librarian could be any one of us who enjoys the moments of solitude when we can read and let our minds wander and our hearts yearn. This is a central element of human joy—to delight in opportunities where we live in our own time and space, no one watching or regulating us. Such individual freedom is a danger to the State. Wandering minds and yearning hearts do not show allegiance, do not pay taxes, and perform no useful service. Hence it is rendered obsolete.

Obsolete stems from the root "no longer used, out of date." Throughout "The Obsolete Man" episode the Chancellor condemns the librarian for a variety of heresies against the State. Echoing Karl Marx's quip that religion is the opium of the people, the Chancellor proclaims that books, poetry, novels are an opiate that endangers the health of the body politic. Worse still, the librarian's interest lies in sacred texts, which makes him as obsolete as all the pastors and priests who have already been exiled or executed. The

Chancellor boasts that the State once conducted 1,300 televised executions within a single six-hour span.

After he's condemned to execution, Wordsworth is granted only one right. He is permitted to arrange his own death. He can pick the mode of death (a bomb), the time (midnight) and his executioner. He invites the Chancellor to his death room to oversee the execution. Wordsworth begins to read Biblical passages, much to the disgust of the Chancellor. Most prominent is Psalm 23. "The Lord is my shepherd," the librarian reads with utter tranquility, "I shall not want . . . he leadeth me in the paths of righteousness for his name's sake." With a quick glance at the Chancellor, Wordsworth continues, "Yea though I walk through the valley of death, I will fear no evil . . ."

According to French philosopher Michel Foucault, in his 1977–1978 lectures *Security, Territory, Population,* the shepherd has been an enduring figure in social and political thought. It is not only a Christian theme, as non-Christian thinkers such as the Ancient Greeks, including Plato, speculated on whether the best leader or government to lead the state is modeled after the attentiveness and devotion of the shepherd who guides his flock.

It's odd that so many Jewish, Greek, and Christian writers have been able to develop this metaphor without really noticing that the shepherd is an early stage in the production of shish kebab. The shepherd's mission, "to serve sheep," has a hidden ambiguity!

Theoretical problems hounded this model. Insurmountable was the shepherd's paradox. If the shepherd is to the flock as the leader is to his people, how does the shepherd decide to care for each and every sheep or focus on the flock itself? Suppose one little lamb wanders off into the woods. Does the shepherd believe every individual sheep has unique worth and go off in search of the little lamb, thus presenting the big bad wolf the opportunity to attack the neglected flock?

On the other hand, suppose the shepherd has to decide which wayward or miscreant sheep does not deserve attention at risk to the flock. On what basis does the shepherd decide who stays and who leaves? Value terms such as freedom and justice are not part of the shepherd's perspective. And regardless of the similarities of the analogy, a just state does not look to its citizens as a flock.

Rod Serling has fun with this paradox. "The Shelter" is one of many episodes that depict human beings' inability to decide who stays and who goes. Here neighbors are friendly and cheerful, often joining each other for weekend barbecues and kids' birthday parties. Suddenly a news flash warns of imminent invasion by UFOs. The radio urges everyone to go home and retreat to their underground shelters. Much like the fable "Three Little Pigs," only one neighbor had the energy and forethought to have actually built a shelter beneath his house to protect his family. His free time was not idly squandered like his neighbors'; he worked and planned for danger while others were amusing themselves.

Within an hour the other neighbors come to his shelter pleading the case for their sick child or aging grandparent. How can the prepared neighbor be so unjust as to dismiss their pleas? Soon they violently threaten to smash through the shelter's thick metal door. Does the well-prepared neighbor allow them in at risk of jeopardizing his own family? He does not. In the background, though, is the idea that the shelter is a microcosm of the State. Serling's twist with this paradox appears in the concluding scenes when everyone learns that the report was based on false signals from radars. With all systems safe again, neighbors nervously reappear and face each other again. Distrust and suspicion have obviously taken over. As with many *Twilight Zone* episodes, the human species is depicted as an unappealing lot.

The Just State

In the early 1970s two American philosophers and their readers engaged in a lively and influential dispute about the nature of a just state. John Rawls, in his *A Theory of Justice,* developed two basic principles of fairness—equal rights and the difference principle—that he considered to be a cornerstone for understanding and seeking a just society. Robert Nozick, in his *Anarchy, State, and Utopia* offered a witty and thoughtful rejoinder to those who supported the central tenets of Rawls's outlook, many of whom believed it offered a framework for a utopian vision of democratic socialism.

While I'm sympathetic to the central purposes of Rawls's vision, and apparently so was Nozick in his younger days, the later Nozick became skeptical of a vision that could be realized only through the expansion of a central authority increasingly invading our personal lives.

Part of Rawls's outlook is based on Aristotle's idea of self-respect as part of the good life. Nozick has no objections to that, except that self-respect should not be part of the State's concerns. A fan of basketball, Nozick asks us to imagine a kid who is the best shooter in his small town. He receives the admiration of fans, teammates, and opposing players. Then Jerry West (one of the greatest shooters of all-time) moves into town. The kid's self-esteem suddenly evaporates. Nozick asks us: do we really want the State to intervene on such a personal matter? A simple but telling case that raises suspicions about the position of Rawls and his advocates, as if they are committed to such intervention or regulation in the name of justice.

An overreaching State is inevitable if we are to ensure that Rawls's two principles are followed. And that commitment is contrary to individual freedom. Serling is quite aware that humans often need a State that can provides guidance, strength, and protection. Let humans decide too much on their own, and, as portrayed in "To Serve Man," they can be so gullible and self-indulgent that they wait in line to visit a planet where humans will be featured on the menu.

Rawls and Nozick did not anticipate the emergence of identity politics, in which individuals aligned themselves primarily within groups rather than as equal citizens before the law or state. Nor could they have predicted the powers and extensions of social media, as their obnoxious and ugly missives often thrive outside the influence and control of a central political or institutional authorities. Both were subject to vitriol. Rawls was accused of being a tacit Marxist as well as privileged male who acquiesced to familiar inequalities despite his humanist inclinations. Nozick was charged with condoning the history of minimalist government that nurtured capitalism's ill-gotten treasures and worldly domination.

These *ad hominems* and distortions aside, both Rawls and Nozick addressed a theme fundamental to Rod Serling:

No State can be considered just that squashes human rights, human dignity and human freedom.

The Freedom to Laugh at Injustice

And supposing that gods, too, philosophize . . . —I should not doubt that they also know how to laugh the while in a superhuman and new way—and at the expense of all serious things. Gods enjoy mockery: it seems they cannot suppress laughter even during holy rites.

—NIETZSCHE, *Beyond Good and Evil*

Would *The Twilight Zone* itself be deemed obsolete in other dimensions?

As the Chancellor awaits the final minutes before the execution, Wordsworth reads and talks with a knowing smile, a smirk, even a stifled laugh. With some embarrassment, I have to admit that I did not catch this the first time I watched "Obsolete Man." Watching it again, and with the help of commentaries from Marc Scott Zittree and Mark Dawidziak, I realize Wordsworth is laughing before the grim reaper who represents an oppressive rule.

There is a photograph taken at a concentration camp where a Jewish prisoner is about to be shot by the guards. The caption emphasizes that we look at the condemned man's face. He is smiling. He is mocking the false powers of the fascists, as if to say: You can shoot me, but you still do not matter. Through the face of actor Burgess Meredith, we see a mischievous grin while he reads passages from the Bible to the Chancellor. The clock is ticking towards the midnight hour. As the bomb is ready to explode, the Chancellor finally panics, realizing that he is about to be blown up with the condemned man. He tries to exit, but the door is locked. In desperation he cries out to Wordsworth, "In the name of God, let me out!"

The Chancellor's utterance of God now makes him obsolete. He has confessed his own betrayal. Anyone who pleads to an obsolete deity has also immediately become obsolete. Yet the Chancellor's utterance sparks a sense of humor among those of us watching this episode. The State now looks pathetic and absurd. As Ambrose Bierce's opening epigraph implies, a cosmic joke has been played upon him and those of us who believe in justice as preached by a higher authority. Hence the humble and condemned librarian indeed has the last laugh. He laughs before the face of death, which is the face of the State.

This laughter can arise whenever a central authority arises from the horizons. Often it emerges in the most informal of settings, such as a friendly neighborhood association, a circle of do-gooders chasing teenage miscreants, revolutionaries attempting to overthrow a despot, faculty committees pledging tolerance. Sooner or later, we no longer see the champions of freedom and justice. We instead recognize a lust for power.

When Serling introduced *The Twilight Zone* in the 1950s, he recognized several enemies of freedom during this time. Psychological and sociological determinists, scientists of human behavior, even lingering religious predeterminists, saw freedom as a trait that could be neither be named nor demonstrated. They have yielded to the current skeptics whose commitment to neuroscience and genetics contends that freedom is an illusion or dangerous myth.

Many liberals and libertarians recognize the ongoing allegations of freedom as illusion. They realize the difficulty of identifying those who use "justice" and "freedom" as weapons for satisfying their own lust for power. The distrust of this lust is poignantly illuminated in the mind and work of Rod Serling.

That we still laugh at the many episodes of his *Twilight Zone* where absurdity reigns is testimony to the show's magic. It is difficult to describe or locate this laughter. It stems from a freedom that cannot be defined. But we know the experience and call it freedom. Since Socrates and Heraclitus, this laughter has been central to a philosophical dimension that we call the Twilight Zone.

In homage to Rod Serling, he gets the last word. "Any state, any entity, any ideology that fails to recognize the worth, the dignity, the rights of man, that state is obsolete."

References

Arendt, Hannah. 1963, *Eichmann in Jerusalem: A Report on the Banality of Evil*. Viking.

———. 1972. Thinking and Moral Considerations. In Jerome Kohn, ed., *Responsibility and Judgment: Hannah Arendt*. Schocken.

Aristotle. 1990. *The Nicomachean Ethics*. Harvard University Press.

Augé, Marc. 1995. *The Non-Places: Introduction to an Anthropology of Supermodernity*. Verso.

Bierce, Ambrose. 2002. *The Unabridged Devil's Dictionary*. University of Georgia Press.

Breton, André. 1969. *Manifestoes of Surrealism*. University of Michigan Press.

———. 1994. *Nadja*. Grove Press.

Brightman, Carol, ed. 1995. *Between Friends: The Correspondence of Hannah Arendt and Mary McCarthy, 1949–1975*. Harcourt, Brace.

Byrne, Peter. 2010. *The Many Worlds of Hugh Everett III: Multiple Universes, Mutual Assured Destruction, and the Meltdown of a Nuclear Family*. Oxford University Press.

Cardin, Matt. 2017. *Horror Literature through History: An Encyclopedia of the Stories that Speak to Our Deepest Fears*. Greenwood.

Carroll, Noël, and Lester Hunt, eds. 2009. *Philosophy in The Twilight Zone*. Wiley-Blackwell.

Carroll, Siobhan. 2017. Atopia/Non-Place. In Robert T. Tally Jr., ed., *The Routledge Handbook of Literature and Space*. Routledge.

Churchland, Paul. 1988. *Matter and Consciousness*. Revised Edition. MIT Press.

———. 1989. *A Neurocomputational Perspective: The Nature of Mind and the Structure of Science*. MIT Press.

Coeckelbergh, Mark. 2012. How I Learned to Love the Robot: Capabilities, Information Technologies, and Elderly Care. In I. Oosterlaken and J. van den Hoven, eds., *The Capability Approach, Technology and Design*. Springer.

Dawidziak, Mark. 2017. *Everything I Need to Know I Learned in the Twilight Zone: A Fifth Dimension Guide to Life*. Thomas Dunne.

Dewitt, Bryce Seligman, and Neil Graham. 2015. *The Many Worlds Interpretation of Quantum Mechanics*. Princeton University Press.

Eco, Umberto. 1995. Ur-Fascism. *New York Review of Books* (June 22nd).

Foucault, Michel. 2009. *Security, Territory, Population: Lectures at the Collège de France 1977–1978*. Picador.

Harmon, Amy. 2010. A Soft Spot for Circuitry. *New York Times* (July 4th).

Hume, David. 1978 [1738]. *A Treatise of Human Nature*. Clarendon.

Kaku, Michio. 2005. *Parallel Worlds: A Journey through Creation, Higher Dimensions, and the Future of the Cosmos*. Random House.

Kierkegaard, Søren. 1992. [1843]. *Either/Or: A Fragment of Life*. Penguin.

Kuhn, Thomas S. 1970 [1962]. *The Structure of Scientific Revolutions*. University of Chicago Press.

Levinas, Emmanuel. 1991 [1961]. *Totality and Infinity: An Essay on Exteriority*. Kluwer.

Lewis, C.S. 1960. *The Four Loves*. Harcourt, Brace.

Lingis, Alphonso. 2004. *Trust*. University of Minnesota Press.

———. 2007. *The First Person Singular*. Northwestern University Press.

Locke, John. 1975 [1648]. *An Essay Concerning Human Understanding*. Oxford University Press.

Neiman, Susan. 2001. What Is the Problem of Evil? In Maria Pia Lara, ed., *Rethinking Evil: Contemporary Perspectives*. University of California Press.

———. 2002. *Evil in Modern Thought: An Alternative History of Philosophy*. Princeton University Press.

Nietzsche, Friedrich. 1997. *Beyond Good and Evil: Prelude to a Philosophy of the Future*. Dover.

Nozick, Robert. 1974. *Anarchy, State, and Utopia*. Basic Books.

Olson, James Stuart, ed. 2000. *Historical Dictionary of the 1950s*. Greenwood.

Parfit, Derek. 1984. *Reasons and Persons*. Oxford University Press.

Peirce, Charles S. 1999. How to Make Our Ideas Clear. In Nathan Houser and Christian Kloesel, eds., *The Essential Peirce: Selected Philosophical Writings*. Indiana University Press.

Plato. 1992. *Republic*, Hackett.

Popper, Karl R. 1972. *Objective Knowledge: An Evolutionary Approach*. Oxford University Press.

Rawls, John. 1971. *A Theory of Justice*. Harvard University Press.

Reid, Thomas. 1975. Of Identity. In John Perry, ed., *Personal Identity*. University of California Press.

Rubin, Steven Jay. 2018. *The Twilight Zone Encyclopedia*. Chicago Review Press.

Sander, Gordon. 2012. *Serling: The Rise and Twilight of Television's Last Angry Man*. Cornell University Press

Serling, Anne. 2003. *As I Knew Him: My Dad, Rod Serling*. Citadel.

Serling, Rod. 1968. The Challenge of the Mass Media to the 20th-Century Writer. *The Quarterly Journal of the Library of Congress* 25:2 (April).

———. 1972. The Commencement Address of Rod Sterling, May 13th 1972. Ithaca College.

———. 1983. TZ Classic Teleplay: The Lonely. *Twilight Zone Magazine* 3:2.

Schumer, Arlen, ed. 1990. *Visions from the Twilight Zone*. Chronicle.

Singer, Peter. 1986. All Animals Are Equal. *Applied Ethics*.

Sparrow, Robert, and Linda Sparrow. 2006. In the Hands of Machines? The Future of Aged Care. *Minds and Machines* 16.

Turkle, Sherry. 1997. *Life on the Screen: Identity in the Age of the Internet*. Simon and Schuster.

———. 2005 [1984]. *The Second Self: Computers and the Human Spirit*. MIT Press.

Walton, Kendall. 1978. Fearing Fictions. *The Journal of Philosophy* 75:1.

Zicree, Marc Scott. 2018 [1992]. *The Twilight Zone Companion*. Silman-James.

About the Authors and Editors

EMILIANO AGUILAR has published chapters in *Orphan Black and Philosophy: Grand Theft DNA* (2016), *The Man in the High Castle and Philosophy: Subversive Reports from Another Reality* (2017), *Giant Creatures in our World: Essays on Kaiju and American Popular Culture* (2017), and many more. But Emiliano's bedside book is an interesting cookbook that only has three words on the cover. Fortunately or unfortunately, he has not yet put the book into practice. However, he does not rule it out for the future.

JOHN ALTMANN is an independent scholar of Philosophy with a star rating of 2/5 stars who lives among the Monsters on Maple Street.

FERNANDO GABRIEL PAGNONI BERNS is a profesor at Universidad de Buenos Aires (UBA), where he teaches seminars on international horror film. He has published chapters in the books *Divine Horror* (2017), *To See the Saw Movies: Essays on Torture Porn and Post 9 / 11 Horror* (2013), *Critical Insights Film: Alfred Hitchcock* (2016), and many more. In his free time, Fernando likes to create worlds in which all of his co-authors are no more than figments of his imagination. That includes Juan and Emiliano.

LARRY ALAN BUSK is currently completing a PhD in philosophy at the University of Oregon. This is the second time he has written about *The Twilight Zone* and the Frankfurt School—the first was in an essay for the academic journal *Constellations*, where he analyzed the episode "It's a Good Life." He considers watching *Twilight Zone* marathons as a teenager a crucial part of his philosophical education. For his Transformation, he chose Number 17—a very popular model.

DON FALLIS is Professor of Information and Adjunct Professor of Philosophy at the University of Arizona. He has written several acclaimed philosophy articles on lying and deception, including "What Is Lying?" in the *Journal of Philosophy* and "The Most Terrific Liar You Ever Saw in Your Life" in *The Catcher in the Rye and Philosophy*. (2012). He thinks that it is particularly important to get these issues in the philosophy of testimony straight. After all, Mr. Garrity's "next stop is Tucson."

ALEXANDER E. HOOKE is a philosophy professor at Stevenson University. He's a bit of a wimp when it comes to dangerous dimensions. However, he once dared to enter the zone of the Nietzsche Haus in Sils Maria, Switzerland. The good-hearted proprietors even allowed him to sleep in Nietzsche's room one night. Was it his imagination that sensed the eternal recurrence of the strange? Did his visions of the Übermensch emerge from light or shadow? Did he really encounter the ghost of Nietzsche hovering beyond the windows, or were they merely frosty forms shaped by the Alpine chilly nights? In any event, he survived the trauma to write about Nietzsche, Foucault, Lingis, and others who more vigorously dared to encounter the dangerous dimensions.

TIM JONES lives in the United Kingdom, where he teaches Literature and Foundation Year Humanities. His first thought of writing for this volume, however, arrived when he was staying with his partner's family in another realm entirely, in the middle ground between light and shadow, between science and superstition, lying between the pit of man's fears and the summit of his knowledge. At least that's how America can feel these days.

JUAN IGNACIO JUVÉ usually takes pictures of blank pages at night. When he later develops them, he receives the text he needs to write. This is how he earns his living. What a useful camera . . . Thanks to this uncanny process, he has published in books such as *Science Fiction and the Abolition of Man. Finding C.S. Lewis in Sci-Fi Film and Television* (2016), *Requiem for a Nation: Religion and Politics in Post-war Italy* (2017), and *The*

Rwandan Genocide on Film: Critical Essays and Interviews (2018).

JOHN V. KARAVITIS has been a fan of *The Twilight Zone*, and its twist endings, since childhood. But he knows that watching too many episodes in a row could leave your mind tied up in knots. So John created a step-by-step procedure that you can mechanically follow which will untangle those knots and give you a second chance to really enjoy this television series. Step one: Read both of John's chapters. Step two: Binge-watch every episode mentioned in John's chapters in *The Twilight Zone and Philosophy*. Step three: Go back to step one.

CHARLES KLAYMAN received his PhD from Southern Illinois University Carbondale and is a term instructor of philosophy at John A Logan College in Illinois. His research interests include classical American philosophy, the relationship between epistemology and aesthetics, as well as discovering an alternate dimension that furiously recruits philosophers and pays them ridiculously large sums of money.

CHRIS LAY is a PhD candidate and teaches at the University of Georgia. He has published in several other pop culture anthologies, including *Alien and Philosophy* (2017), *Rick and Morty and Philosophy* (2019), and *Westworld and Philosophy* (2018). Or maybe his doppelgänger wrote those? The struggles of dissertation writing have left Chris suspicious that he is caught in a time loop in a *Twilight Zone*-esque parallel dimension, and he hopes that someone reading this can rescue him.

TRIP MCCROSSIN teaches in the Philosophy Department at Rutgers University, where he works on, among other things, the nature, history, and legacy of the Enlightenment. "It's a good life, yes," he wonders sometimes, "but is it a *wonderful* life?"

DAVID MORGAN received his PhD in theoretical physics from the College of William and Mary, and is currently the Associate Professor of Physics and Astronomy at the Richard Bland College of William and Mary. His writing on popular culture and the philosophy of science has appeared in three earlier Open Court books, *Planet of the Apes and Philosophy* (2013), *Jurassic Park and Philosophy* (2014), and *Jimi Hendrix and Philosophy* (2018). Dr. Morgan has taught, written, and presented extensively on the ideas of parallel universes and time travel, and recently did a bit of consulting on the topic with the producers of

a major science-fiction project that he can't talk about because it's top secret.
.

CLARA NISLEY has taught courses in ethics and political and social philosophy. She has written chapters in *Downton Abbey and Philosophy* (2016) and *Iron Man vs. Captain America and Philosophy* (2018). In the twilight of dusk, her identity is veiled in shadows. Thoughts of David Hume give her a glimmer into beliefs about personal identity and existence.

ALAN PICHANICK teaches in the Augustine and Culture Seminar Program at Villanova University. He is especially interested in ancient conceptions of self-knowledge, and is currently working on a book on self-knowledge and love in the Platonic dialogues. He hopes to finish this book when he has time enough at last.

ELIZABETH RARD lives in a house with many doors, each hiding a mystery that can only be solved with a trip through the human heart. Those hearts are in jars in a shop that promises dreams but delivers only nightmares. The shop owner sells a lamp that can grant your every wish. The asking price is your fondest childhood memory. Elizabeth does not make wishes anymore because the lifelike human robot replicas that wait on her, day and night, have taught her that wishes are never answered in the Twilight Zone.

HEATHER L. RIVERA is an independent philosophical writer who has interests in metaphysics, the Problem of Evil, and philosophy of mind. Heather has written numerous philosophy articles and guest lectured at Suffolk County Community College on such topics as *Cindy Sherman's Film Stills* and *Simulacra and Simulation by Jean Baudrillard*, and *Inception* relating to René Descartes's *Meditations on First Philosophy*. She has given lectures annually on Evil, Pop Culture, and Philosophy at the Long Island Philosophical Society Conferences. Heather has been accused of being "A Reader."

FRANK SCALAMBRINO Whether in the rye, the further, the upside down, or the twilight zone, examining surreal experiences—such as *déjà vu*—Frank Scalambrino can be found interrogating the concepts of identity, memory, time, and fate, which may be eclipsing the revelation of a multi-versed existence.

STEPHEN SCALES received his BA in Liberal Arts from the New School for Social Research in 1986, and earned his PhD in philosophy at the University of California, San Diego in 1995. He joined the faculty at Towson University in 1995, and was advanced to Assistant Professor in 1997, Associate Professor in 2002, and Professor in 2013. Dr. Scales is co-editor of the collected volume, *The Ethics of the Family* (2010) and has written several articles in applied ethics and ethics pedagogy.

There's a signpost up ahead and it says: ROBERT VUCKOVICH is an independent scholar who has a fondness for Cynic and Stoic philosophy. He intends to return to some university where he can write research papers on Diogenes of Sinope and Marcus Aurelius. As a kid, he watched *The Twilight Zone* on syndication; his favourite episode is "A Penny for Your Thoughts." He opted to write about "Still Valley," because the expression about "damn Yanks" stuck with him and online reviews for this episode failed to explore a soldier's quandary of having to give up an assured victory and return to a decisive battle where he will likely meet his demise. Who said War isn't Hell?

DENNIS WEISS is a fan of all-things televisual and when he's not watching television he is Professor of Philosophy at York College of Pennsylvania where he regularly teaches courses on the intersections of philosophy, technology, popular culture, and science fiction. He has authored articles exploring the philosophical implications of Buffy, Data, Dick, Alicia, and Sarah (a certain clone) and is the editor of *Interpreting Man* (2003) and *Design, Mediation, and the Posthuman* (2014). He regularly draws inspiration from a variety of twilight zones and is currently at work on a project examining the rise of the posthuman in television.

REBA WISSNER is a music historian who teaches at way too many colleges in New York and New Jersey (four, to be exact). She has literally written the books on music in two great TV shows, *We Will Control All that You Hear: The Outer Limits and the Aural Imagination* (2016) and *A Dimension of Sound: Music in The Twilight Zone* (2013). Her love for *The Twilight Zone* began when her parents first watched it in reruns when she was six, thereby unknowingly creating a monster.

Index

POPULAR CULTURE AND PHILOSOPHY®

DOCTOR WHO

AND PHILOSOPHY
BIGGER ON THE INSIDE

EDITED BY COURTLAND LEWIS AND PAULA SMITHKA